99% PERSPIRATION

ALSO BY ADAM CHANDLER

Drive-Thru Dreams

99% PERSPIRATION

A NEW WORKING HISTORY OF
THE AMERICAN WAY OF LIFE

ADAM CHANDLER

PANTHEON   NEW YORK

For Emily

There has never been an American tragedy. There have only been great failures.

—F. SCOTT FITZGERALD

There are stories that save us, and stories that trap us, and in the midst of an illness, it can be very hard to know which is which.

—RACHEL AVIV

I work a lot and live far less than I could, but the moon is beautiful and there are blue stars. . . . I live the chaste song of my heart.

—FEDERICO GARCÍA LORCA

CONTENTS

99% PERSPIRATION

INTRODUCTION

THE AMERICAN ABRACADABRA

ONLY WHEN THE TIDE GOES OUT
DO YOU LEARN WHO'S BEEN SWIMMING NAKED.

—WARREN BUFFETT

It wasn't a perfect job. In the scheme of the universe, it wasn't even a great one. But for two years, Nakitta Long had been working part-time at an automotive plant in Winston-Salem, North Carolina, manufacturing car parts. Though she'd gotten a dollar bump to $15.25 an hour—nearly twice the state's minimum wage—it was still hard to get by. "Wages never match the cost of living. The cost of everything," she told me.

Like tens of millions of other American workers, Long relied on food stamps. And like tens of millions of American jobs, Long's was a temp gig with few benefits, another casualty of old, sturdier, middle-income work lost to automation and offshoring. Still she stayed on, hoping that the frequent but unfulfilled promises of becoming a permanent full-time employee there would pan out.

But then, in March 2020, Long was about to fire up the grill on a day off when she received a call from her manager at the temp agency. She was instructed not to go back to the plant and to return her work badge ASAP. She was being let go. Immediately, Long began panic cycling through scenarios, wondering if she had made some mistake at work, maybe messed up a part.

It was nothing that specific. With the pandemic suddenly raging, markets quaking, economies cratering, and consumers everywhere shrink-wrapping their wallets, businesses were shedding employees from their ranks with abandon. Around the country, mass layoffs were disproportionately affecting hourly workers, women, and people of color; Long happened to be all three. As she quickly discovered, even after two years, there wouldn't be time for pleasantries, well-wishes, or basic separation benefits. She went from being paid every week to not being paid at all. "I knew that I didn't have any type of resources that, if my job was to shut down, I could fall back on," she explained. "I wasn't at retirement age, I didn't have any savings, and I was living paycheck to paycheck like I've done pretty much most of my working life."

Long was forty-four, with two kids she was raising alone and without the time to luxuriate in her bad fortune. Steeling herself for a crisis ahead, she passed through denial, anger, acceptance, and then contingency plans at warp speed. In the short term, she planned to live off her tax refund until government unemployment benefits came through. In the early months of the pandemic, even that didn't seem like a sure bet.

"It was just like what everybody else was experiencing across the country," she recalled. "Unemployment offices were not able to handle the number of applications coming in. Systems were down. You couldn't get anybody on the phone to talk to, and if you did, they didn't know what was going on." Long caught what qualified as a lucky break because she knew someone at a government office who helped her sort through a technicality and receive benefits in less than a month. (According to U.S. Department of Labor data, only 14 percent of the roughly 12 million Americans who filed for unemployment in March 2020 received their payments that same month. Within six weeks, 30 million Americans—nearly 20 percent of the country's workforce—would apply.)

In addition to state unemployment benefits, a temporary $600 weekly boost had been issued under the CARES Act, the controversial federal aid package passed by Congress in the early days of the pandemic when America's financial footing was skittering on black ice. When those benefits kicked in for Long, there was relief, but also a sense of deflation; she was making considerably more on unemployment than she had at the job she'd worked for two years. "That's what was sad about it; it was $300 more per week, an additional $1,200 to $1,400 a month."

Nakitta Long's predicament reflects our biggest, most troublesome, most outrageous, most urgent, and most definitional social misperception: our belief in what I'll call the "American Abracadabra," a swaggering bit of magical thinking that asserts that through hard work, self-reliance, and heroic grit, each person determines their own fate.

This idea makes up the marrow of the American self. It's an inborn, anti-aristocratic, uniquely American code that gets reinforced each generation—in education, in policy, in religion, in everything. It's under our fingernails, evident in our heroes, holidays, and history; it provides the score to our rituals, customs, and mythologies. From Thoreau's Walden to Gatsby's West Egg and beyond, it lurks in the contours of our popular culture, and from Manifest Destiny to minimum wage, it whirls in the whiplash of our politics. Its cutthroat, winner-take-all logic—anyone who fails to make it here in the Land of Opportunity must not be trying hard enough—lifts the enormous needs of communities and heaps them entirely onto the shoulders of individuals. As a feat of branding, the American abracadabra is undefeated. It's the first slide in our sales deck, the first bullet point in our citizen handbook. As a channel of collective aspiration, it's durable and bipartisan, and so ingrained that it's practically invisible. "My grandfather," the elevator pitch begins, "came to this country with a dollar in the pocket of his only pair of pants." I don't need to tell you the rest, you already know how it goes.

For centuries now, this bit of fantasy has been proclaimed as the lodestar that guides our salvation ship across the blinding sea. Here in America, we get it done by ourselves, goddammit, and we take pains to note that this is what makes us different and exceptional.

The promise of mobility and untrammeled possibility here has beckoned tens of millions from around the globe to seek our shores, pass through our golden doors, forge a gritty path forward, and inhabit a bootstraps story to be uttered with soft reverence by future grandchildren. The ideal of self-propelled achievement guides practically everything we do (except maybe corporate tax policy).

Against all reality, this blurry, seductive legend thrives. The abracadabra remains America's greatest hit—part Rosebud, part Excalibur, part Sisyphus, and part "Free Bird." It's that dab of radioactive spider venom that supposedly endows us with our superpowers, the wind beneath our wings. Blessed as miraculous by its true believers, the abracadabra has come to define us; we are what we do, and our successes are an assertion of our own moral and social worth.

———

The title of this book, *99% Perspiration*, comes from the often posterized Thomas Edison quote about industriousness: "Genius is one percent inspiration, ninety-nine percent perspiration." But there's always been more to this quote than meets the eye. One of the first known renderings of Edison's famous aphorism appears in a story titled "Doing One's Best" in the *Idaho Daily Statesman* on May 6, 1901. In a way that will feel eerily familiar for being nearly 125 years old, Edison's iconic chestnut about hard work is part of an editorial instructing readers to push themselves beyond the limits of their responsibilities (and their compensation): "Genius is another name for hard work, honest work," it reads. "'Genius,' says Edison, 'is 1 per cent inspiration and 99 per cent perspiration.' People who take pains never to do any more than they get paid for, never get paid for anything more than they do."

Later, in the 1910 book *Edison: His Life and Inventions*, the inventor's biographers recount a conversation at Edison's laboratory in which he deflects praise for his life's brilliant, world-shaping output by attributing it mostly to hard work. "Stuff!" Edison apparently shouted. "I tell you genius is hard work, stick-to-it-iveness, and common sense."

Genius for the sake of the genius, in other words, is a less-than-cherished concept in a culture that spawned the bland efficiency of nutrition bars and the ten-thousand-hour rule. Edison's enduring maxim about work is just one prominent entry in a catalog of cultural and historical artifacts that promote the primacy of mettle and hard-won results in America.

You can find *The Muses* at the Prado in Madrid or *The Thinker* in Paris, but America beatifies doers. Edison's image and words still live on high school murals and in Boy Scout handbooks. In a telling (and creepy) legend, the fellow efficiency stalwart and inventor Henry Ford so admired his friend Edison that he arranged to have the inventor's last human exertion—his final breath—captured in a glass tube and put on display in his museum in Detroit.

More recently, the modern-day Edison wannabe Elon Musk channeled his role model when describing the taxing working culture at his companies. "There are way easier places to work," he posted in 2018, "but nobody ever changed the world on 40 hours a week." Musk's workweek formula, he added, "varies per person, but about 80 [hours] sustained, peaking above 100 at times. Pain level increases exponentially above 80."* (Owing in part to those long hours, Reuters documented more than six hundred serious workplace injuries at Musk's SpaceX facilities between 2014 and 2023, a previously unreported fraction of the total deaths and injuries at his facilities.)

The belief that the grind alone has powered the genius or success of tinkerers like Edison and Musk is a cornerstone American

---

* Despite naming his most celebrated product after the inventor Nikola Tesla, Musk actually favored Edison in the famous rivalry between Edison and Tesla. His reasoning: "Edison brought his stuff to market and made those inventions accessible to the world."

Edison, for his part, applied a cold transactional logic to his approach to work. "Anything that won't sell, I don't want to invent," he once explained. "Its sale is proof of utility, and utility is success." His rival Tesla, meanwhile, died alone and penniless in a hotel near New York's Penn Station.

myth; part of an individualistic belief that the first part of this book—"The Inspiration"—will trace back to America's beginning. We'll also dig into how for countless others without the benefit of benefactors, teams of unsung subordinates or unpaid labor, or, in Musk's case, family wealth, massive government loans and contracts, and billions of dollars in taxpayer-funded subsidies, hard work has never been the single galvanic force with which the hand of destiny has lifted up the deserving.

On balance, we seem to understand (however quietly) that the abracadabra isn't true. And yet, as we'll explore in the second part of this book—"The Perspiration"—this line of thinking not only still enchants us but casts an unshakable spell on American life. That spell makes our communities wobbly, our faith weak, our lives lonely, our politics toxic, and our relationship with work masochistic and unsustainable. As we journey around the country, we'll meet smart, dedicated people who are already finding solutions that show us another way.

Over the past few years, we've experienced the false notes of this American promise in some of the starkest of terms. We saw up close who suffered the most during the pandemic, who helped the most, who profited the most, who was suddenly deemed *essential*, and who, right from the jump, was shockingly comfortable with death for the sake of the economy.

"Those of us who are 70-plus, we'll take care of ourselves, but don't sacrifice the country," Texas lieutenant governor Dan Patrick declared on national television in March 2020, while arguing that seniors should be willing to put themselves in mortal danger to help younger generations remain at their jobs. "The message is that the American people have gone through significant death before," former New Jersey governor Chris Christie (who would later spend seven days in an intensive care unit after contracting COVID-19 at a White House event) replied when asked what he would tell Americans about reopening the economy if he were president. "We sent our young men during World War II over to Europe, out to the Pacific, knowing, knowing that many of them would not come home alive. And we decided to make that sacrifice because what we were standing up for was the American way of life. In the very same way now, we have to stand up for the American way of life."

But the pandemic exposed just how shabbily that vaunted "American way of life" compares to that of other countries. According to census data, more than 10 percent of nonelderly Americans (27.4 million) went through 2020 without health insurance, including many who lost their jobs and whose coverage had been anchored to their employment.[*] That figure in all other industrialized countries, which have the basic guardrails of universal healthcare: 0.0 percent.

Depending on whose data you consult, Americans working from home saw their workdays expand by anywhere from one hour to three, despite a boom in remote work and limited commutes for millions. As for those workers who couldn't work from home, many kept clocking shifts at restaurants, factories, fulfillment warehouses, and other environments where jobs typically don't offer paid sick leave and adequate health precautions and became the highest percentage of COVID casualties by profession. Sure, those performing indispensable functions were sprinkled with nightly applause and "hero pay," small, short-term wage boosts meant to offset dangers that many frontline workers hadn't signed up for. But then the applause died out, the hero pay bumps expired, and we all moved on.

Within a year of the start of the pandemic, the Federal Reserve Bank of Minneapolis reported that 3 million U.S. women had dropped out of the workforce, turning the slow-boil crises around gender pay inequality, childcare policy, and outdated caregiving expectations into an outright grease fire. In December 2021, Congress failed to renew the Child Tax Credit, an expanded tax

---

[*] Research published in *Proceedings of the National Academy of Sciences of the United States of America* suggests that universal healthcare could have saved the lives of more than 338,000 Americans from COVID-19 in the first two years of the pandemic alone. Americans could also have saved more than $105 billion in healthcare costs.

credit that implicitly acknowledged that childcare is work *and* kept 3.7 million U.S. children out of poverty. (The rate of child poverty would jump 41 percent the following month.)

As for the temporarily boosted unemployment benefits by which tens of millions of people including Nakitta Long were sustained during the early months of COVID: When they neared expiration a few short months after they first took effect, a majority of the Senate seemed to take offense at the idea of extending them. Or as Senator Lindsey Graham put it, "I promise you over our dead bodies will this get reauthorized." Their demise helped beget the largest single-year spike in poverty levels in sixty years. By the end of 2020, just a few months later, 8 million Americans had newly fallen into poverty.

Even after a new president took office and a new party took over Congress in 2021, the will to build a permanent, durable safety net out of the tumult and obvious need of the COVID crisis didn't materialize. We had learned nothing. And once a new relief spending spree ended and the last of the stimulus checks were cashed, Americans were left waiting (as they had done before previous recessions, depressions, disasters, and panics) for the next calamity to hit before hastily conceived, tonally disdainful, after-the-fact action could follow.

Simply put, even during the most extreme crisis in nearly a century, the dark, go-it-alone tenet of the American abracadabra won out again. Those who struggled to stay afloat, who had been laid off, who were immunocompromised, who had to remain at home to care for family or double as substitute teachers for their suddenly homebound kids, or who simply wished to avoid exposure to a potentially deadly disease were cast by many as freeloaders who didn't want to work for a living. Despite the precarity of those prevaccine pandemic days, some officials claimed an obligation to *not* help.

To justify this inaction, political and business leaders alike leaned on a timeworn, contested line of thinking that government-provided financial aid created dependency, disincentivized work, and, most paternalistically of all, promoted or supported poor character and a bad work ethic. "If a person is making $23 an hour on unemployment," Graham explained, "it's going to be hard to get you to go back to work for a $17 an hour job." In addition to not addressing the core problem of workers not being paid enough to live, Graham's words echoed those of generations of national leaders, stretching from Thomas Jefferson to Joe Biden.*

Yet back in Winston-Salem, not far from where Graham had grown up, there was Nakitta Long, whose character and work ethic were intact and who had *tried* to fulfill her American Dream before her path went astray. Long had first started work in manufacturing while pushing her way through college and then a master's degree in criminal justice, all while raising her kids. From there, she had planned to go on to law school and earn her JD. "I wanted to be a judge, I wanted to be a lawyer, I wanted to be a police officer," she said, recalling her early career goals during a Bronx childhood that bore witness to a disproportionate share of injustice, neglect, and police brutality. "I wanted to be anybody that was influential in changing the lifestyle of the people that I saw every day."

But when the time came to graduate and look for a job, Long found that her degrees—those vaunted skeleton keys to American dreams—made her a liability. Potential employers told her either that she didn't have enough work experience in the criminal justice field or that she was *too qualified* for entry-level jobs and would probably leave as soon as she found something better. In those rejections, she sometimes detected elements of an unsaid code, an invisible criterion popularly euphemized in HR-speak as being a "cultural fit."

An element of betrayal came embedded in every setback. Long would think back in frustration to the posters that used to line the walls of her high school and many others across the country—you might remember them, the ones that linked educational attainment to certain salary thresholds. She had earned a master's degree and had still never seen $50,000 a year. "I did everything I was supposed to do," Long said of her bind, "and I

---

* In an earlier variation on this theme, then senator Joe Biden cast his vote for the infamous welfare reform bill, titled the Personal Responsibility and Work Opportunity Reconciliation Act of 1996, declaring, "The culture of dependence must be replaced with the culture of self-sufficiency and personal responsibility."

didn't really know at that point where I could fit in. I knew I had to start somewhere, but I kept getting the same responses. I'm like, 'Well, what am I doing wrong? Why is this not simple?'"

Her experience is a small but revealing capsule of a collective national paradox, the unforgiving American way that defines us by our industry and judges us by our achievement while simultaneously making it incredibly difficult to climb the economic ladder. In a country where work and utility dominate life and culture, reducing success and failure into matters of character traps millions of people between abstract ideals and punch-clock realities.

———————

Writing this makes me feel a bit like the most stoned kid on an ultimate Frisbee team, but America isn't what we're told it is. I'm not saying anything that you don't already know. Aided mightily by bad weather and handouts from the French, we fumbled our way into independence despite not having a set goal of nationhood or even a common conception of it. And we've remained a jumble of competing energies and priorities ever since. Observers at least as far back as Alexis de Tocqueville in the early 1800s have noticed the clash between the forces of individualism and conformity in American life and culture. We're now a diverse, self-proclaimed melting pot composed of communities that are increasingly separated or gerrymandered apart by factors like race and income and political ideology. We've had countless chances to make something real and resilient of our opportunities, and we've screwed the pooch on a lot of them. We've also done and continue to do things that make people the world over look on us with hope, admiration, disappointment, and disgust. We remain both utterly predictable and full of surprises.

This book is about the why of all of these phenomena, glories, infuriations, and inconsistencies and what we can do to fix them. In spite of its remarkable staying power, it's not a stretch to suggest that the warm sentiments about the celebrated American way of life have started to cool off a bit. Life expectancy in the United States lags behind that of its counterparts and has even declined in recent years; income inequality remains dangerously high for a functional democracy.

A great reconsideration is under way. The old tropes and reflexive optimism on which generations were brought up have been replaced by bad vibes. A 2023 economic opportunity poll by Gallup found that 39 percent of Americans believed that they were failing to get ahead despite working hard. That figure in 2002: 23 percent. There is a growing sense of dysfunction that can't be masked, regardless of what the stock market or unemployment rate tells us.

As a result, workers have begun to risk more to demand better, and more people than ever have begun to understand how selective opportunity in America has been all along. In the past few years alone, several excellent revisionist histories of the United States have been published, each offering a new way of seeing the trajectory of the country through its thirst for land (Greg Grandin's *The End of the Myth*), its love of wild-eyed conspiracy (Kurt Andersen's *Fantasyland*), or its foundational disdain for Black life (Nikole Hannah-Jones' *The 1619 Project* and Isabel Wilkerson's *Caste*), to name a few. The need for these books, the appetite for them (and the passionate resistance to them, for that matter), come from a shift that's happening beneath our feet. Many of us are newly reckoning with the reality that we've been sold a rotten bill of goods, and for our own sanity, we're trying to understand why. The abracadabra, or the myth that hard work equals destiny, intersects with all these themes. It explains why plenty of people for plenty of good reasons have never bought into the conceit that gumption, moxie, get-up-and-go, whatever, is the secret sauce that powers the big, beautiful American machine.

The germ of this book came from the experience of meeting some classic American success stories while reporting on the culture and history of fast food in America for my first book, *Drive-Thru Dreams*. Driving across the country, I heard the testimonies of store owners, industry titans, and corporate figures who all believed, with unshakable conviction, that they had arrived at their American Dream strictly by the dint of their whatever-it-takes work ethic.

Their decades-old war stories about starting on the fryers

at sixteen for $1.25 an hour and hustling their way up to great wealth were held as articles of faith, even as they cut a strange contrast to the lives of their own current-day employees, many of whom were also tirelessly scrambling—not to win the Horatio Alger Award, bestowed upon those who supposedly rose from nothing, but to barely keep their lives together on minimum wage. (This particular flair for mythmaking, by the way, exists across all industries, not just the one serving two-dollar burgers to a stressed and overworked customer base.)

The truth is that regardless of whether we're high on the hog or low in the sty, we give and have given way too much for this myth. Held against our peer countries, Americans are all but alone in how we work longer hours, take fewer vacations or less time off, move more frequently for opportunity, and retire later in life. It's who we are. In 2023, an astounding 71 percent of Americans listed having a job or career they enjoyed as the top measure of what makes for a fulfilling life, more than close friendships, having children, or marriage. Work, self-determination, the concept of dignity earned, and American exceptionalism compose much of the foundation of our shared identity. When this promise doesn't produce, we don't just float adrift, we head right into danger's way as political opportunists exploit the disillusion.

As has recently become more apparent, the growing distance between our reality and our professed ideals puts everyone at odds, as we've fallen deep into traps of tribalism, xenophobia, racism, despair, conspiracy, and extremism. At least some of those within the hordes of insurrectionists who stormed the Capitol on January 6, 2021, might never have felt compelled to do so had they not been drunk on the belief that others were cutting ahead of them in line. Four years later, the fever still hasn't broken.

———————

All of that said, I'm not here *exclusively* to bum you out. The American way of life and our relationship with it are fluid—and that's what's so fascinating about it! At various points in our history, we've flirted with holding true to our proclaimed principles, only to fall short when it came to uplifting all people. We've created mechanisms to protect workers from harm and exploitation as well as safeguards for the aged and the poor and the sick. We've electrified rural areas and devoted resources toward free high school and local higher education. The Freedmen's Bureau, for example, helped build schools, enforce civil protections, and alleviate poverty and sickness (however briefly) in the aftermath of the Civil War. The GI Bill, though structured by Southern Democrats to be widely exclusive of Black veterans, invested in education, housing, and infrastructure and helped build an imperfect middle class that reliably encompassed the majority of Americans until about a decade ago. (The bill was also a rare, uncamouflaged example of how the government can directly serve and benefit its citizens.)

The battle to live up to our creed has inspired everything from the abolition of slavery to universal suffrage and civil rights. You can tie the imagination that's endemic in the American belief in boundlessness to the first footprints on the moon or the invention of everything from the transistor and the polio vaccine to the Slinky, the Slanket, and the microwave popcorn bag. We've speculated gamely on a hopelessly bright future, selectively advocated for freedom and democracy, and created art, tech, and forms of expression that are beloved the world over.

Warts and all, America has, at times, served as a byword for ingenuity and democratized opportunity. In his book *Travels in Siberia*, the writer Ian Frazier describes being led through the house of his Russian host and encountering a lightless kitchen. "He reached up and screwed the new bulb into the socket," Frazier writes. "After a few twists, the light came on. He turned to us and spread his arms wide, indicating the beams brightly filling the room. *'Ahhh,'* he said, triumphantly. *'Amerika!'*" The American way can inspire once again.

Even as we face some of the direst challenges to our near-term stability and far-term viability, there are people at every level of society devoting their lives to making communities stronger, safer, healthier, and happier. Workers have started to walk away from bad jobs and band together to force the hands of their employers toward a more sustainable reality. This book is about them as well as the very attainable versions of an American future where jobs will fit naturally into the order of life, community strength will outstrip individual destiny, empathy won't be weakness, and work will have dignity.

Ultimately, this is a work of nonfiction that's about a work of semifiction.

Let's get into it.

PART I

THE INSPIRATION

CHAPTER ONE

COLUMBIA

THE BIRTH OF THE AMERICAN ORDER

ONE CANNOT CLAIM THE BIRTHRIGHT
WITHOUT ACCEPTING THE INHERITANCE.

—JAMES BALDWIN

One day in early 2001, according to legend, the comedian Lewis Black was walking down a city street in Houston, Texas, when he came upon a Starbucks. Then and there, an eerie despair set in; the store was sitting directly across the street from another Starbucks.

In his mind, this was an omen that he had reached the edge of civilization. "Go there! Stand between those two Starbucks, look at your watch. Time stands still," he later told crowds in disbelief. "If you turn this way and look, just at one Starbucks, immediately you think, 'You know, when I turn around, there cannot possibly be a Starbucks behind me. No one would have been that stupid to have built a Starbucks across from a Starbucks, and if there was a just and loving God, he wouldn't allow that kind of shit to go down.'"

Whether your outlook is secular, religious, or guided by zodiac signs, plenty of us worry that we've lived to tumble smack into the end of our civilization; the place where the universe ends. In 2021, a Public Religion Research Institute poll found that a majority of Americans said that the "culture and way of life" in the United States have gotten worse since the 1950s. Escalating matters a bit, almost a third of Americans believe in the apocalypse. Across the sweep of U.S. history, various groups have claimed to see signals of end times in things like alcohol, rock music, women's lib, vaccines, or the designated hitter rule. For some, it was the MTV reality show *Jersey Shore* that broke them. For Lewis Black, he felt doomsday vibes in the sterile corporate sameness of an early-aughts American life that had seemingly run headfirst into its own commercial extremes.

Whatever the theory, if there's a subjective end of this universe, it means there must also be a beginning, a place where the cosmography first began to take its distinct form and the story of what followed afterward starts to make a little bit more sense. To understand how the American way first took root, I trekked to St. Croix in the U.S. Virgin Islands. Better known now for its white sand beaches, rum exports, and bioluminescent lagoons, St. Croix holds the historic distinction of being the first place in the present-day United States where any of Christopher Columbus' ships actually landed.*

As it turns out, despite the outsized place of Columbus in America's origin story, his landing spot isn't much of a draw. "The Columbus landing . . . there's not too much to see," Sweeny Toussaint, a local Crucian tour operator, explained when I asked about the popularity of the island's physical link to Columbus. Beyond stray outfits like Celebrity Cruises, which occasionally offers the option to trace the end of Columbus' voyage to St. Croix via kayak as a tacked-on $139 shore excursion, it's not a highly touted attraction. (A pitch from one of the few local businesses promoting the landing spot online felt kind of phoned in: "He stopped in search of fresh water . . . he didn't find any!") In fact, the Columbus landing spot has grown so obscure that it appeared on the very first list of endangered American historical places set forth by the National Trust for Historic Preservation in 1988. Nowadays, vacationers, cruise ship throngs, and Broadway nerds lighting out for St. Croix are more apt to devote precious

---

* Columbus famously never hit the mainland.

holiday time to the island's fixture as the birthplace of Alexander Hamilton, leaving the real Columbus-heads out there to grab their passports and venture to San Salvador, the Bahamian island where the Columbus name can be found on the marquees of museums, beach bars, and a Club Med resort, even on currency.

By now we know that Columbus didn't *discover* America. Moreover, he went to his grave arguing that he had hit the outskirts of the Far East. The reason the United States is known as *America* instead of *Columbia* or something else is because a prominent German mapmaker named it after Amerigo Vespucci, the first acknowledged European explorer to grasp that the faraway grounds that Europeans had just started tripping over in the later 1400s were in fact an entirely separate landmass from Asia. (To be clear, Vespucci didn't *discover* America, either. And the mapmaker had apparently intended only to christen a section of modern-day Brazil with Vespucci's name, but these things have a way of getting out of hand.) Ultimately, the name *America* is a historical fluke in the way that July 4, the day the Declaration of Independence was adopted and sent to the printers, became the national holiday rather than July 2 (the day independence was actually declared) or July 8 (when the declaration was read to the public) or August 2 (when it was finally signed by most of the delegates).

All trivia and pedantic technicalities aside, there are still reasons that Columbus holds such sway in the national mythos. While he didn't achieve much of what he set out to do—discover a western sea route to Asia, amass enough gold for an infinity coin pool, convert everyone to Catholicism—his arrival did change everything. "His voyages were significant because they were the first to become widely known in Europe," Russell Freedman wrote in 2007. "They opened a pathway from the Old World to the New, paving the way for the European conquest and colonization of the Americas, changing life forever on both sides of the Atlantic."

Not one of those things was guaranteed. Columbus' inaugural journey west in 1492 had been skeptically and half-heartedly sponsored by Spain with two measly ships, plus another he'd raised funds for on his own. That mood shifted considerably after he returned to Spain with stolen riches, exotic animals, spices, and kidnapped natives.* For the second expedition, which would briefly bring Columbus' fleet to St. Croix in 1493, he scored seventeen ships and well over a thousand men, including a cadre of padres for conversion efforts.

Continental naming rights may have eluded him, but Columbus secured a legacy arguably more meaningful than that: He "reknit the torn seams of Pangaea," as the historian Alfred W. Crosby argued, setting off a flurry of exploration, trade, and exploitation in the parts of the world previously unknown to Europe. After Columbus, crops and diseases became globalized and far-flung commodity chains were launched. "With the Columbian Exchange," the journalist Charles C. Mann wrote in *1493*, "places that were once ecologically distinct have become more alike. In this sense the world has become one, exactly as the old admiral hoped."

The Columbian Exchange made the known world bigger and smaller at the same time, in terms of the luxuries we now take for granted as well as the cultures and crafts whose origins and histories have been lost. Corn, for example, along with the potatoes often associated with Ireland, the tomatoes we crave in Italian red sauces, and the chocolates we romanticize as Swiss, were all grown exclusively in the Americas before they made their way abroad to become cures for famine or sadness. The coffee beans that make up the base layer of the syrupy, 2,200-calorie drinks served at Starbucks stores directly across the street from each other originated in Africa and came here through the pathways of commercial trade and settlement that exploded following Columbus' return to Spain. As for the underpaid baristas customizing those finicky drink orders, they're the downstream result of an enduring connection between cheap human labor and profit

* Historians rightly love to link Columbus' voyages with Johannes Gutenberg, who, fifty years earlier, had invented the first known printing press (in Europe, at least). Printing presses would disseminate tales of Columbus' travels as well as the religious edicts and political texts that were often used to justify the horrors in the Americas that followed.

making that made its way west to the Americas from Europe in that era.

National histories tend to steer us toward what gets found and built, rather than what gets lost and disinherited. One long-standing estimate of the total population of the Americas at the time of Columbus' voyages was 75 million people, significantly larger than the 60 million or so who were thought to live in Europe. The calamine myth of an empty, primitive New World doesn't hold up to scrutiny.

Walking around the Columbus landing point in St. Croix, I passed markers chronicling the artifacts of pre-Columbian societies there that have been unearthed on the island in the last century alone: a court for civic gatherings marked with petroglyphs, a place of worship, a burial site to honor the dead. The groups who lived on the island prior to Columbus' arrival had created rituals to resolve their disputes and built intricate irrigation systems for farming. (Columbus, by the way, never saw those; he didn't leave the ship.)

Near the landing point, I looked out at the Cape of Arrows, which got its name after the local Carib population encountered the well-armed expedition from Columbus' ships in the water and launched a fusillade of poison-spiked arrows at them. "Columbus got his heinie handed to him," Ralph Simpson, a Crucian local and retired naval officer, later told me at a bar. Though minor and not well known, the scrap at the Cape of Arrows carries a big symbolic weight. It was the first documented skirmish between the people of Europe and those of the Americas. The fight cuts against the perception that the Indigenous populations encountered by European voyagers or settlers were compliant or subservient or in search of help or enlightenment. "This is part of history that's not always told," Celeste Fahie, a local academic, told me, "but it's true."

Like those of many of the kingdoms, tribes, villages, and nations across the Caribbean and the Americas, the world of the Indigenous people of St. Croix would be dissolved—quickly, by disease and forced labor, and slowly, through foreign domination of Indigenous women and bloodlines. After Columbus, European speculators would establish colonies and build sprawling sugar and tobacco plantations across the region that, like those in the fields of America's first permanent English settlement in Jamestown, Virginia, they were too weak, too fancy, too aristocratic, or too untrained to work themselves. "A startlingly large proportion of the colonists were gentlemen," Charles C. Mann wrote of the settlers of Jamestown, "a status defined by not having to perform manual labor." Lacking a bench of able workers and indentured servants, the colonists traded for or imported enslaved people and forced them to produce the cash crops in order to make the colonies profitable. And so began a catastrophic, world-shaping system of abuse.

———————

Somewhere in the Pantheon of Historic Understatements, sentences like this are etched into the marble: The transatlantic slave trade endures as one of the most incomprehensible historical cruelties—not just of staggering depth and atrocity and criminality but of dispassion, velocity, and repetition. Between 1600 and 1800, around 2.5 million African men, women, and children were forced to British America, while about 1 million Europeans arrived during the same time period as immigrants and settlers. (Altogether, that first figure comprises only about a fifth of the 12.5 million people thought to be captured and sent west by the countries involved in the slave trade.) One outcome was a ubiquity of enslaved people in America. In 1860, the enslaved population made up nearly a third of the population of Virginia, the place where, in 1619, roughly twenty African people had first arrived on the mainland of the continent in bondage on a privateer called the *White Lion*. In Mississippi and South Carolina, the ranks of the enslaved reached 55 and 57 percent of the total population, respectively.

Numbers like these seed a larger truth about slavery in America: despite often being localized to the plantations of the southern United States in popular imagination, the institution thrived nearly everywhere. Massachusetts was the first British colony to legalize slavery, while many across the North (including several members of Congress) legally held and exploited captive populations well into the mid-1800s.

Moreover, slavery cut furrows across the entire economic landscape, enmeshing and entangling itself in markets and communities the world over. Nearly half of the wealth in colonial New England, for example, came from the sugar produced by workers enslaved in the Caribbean, where islands like Cuba and St. Croix were standout producers. As the sociologist Matthew Desmond noted, enslaved workers were calculated as assets by their captors, assets whose collective value at one point in the 1800s "exceeded that of all the railroads and factories in the nation." Thomas Jefferson financed his fabled Monticello homestead by mortgaging 150 of his enslaved workers.

Following early pursuits of profit in gold and sugar and tobacco, the rise of the cotton economy in the United States created a special class of southern enslavers who would become wealthy beyond reason; in 1860, as the country tumbled toward civil war, there were more millionaires per capita in the Mississippi Valley than anywhere else in the United States. But cotton also fueled the fortunes of an unknowable number of textile mill owners in the North and abroad. (It's poignant that Simon Legree, the sadistic cotton plantation owner in Harriet Beecher Stowe's influential novel *Uncle Tom's Cabin*, hailed from the North, where "the unchristian prejudice . . . is an oppressor almost equally severe.")

In short, whatever distortions or deflections exist about the geography or reach of slavery in America, they tend to collapse spectacularly in the details. "It is uncanny, but perhaps predictable," the historian Tiya Miles wrote about the nation's financial center, "that the original wall for which Wall Street is named was built by the enslaved at a site that served as the city's first organized slave auction." Indeed, Lower Manhattan's piers, now popular for raves, bike paths, and tourist cruises, once hosted a sprawling slave port, and in 1730, the percentage of New Yorkers who held enslaved people was second only to Charleston, South Carolina.

Through a wider aperture like this, it's easier to connect the line running from the imperial speculators who followed Columbus west to the predators and dealers of the modern U.S. economy. Both models involve a select few leveraging power over the vulnerable and extracting profits from the poor, often without getting their own hands physically dirty.

On some level, this through line is easy to follow. After the Civil War, the dark horrors of slavery transformed into atomizing forces such as Jim Crow and economic exclusion, redlining and housing discrimination, disinvestment and mass incarceration. As recently as 2019, a majority of Americans (63 percent) acknowledged that the legacy of slavery still affects Black Americans.

And though we may acknowledge that fact, we avoid grappling with it effectively as a country. A single, damning statistic—that, in 2022, for example, the median wealth of white households in the United States was $285,000, compared to $44,900 for their Black counterparts—has the power to make plenty of us shift defensively in our seats, switch the station, or close the tab. Policies that would address the long-standing imbalance of opportunity are regularly met with fury. Advocating for a national monument dedicated to the horrors of American slavery, the writer Clint Smith explained that while the institution lasted for a total of 250 years, including the time of British rule, it has only *not existed* in the United States for about 160 years. "So you have an institution that existed for almost a century longer than it hasn't, an institution that was so economically, socially, politically entrenched in the founding of this country."

Every nation struggles in its own way to reconcile its past, but there are profound reasons why the American fuse is so short when it comes to the sins of slavery and its stubborn vestiges: the legacy strikes forcefully against the idea of the United States as a self-made country built and sustained by self-made people. George Washington, celebrated for his virtue and humble ambition, set the (mostly upheld) democratic precedent of relinquishing power. But he was also the first of at least eight presidents to rely on slave labor while serving in office.

The lasting social and structural imbalances in American life also make our perpetual worship of the odds-defying achievers in national culture look hollow. "Our journey has never been one of shortcuts or settling for less," President Barack Obama argued at his 2009 inauguration in the city named for Washington in the district named for Columbus. "It has not been the path for the faint-hearted, for those that prefer leisure over work, or seek only the pleasures of riches and fame. Rather, it has been the risk-takers, the doers, the makers of things . . . who have carried us up the long, rugged path towards prosperity and freedom." In this telling of the American story, the bold and industrious tend not to cast many shadows on their way to the top.

Or maybe the biggest reason we flinch at the counterevidence to our blameless greatness is because, unlike the Old World, America came alive singing paeans to liberty, fairness, and universalist principles. And cutting against the foundational American themes of freedom and hard work will never be popular, whether in once-segregated schoolrooms or in the White House and the Capitol, two buildings constructed in part by the hands of two hundred enslaved workers.

Not only can we connect our modern, messy relationship with work to what Columbus' arrival wrought, but his biography also plucks at some timeless American themes that we love to uphold. By most scholarly accounts, Columbus came up in Genoa, humbly and separate from the city-state's swaggering merchant stock; in other words, he was a striver and outsider in one of the wealthiest cities in the world. "He was also a weaver's son with ambitions to outdo his father and bequeath his sons not only money but also a title," the historian Carrie Gibson put it in *Empire's Crossroads*.

The streets of Genoa were filled with traders and enslaved people of all backgrounds and origins and suffused with tall tales about the far-flung voyages of its most famous prisoner of war, Marco Polo. Being a mariner in Columbus' time was on trend, akin to being an airline pilot in the 1950s or a depressive singer-songwriter in 2005. His long-nurtured dream of finding a new route across the ocean blue to the treasures of Asia—dismissed as crazy by nearly all the courts of Europe—wouldn't sound out of step with the poetry of the American frontier and the gold rushes. (Nor would Columbus' horny madness for wealth and status and his go-it-alone willingness to risk it all.)

All of those refrains—Columbus' modest roots and underdog endeavoring, his steadfast self-belief in the face of constant rejection, his unrelenting faith and determination, his hazarding of everything to face down the unknown of uncharted spaces—fasten neatly into the national culture that materialized on the other side of the ocean. That various royal establishments thought his nautical calculations were bunk or that everyone believed the Atlantic Ocean was full of monsters and enormous ship-crushing crabs or that his Spanish crew deeply distrusted and disliked him because he was a foreigner (and an ill-tempered redhead to boot) only enhance the mystique.

Those ideals have carried all the way through to present day. In 1803, exactly three centuries after Columbus was muddling through his final voyage west, the Louisiana Purchase was finalized. The deal would double the size of the United States, expand slavery, and send hordes of reckless, desperate, fortune-seeking speculators adventuring westward into already inhabited lands. A hundred years later, the biggest literary sensation was Jack London's 1903 novel *The Call of the Wild*, a book about a sweet, domesticated Scotch Collie mix that transforms into a murderous alpha dog in the middle of a gold rush. And a century after that, in 2003, the rapper 50 Cent's classic *Get Rich or Die Tryin'* became the runaway bestselling album of the year. Columbus' westward gambit typified the type of moon shot thinking that has fueled human flight, world-shaping innovation, and, more recently, the mass burning of venture capital cash piles in Silicon Valley over unproven concepts with unconsidered consequences.

———————

America's curious case of Columbus Mania didn't fully crystallize until it came time for the colonies to break away from their stifling British overlords. Ahead of the revolution, Columbus began to inhabit a heroic symbol of the New World, an enlightened place that aspired (well, sort of) to be free of the old European repressions. The term *Columbia* started to appear as a shorthand for the colonies in popular poetry.*

After winning independence, "Americans were actively looking to create a new shared national identity that would distinguish them culturally from the former mother country," the historian Michael D. Hattem wrote. "One historian has described this process as 'unbecoming British' and the memory of Columbus played an important role." In New York, the prestigious King's College changed its name to Columbia University in 1784. And with the arrival of the three hundredth anniversary of Columbus' voyage in 1792, public campaigns in the young country would contort Columbus from a symbolic voyager into America's actual *discoverer*. And the idea stuck.

"The strength of the Columbus symbol lies in its pliability," the historian Timothy Kubal argued in a book about American national memory. And since the revolution, Columbus has served many unlikely and even competing functions as a national emblem. Many celebrations of Columbus in the United States were organized, at least partially, to defend against the rampant discrimination faced by Italian immigrants and Italian Americans, who were disparaged as secretly loyal to the pope and often faced exclusion, bigotry, and violence.[†] A few of the many other diasporic groups to dubiously claim him as their own in America include Greeks, Poles, Spaniards, and Portuguese. (As a kid in Hebrew school, I was introduced to the theory that Columbus might be Jewish, an idea perhaps buttressed by the fact that he got lost easily and was exceedingly determined to outshine his father.) There's a powerful subtext here: for some, to have Columbus in your tribe provided a glimmer of social acceptance in America.

By 1892, four hundred years after his first voyage, Columbus had mutated into a symbol of assimilation. On New Year's Day

---

* "Fix'd are the eyes of nations on the scales, / For in their hopes Columbia's arm prevails," the formerly enslaved poet Phillis Wheatley wrote in a tribute received by George Washington in 1775. (Honored by her words, Washington wrote back, and the two later met IRL.)

† In 1899, for example, *The New York Sun* cited an unspoken rule of the South, in which "white men could not be lynched—with the exception of the Italian."

1892, Ellis Island opened its doors to handle the growing waves of new immigrants alighting at New York Harbor. The immigrant boom had inspired a nativist backlash, and so, in July, President Benjamin Harrison created the first national Columbian-themed celebration, which would merge Columbus ("the pioneer of progress and enlightenment") and patriotism ("the great achievements of the four completed centuries of American life"). With credit for discovering America now a "settled fact"—Harrison's presidential proclamation was titled "400th Anniversary of the Discovery of America by Columbus," after all—he decreed, "Let the national flag float over every schoolhouse in the country and the exercises be such as shall impress upon our youth the patriotic duties of American citizenship."[*]

As the first Columbus national celebration approached, churches, local governments, and civic groups planned their ceremonies. Schools began to install American flags and institute the regular reciting of the Pledge of Allegiance, which had been written by a Baptist minister and socialist named Francis Bellamy with the four hundredth anniversary and the need "to assimilate . . . children to an American standard of life and ideas" in mind.[†] Over at Thomas Jefferson's historic home at Monticello, the newly founded Daughters of the American Revolution, created to flaunt its genealogical links to America's founders, put on a colonial ball in Columbus' honor.

The grand mother of all Columbus Day celebrations took place in New York City, where forty thousand men in military uniform marched, along with nearly twenty thousand children from the city's schools, including its public schools and Catholic parochial academies, secular and Italian colleges, and a Hebrew

---

[*] Harrison's motives for boosting Columbus were also diplomatic in nature. One year before, in 1891, eleven Italian Americans and Italian immigrants, who had been accused and mostly acquitted of killing the police chief of New Orleans, had been murdered when a mob led by civic leaders had stormed the jail where they were being held. The episode, the largest lynching in American history, was met with wide approval in the national press and caused the United States and Italy to break off relations and even talk of war.

[†] Conveniently enough, the magazine that published Bellamy's pledge just happened to sell American flags as well.

orphan asylum, as well as "300 marching Indian boys and 50 tall Indian girls" from a Native American boarding school in Pennsylvania. A flotilla of warships paraded down the Hudson while the vice president, governor, and New York's mayor looked on and "smoked incessantly." Bandwagons and themed floats celebrating music, electricity, the cosmos, science, and the oceans passed through the city as crowds packed the streets and windows overhead. A rider dressed as Columbus waved an American flag while, bringing up the rear, came a thousand people attired in "the regulation, every-day, stage style of Indian costume, with red blankets, painted faces, and feathered head gear." *The New York Times* pronounced the estimated 1 million spectators to be "the greatest crowd New York ever held."[*] Throughout the country, statues of Columbus would be cast, set, and unveiled, including the landmark that still stands near Central Park in New York, seventy-six feet tall, with the marble mariner staring defiantly in the direction of the West 59th Street Starbucks, just across Columbus Circle from yet another Starbucks.

––––––––––

The whiplash over Columbus remains a decent barometer of America's evolving social disorder. When Columbus morphed into a nineteenth-century folk hero, nativist forces pushed back and promoted the lily-white Nordic beefcake and explorer Leif Erikson as rightful holder of the title of America's discoverer, even though he obviously didn't discover America, either. "The celebration of Erikson," the historian and journalist Yoni Appelbaum has noted, "often crossed over into explicit denigration of Catholics in general, and of Columbus in particular." In the mid-1930s, the Knights of Columbus, a Roman Catholic organization, successfully lobbied President Franklin D. Roosevelt to create a federal holiday for Columbus. Nevertheless, a few short years

––––––––––

[*] One conspicuous absence was President Harrison, who missed the event because his wife, Caroline, was ailing with a terminal case of tuberculosis. Former president Grover Cleveland, whom Harrison had beaten, attended and, the following month, would become the first and possibly only president to be elected to nonconsecutive terms.

later, during World War II, Roosevelt would designate masses of
Italian immigrants and Americans of Italian descent as "enemy
aliens," with thousands forcibly relocated and hundreds placed in
internment camps.* In a Columbus Day proclamation weeks after
the 1969 moon landing, President Richard Nixon, who had once
privately sneered that Italians "don't have their heads screwed on
tight," honored the feats of both Columbus and the astronauts as
"expressions of man's great ambition to confront the unknown,
and to master the challenges of distance and space."

By 1992, the five hundredth anniversary of his first voyage, grunge-era reassessments of American life and institutions
had begun targeting the legacy of Columbus for greater scrutiny. In communities around the country, Columbus Day had
been replaced by Indigenous Peoples' Day (Berkeley, California), Native American Day (South Dakota), or Discoverers' Day
(Hawaii). Yet at the same time, the U.S. Mint, never known for
its aesthetic restraint, issued more than a million commemora-
tive coins for the Columbus quincentenary that displayed him
posing nobly beside a globe on the front side and a bifurcated
mash-up of the *Santa Maria* caravel and space shuttle *Discovery*
on the back.

Even recently, the rickety themes of enlightenment in Columbus' voyage remain a useful way to rail against outdated thinking.
Speaking on the stump in 2012, President Barack Obama used
Columbus to pillory political opponents of alternative energy.
"Let me tell you something," he began. "If some of these folks
were around when Columbus set sail"—he trailed off into a the-
atrical shrug—"they probably must have been founding members of the flat earth society. They would not believe that the
world was round."

Clever though it was, that bit of political theater preserved
the popular myth of Columbus as a rational heretic who had

---

* In one ill-famed 1942 case, a man named Giuseppe DiMaggio was designated as an
enemy alien, banned from working the San Francisco docks, and had his fishing boat
seized by the government. One year later, his son, New York Yankees slugger Joe
DiMaggio, sat out the first of three seasons during his playing prime to serve as one
of the 500,000-plus Italian Americans in the U.S. armed forces during World War II.

embarked on his voyage to prove that the earth was round, even though most educated people in his time had known for centuries that it wasn't flat. A fascinating 2014 project by Professor Christina M. Desai dissected the stubborn survival of this narrative in contemporary children's books about Columbus, where the triumphal myth of Columbus proving the flat-earthers wrong is still favored over the truths about his real transactional motives. "Powerful interests," she lamented, ". . . can more easily abuse power when citizens accept inequalities and fail to think critically about their history or insist on its ideals."

Ultimately, it's a lose-lose deal to adopt Columbus as a symbol of freedom from British repression, of American social and scientific progress, or, for certain groups, as a shield against oppression and racist omission. After all, his success came at the expense and misfortune of countless others. "It is difficult to grapple with the complete accomplishments of individuals and also the costs of what those accomplishments came at," Mandy Van Heuvelen, a member of Cheyenne River Sioux Tribe in South Dakota, once explained of the Columbus dilemma and, by extension, the American one.

One feature of the great social upheaval of the past several years is not that some are *finally* seeing the brutality of what Columbus did or set in motion but that some are very slowly starting to reckon with how these features still exist in everyday life. It's neither a simple nor a straightforward truth to absorb. "For generations, Federal policies systematically sought to assimilate and displace Native people and eradicate Native cultures," President Joe Biden offered in the first-ever presidential proclamation of Indigenous Peoples' Day in October 2021. "It is a measure of our greatness as a nation," he added in a Columbus Day proclamation on the same day, "that we do not seek to bury these shameful episodes of our past—that we face them honestly, we bring them to the light, and we do all we can to address them." Though Biden kept the federal Columbus Day holiday intact, his statement was a surreal departure from President Donald Trump, who, in a proclamation issued 364 days earlier, had directed the government "to root out the teaching of racially divisive concepts from the Federal workplace, many of which are grounded in the same type of revisionist history that is trying to erase Christopher Columbus from our national heritage."

Nearly 250 years after declaring independence, we're nowhere close to sorting out how to handle the particulars of Columbus or the paradoxes of our founding. It's telling that Columbus and Indigenous Peoples share a joint holiday in some cities (not to mention that in at least two states, Martin Luther King, Jr., and Robert E. Lee share another).

I'd argue that the most American interpretation of Columbus Day isn't about the who (Columbus or gold-hungry Europe) or the where (the Western Hemisphere) but the what. Eclipsed lately by sales on fall fashion and direct-to-consumer mattresses, Columbus Day was initially established to memorialize an act, a professional deed, the fulfillment of a contracted goal. "It sometimes gets overlooked in current discussions that we neither commemorate Columbus' birthday (as was the practice for Presidents Washington and Lincoln, and as we now do with Martin Luther King, Jr.) nor his death date (which is when Christian saints are memorialized)," William J. Connell noted in *The American Scholar*. Instead, we mark Columbus Day around the date of his first western landfall in October 1492. Neither saint nor hero, Columbus represents a striver for whom the journey was meaningless without the destination.

CHAPTER TWO

EXCEPTIONAL AND EXCEPTIONALLY VAGUE

THE DANGERS OF A SAFE FOUNDING STORY

IT SAYS HERE IN THIS HISTORY BOOK THAT LUCKILY, THE GOOD GUYS
HAVE WON EVERY SINGLE TIME. WHAT ARE THE ODDS?

—NORM MACDONALD

From Sigmund Freud, Frida Kahlo, and Simone de Beauvoir to Jawaharlal Nehru, Nelson Mandela, and the Marquis de Lafayette, a long line of foreign observers has aired fascinating (and often devastating) impressions of what they've seen of American life. "I never knew what it was to feel disgust and contempt," Charles Dickens humbugged, "'till I travelled in America." For my two pence, though, former British prime minister Margaret Thatcher had one of the better insights when she offered that "No other nation has been built upon an idea—the idea of liberty." America's European counterparts, she added, were different. "They are the product of history and not of philosophy."

To be the product of an idea, of course, is incredibly flattering, especially an idea as stirring as liberty. But it *is* vague. While other countries have their shared histories, religions, cultures, rituals, and languages, the United States—even if it was founded on an idea—has never had just one prevailing philosophy.

Even when it came to breaking away from the British (sorry, Maggie), the colonists didn't characterize it as a revolution. In two excellent histories of the era, Robert Parkinson and Joseph J. Ellis used the imprecise titles "The Common Cause" and "The Cause," respectively—two of the most common terms used in the colonies around the time of the revolution, because the resistance against the British had so many different motivations and animating factors among those who supported it. Among the many, many reasons for supporting the Cause: the desire to have full rights as English citizens restored, the desire to have a European-style confederation of independent states, the Columbian desire to speculate and conquer Native American lands west of the Appalachian rim, the (selective) desire for access to universal rights, the desire to preserve slavery, the desire not to be taxed by a condescending Parliament three thousand miles away in London, the desire to end the British occupation of Boston— you get the picture.

Still, despite this wide-ranging spectrum of desires, many future Americans wanted absolutely nothing at all to do with the Cause. Citing John Adams in her book *Liberty's Exiles*, the historian Maya Jasanoff notes that for all the fun "Spirit of '76" language in the national public memory, only about one-third of future Americans actually supported the revolution; the remainder were fairly evenly split between opposition and neutrality. Even Benjamin "American Prometheus" Franklin, who goaded the French to join the war and then ran circles around the British in postwar negotiations, had a loyalist son, William.*

When the war was ultimately won, victory came not from the efforts of a united front but from the fractious combination of a federal fighting force (the Continental Army), the French, and a pu pu platter of militias and local forces (the Minutemen and the Green Mountain Boys, to name two), sometimes fighting in their own backyards, all with their own motivations. And almost immediately after independence was settled, a debate began over which group deserved most credit and honor for defeating the

* So deep was their rift that when William Franklin, who served as New Jersey's royal governor (and as a rat for the British), was set to be arrested by colonial militia, his father did nothing to help him. Near the end of the war, the younger Franklin, who had settled in the heavily Loyalist enclave of New York City, would set sail for Great Britain and never come back.

British. That debate is still carried on today, albeit mostly in academic circles and by uncles at certain holiday dinner tables, and in the related arguments over the appropriate balance of power between federal and local bodies.

———————

Depending upon when and where you grew up, this bizarre, variegated tale of U.S. independence may stray significantly from the smooth, cohesive, muskets-and-grit, liberty-minded rendering of the founding story you were brought up on. (Having taken U.S. history classes in late-nineties Texas, it certainly does for me!) But rather than think of this disunity as something that weakens or undermines or betrays the American story, I wondered what meaning and use could be taken from the less tidy version, especially as it relates to our modern conflict over work and opportunity.

To help me out, I called Dr. Richard Bell, a professor of American history at the University of Maryland. Bell, who grew up in England, was inspired as a young student at Oxford to make U.S. history the focus of his work by some of the very same bottom-up sensibilities of the founding. "I came to American history," he told me, "because I was attracted by the ability of historians to look beyond presidents and generals and people on pedestals and offer a vision of change in American history that was driven by ordinary people." In that spirit of shared exertion, he told me that some of his insights had drawn from a broad body of scholarship beyond his own.*

We began with the dominant account of America's founding. "I would argue that the popular narrative—that this was a broad and cohering coalition of all Americans in a joint struggle against external tyranny—is mythology," Bell said. "Romantic, self-serving mythology."

Obviously, the United States isn't the only country to lean toward a heroic, blemish-free Noxzema commercial of a creation

———————

* He also made a request: "If you end up using anything I say, I hope that you don't make me sound like a dick."

story. The writer Joseph Campbell once described the seductive nature of myth in universal terms as "the depersonalized dream," something more of psychology than actual history. But even if you chose to ignore or play down the darkest motivations that drove some to the Cause, the baseline creation story of the United States still isn't wholly inspirational.

In the scheme of things, for example, it's still a bitter pill to swallow that George Washington spent an excruciating amount of time during the war writing unheeded letters and circulars to the Continental Congress and others begging and pleading to get the states to pony up money to support his malnourished, underequipped, poorly paid army. But that was exactly what happened, and the independence effort, at a few points, nearly fell apart because of it. "We had in Camp," he wrote in one entreaty from the infamous encampment at Valley Forge, ". . . not less than 2898 men unfit for duty, by reason of their being barefoot and otherwise naked."*

Sacrifice in the face of avoidable hardship is just one aspect of the revolution that feels particularly resonant today. Another was the brutal work done by those hoping to overcome their circumstances. Some of Washington's most trusted and highly decorated officers were "low-born" men like Nathanael Greene and Henry Knox, who ascended the ranks through their competence and valor. "Most were working-class Americans—blacksmiths, carpenters, artisans, wagon masters, itinerant laborers," the historian Joseph J. Ellis wrote of Washington's soldiers. "Many were recently arrived immigrants from Ireland and Scotland, indentured servants, and ex-slaves." Meanwhile, farmers made up much of the local militias. (At the same time, Washington and his fellow colonists were fighting an army led by wealthy British officers who'd been bestowed with higher ranks because of their bloodlines and status, an army also aided by Hessian troops, who, despite being cast as "mercenaries" in popular history, were by and large considered to be the property of the German nations that sold them into service for profit.)

---

* Within months, a full third of the camp would be lost to disease, desertion, malnutrition, and exposure.

In 1782, the heroic deeds of those humble, low-ranking striv-
ers would be given their due by Washington through the creation
of the Badge of Military Merit. The honor, which was available
only to privates and noncommissioned officers, came in the form
of purple cloth cut into the shape of a heart and embroidered
with leaves and the word MERIT; it would become the country's
oldest military decoration. "The road to glory in a patriot army
and a free country is thus open to all," Washington's order read.
The gesture epitomized the democratic themes of the Cause
that, though undoubtedly ironic, inconsistent, and incomplete,
would soon inspire revolutions and reforms across Europe and
the Americas.

As we work to understand why current-day American life feels
so overwrought and contentious and to solve what ails us, it's
helpful to recast the founding story. The reality that the independence movement had dissonant and outright evil features saves
us from the collective burden of being beholden to some idealized past era in which everything made perfect logical and moral
sense—or that our understanding of history is fully reconciled.
For every overdue tribute to William Lee, George Washington's
enslaved valet and indispensable confidant, and the numberless
lesser-known heroes of the Revolution, there are stories like
that of Harry Washington, a man enslaved by George Washington at Mount Vernon, who would become one of the twenty-
five-thousand-plus captive Americans to flee to freedom behind
British lines rather than waiting to see what promise American
independence might hold.

To reckon with the political and ideological turbulence of
America's formation also chips away at the grief that the seemingly "unprecedented" times we're in are not all that unprecedented. We've always had social divisiveness, inequality, racism,
and the big, troublesome themes of the founding have real valence
in the here and now. "The American Revolution is driven by a
patriot movement that itself is a very uneasy bundle of interests
and coalitions," Bell explained. "I think class or social-economic

background is an important marker of divisions and tensions within the patriot movement in the American Revolution. I think the rural-urban divide, I think North versus South, I think merchants versus farmers, debtors versus creditors, workers versus employers, are all important markers of division within the patriot movement." Sound familiar?

In this framework, the sources of internal tension in the early fight for America don't really sound all that different from the sources of internal tension that plague modern America. "It's a small miracle that this coalition cohered in a significant way and for long enough to achieve the sort of political and military outcomes that were eventually delivered," Bell noted of the fractious groups within the Cause.

In other words, if a bunch of strangers who distrusted or didn't understand one another managed to defeat an empire with a little help from their friends and (eventually) slap together a working basis for governance back then, maybe we can, at minimum, get to the bottom of why we need an entirely different set of insurance for our teeth today.

Nearly 250 years later, it should be a slightly liberating truth that we're still fastened to the sloppy fallout from our founding. An enormous part of that has to do with the reality that the United States was forged in an oppositional posture, a rebellion fueled by people knowing what they didn't want perhaps more than knowing what they did. The colonies were vastly unlike one another, with different economies, religious affiliations, and historic folkways. Attitudes among colonists varied wildly about everything from war to territorial expansion, abolition, religious freedom, and women's rights, which made coherence and unanimity elusive. John Dickinson, the self-branded Quaker farmer and founder who is often credited with coining the name "The United States of America," fretted that the colonies had little in common beyond hatred of the British. "Every other aspect," he said, "presents to me an Ocean perpetually tempestuous without Bottom and without Shore."

Dickinson's forecast would bear out in fascinating ways following independence. *E pluribus unum* (Out of many, one) may have been approved by Congress as a unity-themed motto on the Great Seal in 1782,* but it would be decades before the word *nation* entered into popular use in the place of *union*. Poignantly enough, it would take a civil war for that to happen. Writing in *Prologue*, the magazine of the National Archives, James M. McPherson explained that "in his first message to Congress on July 4, 1861, Lincoln used the word Union 32 times and nation only three times. But in his Gettysburg Address in November 1863, he did not mention the Union at all, but spoke of the nation five times to invoke a new birth of freedom and nationhood."

More theatrically yet, the United States didn't refer to itself as one body with one voice for generations after the founding. "The United States is considered a plural entity rather than a singular entity," Bell explained. "They would say, 'The United States *are* proclaiming that they are against the war with France' rather than 'The United States *is* proclaiming that it is against the war with France.' So for a long time, the United States was considered the plural collective entity."

Though it's certainly nice that the United States has cozied itself into a singular entity in the sense of its grammatical identity, the battles over who gets to claim the country's "real" voice or who is a "real" American remain vicious quirks of national life. At least some of that, too, goes back to our founding days, when many of the frictions, biases, and paranoias were initially fixed into place. Through our system of checks and balances, the airing of arguments in open court and in a free press, the indirect election of senators and presidents, the quick rise of political parties, and, as AM talk radio hosts remind us way too often, an independence document that asserted the right to rebel, the table was set for a very tense and inefficient family cookout.

Again, not all of the innovations were bad! The Constitution enshrined the consent of the governed, which meant that government power came from its citizens. Meanwhile, federalism theoretically gave Americans across wide territories equal say (with *huge*, obvious, notable exceptions). That the United States banned titles of nobility and separated religion from governance was unprecedented in how it diverged from the stuffy Old World ways.

---

* Adorably, the motto contains one Latin letter for each of the thirteen colonies.

But the problem of being bound by a vague philosophy of liberty never went away. Even the crankiest of historians agree that American unity only ever hits its apexes when there's a common foe, whether it's the Kaiser, the Axis powers, the Soviets, al-Qaeda, or the writer of the final episode of *The Sopranos*. Someday, when a blockbuster Broadway musical is made about the life of John Adams, there's going to be a whole number dedicated to the moment when Adams is asked who contributed most to America's independence and he responds, "King George."

The result of this fundamental ambiguity is that there's no shared vision of what the United States should be. And there's never been one. America's establishing documents are a poetic mishmash of vagaries. All the lofty phrases and lack of specifics are the concession-heavy outcomes of several anguished processes. Depicting the country's first constitution in *These Truths*, the historian Jill Lepore wrote, "the final Articles of Confederation are more like a peace treaty, establishing a defensive alliance among sovereign states, than a constitution, establishing a system of government." Even after the Articles of Confederation were scrapped, many big questions remained unanswered in the Constitution. As Bell told me, "On many important issues, the framers simply kick the can down the road rather than taking a clear stance." And so it was practically a guarantee that disputes over the critical points of contention would boil over or that new issues—whether slavery, women's suffrage, civil rights, the desire of nonlandholders to vote, deindustrialization, or looming environmental catastrophe—would become the centerpieces of popular movements and require urgent attention.*

The United States has the oldest operating constitution in the world, and at the end of the day, its creakiness shows. Its most recent amendments, the twenty-sixth (which set the voting age at eighteen) and twenty-seventh (which set a timetable for congressional pay raises), were inspired by events occurring during the 1940s and the 1780s, respectively. And while life on Earth has become wholly unrecognizable in the past eighty-plus

---

* Some founders sensed those limitations; Thomas Jefferson once suggested that the United States create a brand-new Constitution every nineteen years.

years, Americans are still scuffling over the country's kludgy original terms of service, rather than coming together to solve problems. Two law professors, Ryan D. Doerfler and Samuel Moyn, recently put this much more eloquently: "It has exacted a terrible price in distortion and distraction to transform our national life into a contest over reinterpreting our founding charter consistently with what majorities believe now."

———————

In the absence of meaningful movement, a sorry status quo remains intact; the deadlock and dysfunction and violence of recent years seem like pretty clear indications of a coming breaking point. "Our myths have not served us well," Nikole Hannah-Jones argues early in *The 1619 Project*, a recasting of the American story that was both celebrated by critics and scholars and castigated as "hateful" and banned from schools in various states. "We are the most unequal of the Western democracies. We incarcerate our citizens at the highest rates. We suffer the greatest income inequality. Americans' life spans are shorter than those of the people in the nations we compare ourselves to." (Our inequities and inefficiencies also extend to the countries we usually *don't* compare ourselves to. In 2023, the United States fell to forty-sixth in the World Economic Forum's wide-ranging gender opportunity index, behind countries such as Barundi, Peru, Slovenia, Jamaica, Mozambique, Moldova, and Rwanda.)

What's more, if our myths were true, if the abracadabra had done its magic, we simply wouldn't be where we are. It doesn't take a well-constructed historical counternarrative to show that; the existing language we already use to convey values of hard work and opportunity does it for us. The word *meritocracy* was born out of social satire from the late 1950s. The phrase *American exceptionalism*, by more than a few accounts, originated with Soviet dictator Josef Stalin, of all people, as a dig at the character and economic structure of the United States. The term *bootstrapping*, used in politics and corporate culture to describe the act of self-leveraging, was originally intended as a joke because, well, to pull oneself up by one's bootstraps is a physical impossibility.

The embiggening concept of *rugged individualism* was coined by Herbert Hoover just a year before the Great Depression would render tens of millions of people homeless and hungry. Then there's the *American Dream*, that squishy and most charismatic phrase, which originated with a wealthy academic living abroad in London during the Great Depression. (And that's not even getting into *the pursuit of happiness*, an eleventh-hour edit from *the pursuit of property* in the Declaration of Independence.)

The messages continue to get muddled across the culture. Greed, at the end of the movie *Wall Street*, turned out not to be good. "I love the smell of napalm in the morning" maybe shouldn't be the takeaway line from *Apocalypse Now*. Not to be a schmuck about it, but despite its regular appearance in graduation speeches and ads for financial firms and job search engines, Robert Frost's ever-misinterpreted poem "The Road Not Taken" isn't about individual destiny and intrepid self-assertion, it's about the childish nature of self-mythology. As the American sage and seminal self-reinventor Mark Twain might have said about all of this, "Never let the truth get in the way of a good story."[*]

In early 2022, a few months before I arrived in Indiana, the state's lawmakers had joined most of the other states in the country in putting forward a "divisive concepts" bill. If enacted, it would restrict what teachers could say about certain topics in the classroom and what books and subjects could be included in school curricula. The criteria for what counts as "divisive" are ambiguous; a working definition seems to be an idea that presents any type of grievance about America's past. In some cases, such as Florida's Stop W.O.K.E. Act, any acknowledgment that people are privileged or oppressed by virtue of their race or sex is forbidden. More than a few of these bills or rules or orders have gone into effect—in Georgia, Mississippi, New Hampshire, Texas, Oklahoma, Utah, and so on.

---

[*] In a perfect irony, no one has ever been able to definitively link this quote to Mark Twain.

The first stab at it in Indiana, however, failed. Its specific cause of death was not so much a lack of support but a nuclear-level gaffe by a state senator during the hearings. "One line of questioning from a teacher led Sen. Scott Baldwin (R-Noblesville) to suggest teachers teach Nazism neutrally," the journalists Aleksandra Appleton and Stephanie Wang reported. "Baldwin was lambasted nationally and eventually walked the comments back."

In most cases, what these initiatives speak to are problems that don't exist; there is no sweeping phenomenon, for example, of students being told by teachers that they should feel personal culpability for historic atrocities like slavery or the forced relocation of Native American communities. Florida's Parental Rights in Education Act, known colloquially as the "Don't Say Gay" law, outlaws (in part) the instruction of sexual orientation or gender identity for students in kindergarten through the third grade. "In practice, it is unclear exactly how things will change in the classroom," the journalist Ana Ceballos explained of the bill's effect, "because sexual orientation and gender identity is not something that is being taught in grades K–3 at the moment."

In all cases, however, these bills create a burden, whether it means that teachers avoid aspects of history that are meant to provide a fundamental understanding of the national story. Or that teachers are obligated to qualify some of the worst things ever to happen. Or that students fail to learn the critical context for why so many different communities feel shut out of opportunity in the United States. Or that parents assume that there is a clandestine plot to raise a generation of American kids who are required to hate their country, love drag brunches, and only drink soy milk.

My quest to unpack all of this took me to Frankton, Indiana. A town of about two thousand people, Frankton is surrounded by corn and soy fields and not far from the dead geographic center of Indiana, a handful of former sundown towns, and a kitschy roadside attraction that claims to be the world's largest ball of paint. Outside the town's American Legion hall, there was a road sign for the previous week's chicken noodle dinner and a handsomely painted deposit box for retired American flags. Across the road sat a church, a tattoo parlor, and a firearms shop. (All the town needed to complete the picture was a diner for political reporters to take the pulse of the heartland during election years.)

The official Frankton website features a history of the town written in the late 1940s, all but guaranteeing that the local lore would be rich with good old fables, long-odds feats, and the kind of folksy honorifics you might forgive for feeling out of time. The town, the account explains, was founded in the 1820s by a man named Jacob Sigler, who "lived in a large hollow of a syca-more tree" while clearing the land for settlement. Later, while courageously returning with the town deed, Sigler fended off one of the brutal wolf attacks (!) for which the area had been notorious. The town of Frankton had come up in a familiar way ever since: the building of churches, a gas boom, a gas bust, a train station made of yellow poplar. "Frankton is a community of neighborly, Christian people who live by law and support their common interests," the town's website goes on to say. Today, Frankton is also where Kevin Cline teaches U.S. history and gov-ernment at the local high school, moonlighting in the evenings as an announcer for school football and volleyball games.

"You have trouble finding the place?" Cline joked with a big handshake. "Second cornfield on the left?" Cline is exactly the kind of teacher college applicants and sappy journalists write essays about. The son of two teachers (choir and special educa-tion), his classroom was kitted out with vintage social movement posters, a minilibrary of history books and tchotchkes, and framed copies of authentic newspaper front pages showcasing presi-dential assassinations going back to Lincoln. A dry-erase board by his desk featured an inspiring daily quote; when I visited, it was a verse from the Prince jam "Uptown" about not conform-ing to society's expectations. One particularly bright current student, Cline confided early in our conversation, had recently earned a place on his "Mount Rushmore." Cline also carries around a dog-eared copy of the Constitution in his back pocket and uses a thick brick of tea as a classroom prop to bring the Boston Tea Party story to life. "Physically, the students always think it's boxes of Lipton tea that get dumped into the harbor," he explained.

I wasn't alone in my swooning over Mr. Cline. In 2016, the

Gilder Lehrman Institute of American History, a nonprofit organization that offers history resources for schools and the public,
had awarded him the title of National History Teacher of the
Year. He has since been tapped to serve on a council to create
educational programming for America's 250th celebration in
2026.

I had sought out Cline because for most high school U.S.
history teachers, navigating the squalls of America's founding as
well as finding the relevant links to today's contentious story are
natural parts of the work. After all, narratives help shape identity,
especially for teens, who are already in the process of figuring out
who they are. (For my part, like a lot of spoiled teens who fancied
themselves rebellious in high school, being assigned *The Catcher
in the Rye* placed my own adolescent sense of angst into a social
context and made it seem even more clichéd than it already was.)

When I asked Cline if, given the general mood of dysfunction
and disunity in America, his students felt a sense of disaffection
about learning about the founding ideals, he gently reminded me
what it means to be a teenager. "I don't know that I've felt this
overabundance of feelings like that coming into the classroom,"
he said. "I feel like the biggest feeling that kids are coming in
with is," he added, breaking out a solid Eeyore voice, "'Yeah, I
gotta take another history class.' It's like they haven't even hit
cynicism."

I was already projecting my own nostalgic baggage onto the
kids. To put it another way, when I followed up by asking if students were staging walkouts in protest after they encountered
"life, liberty, and the pursuit of happiness" in the Declaration
of Independence because they see it as a false promise that only
applies to some, Cline again shook his head no. But the topic
had just come up; the week before, Cline had taken his government class through the declaration with the opposite goal in
mind, using the document as a way to impart a lesson on good
citizenship.

First, the class had held a public reading of the document
and then broken it down word by word, digging into how Jefferson had originally wanted the declaration to be presented.
"One of my favorite things to do," Cline explained, "is to look at

the end of that [first sentence], 'We hold these truths to be self-evident . . . life, liberty, and the pursuit of happiness,' and I say, 'You'll find printings of this all over the place, and they'll have periods after "happiness."' And I'll ask, 'What does that mean?'"

The students, he explained, would usually respond that it was the end of the sentence and the end of the thought. "But Jefferson's original draft," he explained, "had no period there. He went straight from there into the phrase 'that to institute such governments . . .' And then I say, 'It's important, I think, that we understand that when you read the line without a period, it means that you have these rights and then you have these responsibilities to maintain those rights. And what you have to do, what is your duty—Jefferson uses the word *duty*—is to maintain those rights. They're given to you, but they're not guaranteed.'"

Cline likened this duty to breathing air. "I'm given the ability to breathe air, but it's not guaranteed. There are always things that can choke that off unless I actively look to maintain it. Those are things I like to stress. The responsibility that comes along with being a citizen."

———————

A few days before meeting with Cline, I pulled up to the grounds of the town cemetery, which doubled as a parking lot for the Frankton Heritage Days, an annual weekend festival of deep-fried food, rides and unwinnable carnival games, agriculture-themed feats of strength and historical pageantry. They included a muzzle-loading rifle competition, a tractor pull, an opening ceremony with cannon shots, and a kids' pie-eating contest. Vendors hawked homemade crafts and anti-Biden apparel. On Saturday night, there were fireworks. Over an Elvis (a funnel cake sandwich made with banana, peanut butter, honey, and powdered sugar), I watched a historical impersonator of Johnny Appleseed, the American legend who grew fruit to get innumerable Hoosiers drunk on apple liquor in his day, rhapsodize about planting orchards around the region. A ripple of undisguised disappointment went out when the greased pig contest, which tasked competitors with catching a slicked-up pig in a grease pit, was unexpectedly canceled. When I asked Sergeant Eric Lamey, a Frankton public information officer, what you get for capturing the grease pig, he gave a verbal shrug. "To be honest," he said, "I think you just win the honor of being the catcher of the grease pig."

The theme may have been heritage, but the specifics of it were austere. Along the farm roads out to Frankton, dozens of properties within five miles of town had set up rummage sales in their yards to capitalize on the arrival of out-of-town visitors. Considerable talk went around about how attendance for the fair had been boosted by a community hospital sponsorship, which covered the regular $2 admission fee for festivalgoers. Meanwhile, one of the prize attractions, a $50 helicopter ride, had been a bit polarizing because of the cost. Before I left, I asked Sergeant Lamey something that had been puzzling me since I'd arrived in Indiana. It was the middle of September, and all the flags I'd seen were at half-mast. "It was a statewide thing," he told me. "They wanted them lowered for Queen Elizabeth," who had died two weeks before.

———————

As a country built on an idea, America is strange and fascinating. In an unexpected callback to my conversation with Dr. Bell about America's founding, Cline described "pedestal-style thinking" as one of the early challenges he faces when it comes to teaching U.S. history. "That's something that we talk about. I tell them, 'I don't know that you're ever going to study anybody in here who is a perfect person.' We deal with that a lot with some of these early founders."

Still, a casual glance around the classroom revealed a deep reverence for those same early founders. "I'm a Washington guy," Cline went on, "but he owned slaves. And pursued slaves who had escaped. So you gotta cover the whole thing. And that's an important thing for me, telling the whole story, not just the part of the story that gets glossed over in a textbook or gets stuck in people's minds."

To Cline, that also means highlighting the voices that haven't been given the pedestal treatment. "We don't have a remarkably diverse student population here, but I try to find ways to weave as many different voices in as I possibly can. We're not going to just hear or read documents that are written by white American men. We're also going to read [Frederick Douglass'] 'What to the Slave Is the Fourth of July?' We're going to read Abigail Adams' letters to John." In recent years, Cline had found joy when his students, after learning about the muckraking exploits of the journalist Nellie Bly, had declared her to be "kind of a badass."

You can set a watch to the hostility toward this kind of approach. It isn't new. Writing nearly ninety years ago, when slavery was still in living memory, W. E. B. Du Bois argued, "Our histories tend to discuss American slavery so impartially that in the end nobody seems to have done wrong and everybody was right." In the Joseph McCarthy–era 1950s, a student-led group called the Green Feather Movement coalesced in Indiana to successfully protest a state commission's effort to ban the book *Robin Hood* over its apparent Communist themes of wealth redistribution. In a sinister but creative pivot, Florida governor Ron DeSantis recently defended efforts to deemphasize racism in his state's African American history curriculum by arguing that slavery had provided enslaved Black Americans with beneficial skills. Meanwhile, the vote on Indiana's "divisive concepts" bill happened during a year in which the American Library Association reported a 467 percent jump in the number of books known to have been targeted for banning in schools and libraries. (The most challenged books either dealt with race or had LGBTQ+ protagonists or themes.) "If it had been passed, and thankfully it wasn't, it was going to demand you have to show both sides," Cline said of the "divisive concepts" legislation. "Perspectives are great. But when I teach fascism, I'm going to teach that the Nazis were bad."

Even as there's a faint awareness that much of the popular discourse is artificially driven by ahistorical outrage, bad faith, cheap points, and deceptive algorithms, the worst of the ideas still get the oxygen. Those claiming to speak for America's core spirit or its founders do so by squelching dissent, stifling free speech, and promoting bad citizenship. "I've taught history now for eighteen years," Cline said with some frustration. "I've never felt more bricks that I have to pull down, of misconceptions and misguided ideologies. I'm not telling my students how to think. I just want them *to* think."

There's no one single loose thread that can unravel this civic tangle. To start, though, Cline offered a simple, straightforward idea: that learning the truth makes us all stronger and better prepared for the world. Before I left Frankton, he told me about a trip he had taken to Jefferson's Monticello homestead with his own sons, where he marveled at how the site reckoned honestly with its legacy of slavery. "I don't love Thomas, but I was floored at how well they owned it all. I was really proud of that," he said. "And it brought up some great conversations, even with my kids. My oldest is just now fourteen. I mean, if the dude's house can own it, I think we can own it here, right?"

––––––

Had I gone to forty-nine other classrooms in forty-nine other states, the experience almost certainly would have been different. From our scattered, decentralized past comes our scattered, decentralized present in which few states teach anything the same way. "Social studies, consisting of Texas, United States, and world history, government, economics, *with emphasis on the free enterprise system and its benefits*," read the very pro-business education guidelines in a Texas law on the books since 1995. (Italics mine.) Meanwhile, California's social studies education goalposts place a totally different weight on what free enterprise has wrought in American life: "The yawning gap between the haves and have-nots and what is to be done about it is one of the great questions of this time."

The timeless problem of an elusive collective baseline is everywhere. And in the classroom, it goes beyond what's being taught. Not long before I'd left for Indiana, a friend had texted me a flyer from his kid's public school in a liberal, well-to-do community in a large city. The academic year had just kicked off, and the school was hosting a college-themed color day where students were instructed to wear the colors or apparel of their target schools. "Let's promote college and career readiness!" the notice read. I should probably mention that this was an elementary school.

The school's fantasy campaign ignored a reality in which an overwhelming majority of Americans, out of either necessity or desire, enter the workforce after high school or seek out a trade school or associate degree instead of going to a four-year college. Instead of insisting on one acceptable vision of the past and present as "divisive concepts" bills do, this school had insisted on one acceptable vision of the future by defining success on extremely narrow terms: college or bust. Good intentions aside, it has an ugly effect on how we gauge worth in terms of pay and social capital—with life-and-death consequences. A jaw-dropping 2023 report by the economists Anne Case and Angus Deaton found that the gap in adult life expectancy for Americans with a four-year degree and those without had widened from two and a half years in 1992 to roughly eight and a half years in 2021.

Bump against these stifling frameworks once, and it's hard not to see them everywhere. When I got back to the Indianapolis airport for my flight home, I was greeted at the terminal entrance by a beautiful, sprawling mural titled *Entrepreneurs Awakening*. It depicted scenes from the life of Madam C. J. Walker, who is touted as the first self-made female millionaire in America. The piece, which spread across seventy-five feet, featured visual references to Walker's biography—a woman laboring in a cotton field as her parents had as formerly enslaved sharecroppers in Louisiana. "I'm not ashamed of my past," read a Walker quote above the image, "I am not ashamed of my humble beginning." It also incorporated images of her Indianapolis-based business, the Madam C. J. Walker Manufacturing Company, which created a line of cosmetics and hair care products for Black women, whom the market had overlooked. Above a rendering of the landmark building that had once housed her factory, another Walker quote declared, "If I have accomplished anything in life it is because I've been willing to work hard."

In learning about Walker's story for this book, I'd come across plenty of compelling facets beyond her tale of individualistic aspiration: how she had capitalized on the isolation of Black consumers in the marketplace and subverted the limitations of Jim Crow by moving north during the Great Migration and how she had emphasized community-oriented entrepreneurship and long-term financial independence for women. But none of those details had made the cut. She'd had little, she'd worked hard, she'd made it big; that was all that mattered.

The shoehorning of Walker's life into a bland, standard American model of ambition seemed to miss the point: It's never as simple as that. While I waited for my flight, I scrolled my way through a whole slew of entries that seemed determined to set Walker in this exemplary bootstrapping context. Her hard-won path to financial triumph had been the basis of a fictionalized Netflix biography titled *Self Made* in 2020. In 2022, Mattel had released a Barbie doll in honor of Walker as part of its Inspiring Women doll line that included Maya Angelou, Ida B. Wells, and Rosa Parks. The doll's accessory was a miniaturized replica of one of her products, while the packaging featured what might be considered a modern #girlboss quote, one that also made an appearance on the airport mural: "Don't sit down and wait for opportunities to come. Get up and make them!" In a bit of fine print that doubled as unintentional metaphor, Mattel's write-up of the toy noted, "Doll cannot stand alone."

What the sanded, varnished, and denuded versions of Walker's story and America's founding share is that their lack of complications makes them less realistic and less instructive as modern-day parables. It's the uglier bits that make them poignant. In Walker's case, ascribing her success to hard work alone undercuts the place of her mentors, friends, church, and hard-built business associations at a time when Black Americans were excluded from trade unions and denied capital and women entrepreneurs remained exceptionally rare. In the case of nationhood, the American storyline is made all the more miraculous by the lengths taken to build coalitions, solve seemingly intractable problems, and find otherwise elusive consensus. Both show us how far we've come and how far we have left to go.

CHAPTER THREE

LANDFALL

THE RELIGION OF WORK

**I THINK I CAN SEE THE WHOLE DESTINY OF
AMERICA CONTAINED IN THE FIRST PURITAN
WHO LANDED ON THESE SHORES.**

—ALEXIS DE TOCQUEVILLE

In one of the less public opinions of his very opinionated life, Benjamin Franklin dished out possibly the hottest, most heretical take ever recorded in U.S. history. In a 1784 letter to his daughter, Sarah, the founding father ranted that the bald eagle—the vaunted, noble mascot of America, that enduring symbol of fortitude, freedom, and beauty and the inspiration for church hymns and country songs alike—was a bird unworthy to appear on the Great Seal of the United States. Old man Franklin's main gripe? That bald eagles were lazy.

"For my own part I wish the bald eagle had not been chosen as the representative of our country," he wrote. "He is a bird of bad moral character. He does not get his living honestly. You may have seen him perched on some dead tree, where, too lazy to fish for himself, he watches the labour of the fishing hawk; and when that diligent bird has at length taken a fish, and is bearing it to his nest for the support of his mate and young ones, the bald eagle pursues him, and takes it from him."

Though some historians have suggested that Franklin's

scorched-nest assault against the bald eagle may have been a joke, Franklin went as far as to compare the bald eagle's "often very lousy" ways to those of the wicked predators of the economy, the "men who live by sharping and robbing."* Whatever the case, his birdly broadside is a tidy summary of his legacy as a man obsessed with utility and action. It was an obsession that would be highly influential in the country he's often credited with cofounding.

Though we adults may quietly chuckle at his whispered battles with syphilis and gout, Franklin is still held up in schoolhouses as much a founding hero for his work as a statesman and diplomat as he is for his eternal restlessness as a rags-to-riches polymath, an inventor (bifocals and the urinary catheter!), an organizer, and a prolific writer. In addition to working on drafts of the Declaration of Independence and the Constitution and not actually discovering electricity, Franklin spent decades writing about the virtue of hard work and individualistic initiative with famous maxims like "Dost thou love life? Then do not squander Time, for that's the Stuff Life is made of." It's impossible to separate the glute-inflaming masochism in the "no pain, no gain" motto of 1980s aerobics videos from Franklin's best-known fictional persona, Poor Richard, who once declared, "There are no gains without pains."

Scholars have been criminally silent about whether Franklin himself flaunted buns of steel, but they generally agree that the man whom the historian Frederick Jackson Turner called "the first great American" stayed busy. In addition to possibly fathering as many as fifteen children outside his marriage, he was America's first and most prominent public practitioner of thrifty life hacks and moral advice. And nearly 235 years after his death, there may not be a thought leadership sermonizer or self-improvement racketeer on social media who doesn't call back to Franklin's mythical habits and enterprise-flavored chestnuts. His productivity rituals remain legendary even today; "I followed

* A better bird of virtue, to Franklin's mind, was the turkey, which he praised as "a much more respectable bird, and withal a true original native of America." And unlike the eagle ("a rank coward"), the turkey was "a bird of courage, and would not hesitate to attack a grenadier of the British guards who should presume to invade his farm yard with a red coat on."

Ben Franklin's schedule for a month," reads one stunt bit from *Fast Company*, which involved waking up at 5:00 a.m. and working for four hours without a break. Moreover, his most enduring sermon, "The Way to Wealth," is still upheld as a "seminal essay on work ethic and frugality" worthy of rigorous study in the gilded corridors of Harvard Business School. Franklin's general approach to acquiring money—do it as quickly as possible and then spend your life pursuing other interests—is regularly cited as a self-justifying mission of the personal finance craze known as FIRE (Financial Independence, Retire Early) that has seduced disenchanted millennials in recent years.

There's a reason his copy endures. Unlike Adam Smith's influential doorstop, *The Wealth of Nations*, a cornerstone text of modern capitalism that "was published in expensive folios and directed at scholars and elites," Franklin's folksier works were written to be practical and accessible to the masses. His annually released *Poor Richard's Almanack*, of which he claimed to sell as many as ten thousand copies each year, was, in his own braggy words, "a proper vehicle for conveying instruction among the common people, who bought scarcely any other books."

In short, the man had a message: an aggressive, coffee-and-creatine style of ambition that connected money with morality. Franklin himself boiled the themes of his almanacs down to "inculcated industry and frugality as the means of procuring wealth and thereby securing virtue." (In his view, it was harder for a person in need to act honestly.) Even Franklin's posthumously released autobiography was, by one account, "written in part to provide a model for the emerging democratic individual and democratic culture of America," a lot of which revolves around work and the accumulation of wealth.

Prominent cultural and political figures of the eighteenth, nineteenth, and twentieth centuries chided Franklin for holding up himself and such a nakedly careerist view of life as models for emulation. The private letters of fellow founder John Adams reveal that he found Franklin tedious and self-important, which, coming from Adams, was really saying something. In an essay on Franklin, D. H. Lawrence critiqued the idealized American figure constructed by Franklin in his autobiography as a "materialistic instrument," and asked, "Why then did Benjamin set up this dummy of a perfect citizen as a pattern to America?" And in a classic piece of satire, Mark Twain ripped on Franklin for building such gigantic lore around his own story and then using it to create a strict and tiresome standard for young Americans to follow. "He was always proud of telling how he entered Philadelphia, for the first time, with nothing in the world but two shillings in his pocket and four rolls of bread under his arm," Twain wrote before adding mockingly, "But really, when you come to examine it critically, it was nothing. Anybody could have done it."*

As we delve into how the past set the stage for the modern woes of work, another critique of Franklin stands out: that he really wasn't selling anything new. The values that he aimed to set for a new country had existed there long before Franklin picked up his quill or whatever. Indeed, America's industry-obsessed, kite-in-a-thunderstorm lifestyle was one of the few things that united the various divided factions of America's founding set. And this attitude goes back even further than that, all the way to the early years of European settlement in North America.

If you're on a quest for pure, uncut American kitsch, you could certainly do worse than the John Carver Inn in Plymouth, Massachusetts. Named for the Pilgrim leader, it houses an eighty-foot water slide that starts atop a chintzy replica of the *Mayflower and* a six-person hot tub set inside an eerily faithful replica of Plymouth Rock. I never made a reservation to stay somewhere faster in my life.

I'd come to Plymouth for the same reasons that most folks usually do: to be a sucker for seaside New England charm, land-

---

* Still, what Franklin understood about that American-style branding paid considerable dividends. While in France serving as a representative of the fledgling colonies at war with England, he conspicuously donned a coonskin hat and a beaver coat to fulfill Europe's romanticized image of Americans as rugged frontiersmen. The ensemble was a hit, and Franklin managed to secure a treaty guaranteeing critical French support for the Revolutionary War. (Never mind that Franklin had copped the hat in Canada.)

marks of wildly varying importance, and over-the-top history-themed marketing. Plymouth, shrewdly branded as "America's Hometown," had all those amenities in abundance. There were lantern tours at night and craft beers on tap at the Speedwell, a tavern named for the leaky ship that had turned back to England, leaving the *Mayflower* to travel west alone; another pub served up baskets of "New World Wings," which were solid. Later, I passed sugared-up kids pounding ice cream on the wharf in the October cool beside *Mayflower II*, a built-to-spec replica of the original *Mayflower* that costs $15 to board. And when I finally took in the sight of Plymouth Rock itself, I was disappointed (as most people apparently are) by its diminutive size, the rock having been broken while being relocated several times and chiseled off by souvenir seekers.* After a family visiting from New Jersey tossed their good-luck coins down into Plymouth Rock's holding pit, a teen driving by on Water Street did what most any teen would do and shouted, "The rock is fake!" Everyone chuckled a bit nervously.

Of the many treasured folktales that populate the American origin story, I'd argue that the details about this one hunk of stone aren't worth fussing over. Okay, so maybe Plymouth Rock wasn't declared as the spot where the Pilgrims had landed until 120 years *after* they arrived. And fine, maybe the person who claimed to know where the Pilgrims had disembarked was a ninety-four-year-old church elder who wasn't even alive in 1620. But let's not dwell on that. Like the desert rock that Moses battered for water in Exodus, the rock in question here is instructive, a channel of simple meaning. "A few poor souls trod for an instant on this rock, and it has become famous, it is prized by a great nation; fragments are venerated, and tiny pieces distributed far and wide," an awed Alexis de Tocqueville wrote of Plymouth Rock in 1835, contrasting it with Europe's inaccessible symbology. "What has become of the doorsteps of a thousand palaces? Who cares for them?"

Besides, the minutiae of the Plymouth landing seem insignificant when it's the story of the *Mayflower* voyagers that is so often told wrong. Pinpointing the two most popular origin sto-

---

* Historians estimate that as little as 5 percent is all that remains of the original rock.

ries of American settlement, the historian Annette Gordon-Reed offered an explanation for why the story of the 1607 establishment of the Jamestown Colony in Virginia ("a moneymaking venture") is less celebrated than the Pilgrims' virtuous escape from religious persecution and subsequent arrival on the Massachusetts shore more than a decade later in 1620. "The latter narrative," she wrote, "is more inspirational and more in keeping with America's sense of moral exceptionalism than the former, which is why it has tended to loom larger in the American mind."

Nevertheless, the settlers of Jamestown and Plymouth had a lot more in common than is generally discussed. Like Columbus and the Spanish and the French and the Jamestown set before them, the Pilgrims had crossed the Atlantic with financial enrichment in mind. Having fled the religious intolerance of the state church in England, many of the future Pilgrims had first, in 1608, ended up in the Netherlands, where they had been free to practice their faith exactly as they wished—in their case, rigidly as hell. But they were former farmers laboring mostly in a foreign textile industry; and it was economic stability that turned out to be elusive in Holland, and the decade-plus of adversity took a toll. Their pay was low, their hours were long, their children had to work, and the low morale and quality of life sapped their ability to recruit others to join their community (or even retain the members they had). They feared that their children would assimilate to the lax Dutch life and become loafers in wooden shoes.

Contrary to popular myth, freedom of worship was maybe *the only thing* the Pilgrims had going for them. "Some preferred and chose the prisons in England rather than this liberty in Holland with these afflictions," wrote the Pilgrim leader William Bradford in his famous history of Plymouth. "But it was thought that if a better and easier place of living could be had, it would draw many and take away these discouragements." And that's when the *Mayflower* sailed into the picture.

Prior to its life as a creaky ship carrying economic migrants across the Atlantic, the *Mayflower* had mostly been deployed to haul cases of Bordeaux from France to England. "Her new assignment was equally commercial," wrote John McPhee of the ship's best-known voyage. "When she sailed from Devon, she was under instruction to go to the mouth of the Hudson River, where her passengers, under a seven-year contract with investors in London, would warehouse timbers, fur, and fish." Under the terms of the deal, the workers each received one share of the venture, and at the end of the seven years, they would be entitled to a piece of any future profits.[*]

Landing in Plymouth had been a late-game audible; the ship had initially set out for what is now New York City and, in a familiar tale, had been blown off course. And that was when things got interesting. Although the Pilgrims had organized the voyage, they accounted for less than half the ship's passengers. The rest were a collection of workers, indentured servants, and children, who were also seeking economic opportunity abroad. (The Pilgrims referred to them with some suspicion as "strangers.")[†] But the whole group, now sick and cold and travel weary, scrapped their grand plans to move to the Big Apple back when the rent was still cheap.

After scouting what would become Plymouth and determining that it could support a viable plantation, they decided to drop anchor. However, since the ship had ended up beyond where the Virginia Company had granted the settlers their charter, the *Mayflower* passengers had to create a whole new agreement for their venture. What followed—the Mayflower Compact—is now hailed as one of the first artifacts of democratic self-rule and a forerunner of America's major founding documents. In it, the passengers agreed to work together to create "just and equal Laws . . . for the general Good of the Colony" and also reiterated their loyalty to King James I back in Great Britain. John Quincy Adams, one of several American presidents to descend

---

[*] Governance over Jamestown, as dictated by its leader, John Smith, had considerably less chill by comparison: "he that will not worke shall not eat," Smith declared, ". . . for the labours of thirtie or fortie honest and industrious men shall not be consumed to maintaine an hundred and fiftie idle loiterers." Many of the Jamestown settlers would starve to death anyway and resort to cannibalism along the way.

[†] The Pilgrims, by the way, called themselves "Saints" and were generally known as "Separatists" rather than "Puritans" who thought they could reform the Church of England. Thus, their moniker, "Pilgrim," is another after-the-fact feat of branding, which didn't come into popular use until long after they landed.

from *Mayflower* stock, hyped the milestone document as "perhaps, the only instance in human history of that positive, original social compact." *Playboy* founder Hugh Hefner, another *Mayflower* descendant, is not known to have weighed in on the merits of the Mayflower Compact during his life, although the fact that only the men aboard the ship were allowed to sign it might have met with his approval.

Details settled, the passengers made landfall at Plymouth Harbor in December 1620. Almost half of them would die before spring arrived.

––––––––––

Whether you believe that it's God or the Devil that lives in the details, it's still a biblical twist that one of the earliest artifacts of self-government in North America was put to paper only after some of the *Mayflower* strangers argued that their contract with London stockholders couldn't be enforced in Massachusetts. Perhaps this was where Americans' trademark love of fine print and litigiousness was born. If so, they weren't the only *Mayflower* properties to spring to life on the land; after all, the *Mayflower* voyagers came here to toil. And the working culture that we all know and love and loathe today brings to mind the one established in Plymouth and in the later Puritan settlements that followed.

"They were among the first to glorify work, not for its own sake or because of the wealth unstinting work could win, but as a sign that one might be among God's chosen," the historian James T. Kloppenberg wrote of the familiar Puritan link to modern capitalism. This attitude toward industriousness created a formidable social norm, one that could determine as much about the moral worth of those who worked as hard as possible and accrued riches as it did about those who did not. "Wealth did not guarantee membership in the elect," he continued, ". . . but the failure to prosper, if attributable to the failure to work hard, could be taken as a reliable indicator that one remained unregenerate" or unable to be reformed for salvation.

It was a perfectly circular philosophy, the earliest incantation of the American abracadabra. If God could be fickle and the church could be corrupt, the only surefire way to pay the toll of salvation was to work (endlessly and unceasingly) at what you were meant to do. And, as these new communities flourished, their success seemed to provide divine proof that they were on the right path. It's in the Puritan system of belief that your chosen work became synonymous with your *calling*—a religious term that today is often reserved for jobs that are emotionally taxing and underpaid but have fulfilling aspects that are meant to compensate for those shortcomings.*

For many of those fleeing England or simply seeking profit in the sprouting colonies, the arrangement felt like a reward. In it, there was a liberating sense that the religious and economic baggage of the Old World had finally been shed. As Edward Winslow, the third governor of Plymouth Colony, described it in 1624: In America, "Religion and profit jump together (which is rare)."

Now, in case anyone gets inspired enough by this story to bring back knee-length breeches and scurvy, it's not like the Pilgrims and Puritans landed, mustered up some elbow grease, and immediately made Dorchester bloom. The Pilgrims, in particular, were in way over their heads, having arrived dangerously close to winter with few appropriate supplies to farm and fish and possibly even less know-how. One of the many *Mayflower* passengers who didn't survive a full year was John Carver, whose namesake hotel has the killer Plymouth Rock hot tub. The first governor of Plymouth, the first signer of the Mayflower Compact, a key negotiator in agreements with both the Virginia Company in England and the nearby Pokanoket tribe, Carver met his end less than six months after arriving. Tending a field on a hot day, he collapsed and died a few days later, quite possibly having worked himself to death.

---

* For example, one 2017 study of employees at dozens of animal shelters highlights the obvious perils of seeing work as a higher calling. Workers who *followed their passion* for animals often burned out quickly and left disenchanted as the reality of the work revealed itself, while those who treated their employment at a shelter as a traditional job were not only more effective but tended to stay at the job longer. (More on this later.)

If anything, Carver's death proved that toil and sheer force of will wouldn't save Plymouth Colony. Fortunately, around the time that Governor Carver expired, the colony was introduced to Tisquantum, known to history as Squanto.* In a confounding turn of dumb Pilgrim luck, Tisquantum happened to speak terrific English as a result of his having been abducted by earlier English visitors and having manufactured a Tom Ripley–esque escape home from Europe. Along with other local Native American neighbors, he would show the Pilgrims where to fish and how to hunt, how to plant crops and avoid poisonous plants; as an interpreter, he would steer them toward commerce and peace and (generally) away from conflict with their neighbors. He also facilitated the Pilgrims' way into the fur and beaver pelt trade that became a centerpiece of Plymouth's economy and a key part of how the Pilgrims paid off their debts to their London shareholders.

Naturally, Tisquantum, who lived among the Pilgrims until his death, had his own motives. Nearly his entire tribe had been wiped out by a plague while he had been captive in Europe, and his position as consigliere in Plymouth Colony elevated him to relative safety from the complex tribal tensions that existed in North America long before the *Mayflower*'s mast could be spotted on the horizon. From his perch of favor among the Pilgrims, he could also plot how to keep his rivals in check. Yet the Pilgrims didn't exactly see him or their Native American allies that way. William Bradford, the Pilgrim stalwart and eventual governor, saw Tisquantum as "their pilot to bring them to unknown places for their profit." Bradford also depicted him as "a special instrument sent of God for their good, beyond their expectation," freezing Tisquantum in a similar kind of carbonite as the folktales that cast him as one of the "friendly Indians" (see also: Pocahontas, Sacagawea) and cast most other Native American figures as savage brutes. Here, like many stock figures of history, a vital, savvy, and multifaceted figure like Tisquantum ultimately

* By some accounts, Squanto was either a fratty nickname like the ones often dished out by *Mayflower* descendant George W. Bush or possibly the result of the Pilgrims' inability to pronounce Tisquantum's name. Or both.

reduces into a one-dimensional Squanto—either a helper of civilization or an obstacle to it.[*]

This interpretation has been difficult to shake. The Saturday-morning cartoon version of the Pilgrims has long set a tone for a national culture that lionizes them for their self-reliance and work ethic, affirms them as the continent's benevolent, liberty-seeking founders, and overlooks how Native American people enabled their survival or simply had their own inner lives. The legend of Thanksgiving is another distortion. Through some thoroughly discredited storytelling, the holiday honors the forging of a harvest bounty, collective harmony, and the all-American concept of abundance. But walking through Plymouth a few weeks before the four hundredth anniversary of the very first Thanksgiving, I stumbled upon another noteworthy rock—this one marking where, for the past five decades, members of Native American communities have met at noon every Thanksgiving to grieve the loss of their lives, land, and culture in the aftermath of the Pilgrims' arrival.

Despite the warm fuzzies often associated with Thanksgiving and its traditional culinary theater, tryptophan, and Dallas Cowboy failures, the original Thanksgiving didn't exactly have the block party vibes that get elevated in the retellings. In a different reporting of the story, the first Thanksgiving became communal only after some Pilgrims fired off their muskets in celebration, causing nearly a hundred Wampanoag warriors to scramble over to honor their defense pact with the colony. "That being smoothed over, they stayed for a tense, diplomatic meal," Paula Peters, a member of the Mashpee Wampanoag of Cape Cod, explained in 2021. "For hundreds of years it wasn't mentioned again." (Also, in a less meaningful bummer, it's unlikely that turkey was on the menu.)[†]

---

[*] In a related and depressing reflection of this attitude, the original 1629 seal of Massachusetts Bay Colony, which later absorbed Plymouth and much of New England, featured a Native American man in the buff (save for a leafy loincloth) beseeching others to "Come over and help us."

[†] Not to dump more on my own favorite holiday, but apparently the first Thanksgiving didn't involve a massive feast. The concept of a big Turkey Day meal was created as a way to stoke tourism to New England much later, and the holiday itself

A truer, better, more aspirational Pilgrim parable is one of collective responsibilities and shared fates among disparate groups trying to survive and flourish under exceedingly hard conditions. The creation story of Plymouth is both incomplete and impossible without the Pilgrims' dealings with (and help from) the strangers on the *Mayflower*, their reliance on Tisquantum and others, and their strategic relationships with their tribal trading partners, which would hold agreeably for decades before finally descending into war. "For peace and for survival, others must be accommodated," wrote Nathaniel Philbrick of this interdependence in his book *Mayflower*. "The moment any of them gave up on the difficult work of living with their neighbors—and all of the compromise, frustration, and delay that inevitably entailed—they risked losing everything."

The love of work and the individualistic culture that permeate the early history of America materialized from a mash-up of righteousness and necessity. Among many influential religious leaders and thinkers in the lead-up to the *Mayflower* voyage, there was a shift of focus away from spiritual sins like greed and pride toward what were considered observable sins of the flesh. "Thus the true sinners," the historian Robert S. Michaelsen explained, "were those who were sensuous, lazy or idle."

One way to view how this played out is through New England's top-tier confederation of killjoys who railed against the evils of sloth and gratuitous merriment. For example, when the Englishman Thomas Morton, who'd arrived in Massachusetts to engage in trade, erected a maypole to celebrate May Day in 1627 in nearby Quincy, the diminutive Pilgrim military hawk Miles Standish led a group there from Plymouth to chop it down, arrest Morton, and throw him out of New England. Later, describing his 1622 arrival in a land populated by Native American groups

---

wasn't even established until President Lincoln used it as a way to unify the country during the Civil War. In other words, we've long bent our history to suit our ideological and commercial purposes. Even "Honest Abe" did it.

and religious communities, Morton wrote that he had found the former "most full of humanity and more friendly than the other" and was said to have been ostracized for treating them as equals. In another classic piece of humbug in 1659, the long-standing animus toward Yuletide loafing was taken up by Massachusetts Bay Colony lawmakers, who formally banned the celebration of Christmas, even as a day off. Anyone found "observing any such day as Christmas or the like, either by forbearing of labor, feasting, or any other way" would be subject to a hefty five-shilling fine, payable to the county. Easter also got nixed. Like a modern-day Peloton instructor screaming "No days off!," the old Puritan maxim rang out to the faithful: "They for whom all days are holy can have no holiday."

It's not hard to beat up on the Puritans, whose way of being was once roasted by the critic H. L. Mencken as "the haunting fear that someone, somewhere, may be happy." Still, all of their sweat equity, piety, and focus had a democratizing sheen. In New England, as the historian Joseph J. Ellis explained, "there was no titled aristocracy, mandatory support for public education had created nearly universal literacy, ministers were selected by their congregations, local leaders were elected by their neighbors, and knowledge was [in the words of John Adams] 'diffused thro' the whole body of the people.'" It's a little on the nose that Horatio Alger, America's foremost practitioner of individualistic boot-strap fables, could trace his lineage to the second ship that landed at Plymouth in 1621.[*] Meanwhile, back in England, common citizens had nearly none of those rights and little of that access— a potent difference maker when the cause of independence began to stir in the colonies.

As noted before, any admirable leveling of opportunity in New England still excluded groups that had been locally enslaved or imported in the slave trade, practices that were also carried out by the righteous Puritans. The founding spirit of opportunity and betterment also contained—and still contains—a corresponding built-in disdain for those who needed help. Copying

---

* In an excellent narrative flourish, the ship was named *Fortune*, and on its return voyage to England, all of its cargo got jacked by the French.

the design and cynicism of English poor laws, the colonists generally assessed people who received relief or charity as either deserving (disabled, elderly, orphaned, widowed) or undeserving (sluggards, drunks, etc.) and could eject them from the colony or refuse help to those deemed unworthy.

Thanks to Nathaniel Hawthorne, the scarlet *A* retains the title of the Puritan era's most culturally enduring emblem of social shame, but attitudes toward the poor were similarly punitive from the jump. "Some colonies required [welfare] recipients to wear a badge bearing the letter 'P' for 'pauper,'" wrote the economist Randy Albelda and the professor Chris Tilly, while "others denied recipients the right to marry or made them subject to jail, slavery, or indenture." This outlook proved to be foundational. They added that all the way until the 1930s, fourteen states banned welfare recipients from voting or holding office. And then there's the more contemporary conjuring of the "welfare queen," one of many ways in which the working poor, the elderly, and the disabled have been demonized as an entire category of undeserving people by political leaders on both sides of the aisle since the 1970s.

Ultimately, a core national tenet drawn from those early attitudes about work and worthiness is that to be an American (or become one), one has to earn it. Benjamin Franklin's witty but tedious encomiums to moneymaking and productivity later came under fire in part because critics saw them as a narrow-souled Puritan rehash. In the context of providing a young nation with popular guidelines for good citizenship, Franklin's secular sermonizing, in essence, shows us how wealth and unstinting busy-making stopped being strictly a Puritan value and became the American way. As one scholar argued, "the separation between religion and business was completed with Poor Richard," Franklin's most popular pen name.

In a way that's strange and singular, we have broadcast the virtues of work to new arrivals reaching our hallowed shores as a means of cultural integration. Even as the details of the treaty that ended the revolution were being ironed out, civic obligation struck Franklin enough for him to publish a pamphlet in response to the growing number of inquiries he received from Europeans jonesing to emigrate to the United States. In it, he dashed the fantasy of America as a place for noble folks and nepotism babies to comfortably land and expect riches and well-paying appointments. In a few hilarious turns of phrase that resemble the country folk standard "The Big Rock Candy Mountains," Franklin summed up America as the "Land of Labour"; unlike an imagined idyll of ease and luxury, he said, the country was not a place "where the Streets are said to be pav'd with half-peck Loaves, the Houses til'd with Pancakes, and where the Fowls fly about ready roasted, crying, *Come eat me!*"

More important, he warned would-be arrivals that "much less is it adviseable for a Person to go thither who has no other Quality to recommend him but his Birth." In Europe, he added, "it has indeed its Value, but it is a Commodity that cannot be carried to a worse Market than that of America, where People do not inquire concerning a Stranger, *What is he?* but *What can he do?*"

CHAPTER FOUR

EARN THIS

THE IMPOSSIBLE IMMIGRANT BINARY

AND IF THERE HAD TO BE CITY WALLS,
THE WALLS HAD DOORS AND THE DOORS WERE OPEN
TO ANYONE WITH THE WILL AND THE HEART TO GET HERE.

—RONALD REAGAN

From the Pilgrims onward, America's fixture as a place for immigrants to find refuge and prosper has been its global calling card. Today, the United States has (by far) the biggest immigrant population in the world, a fact that certain leaders tend to celebrate in campaign biographies and then condemn on the stump. In this way, immigrants appear on a split screen of absolutes, either as star-spangled success stories or as pernicious villains—an update, perhaps, of Squantos and savages.

Nearly each wave, and even potential wave, of immigration has produced intense domestic backlash. Whether it was the targeted exclusion of Chinese laborers in 1882, the loyalty-tinged birth of the Pledge of Allegiance in 1892, the generalized southern European xenophobia of the early twentieth century, the mass deportation of Mexicans (and even Mexican Americans) during the Great Depression, the Jewish quotas in the run-up to World War II, the federal responses to the various humanitarian crises of the 1970s, or the present-day fearmongering around Central American caravans, two key cries from immigration opponents are that newcomers will impede opportunity for U.S. citizens or make the country unsafe.

In recent times, though, a solid majority of Americans has said year after year that they believe that immigration strengthens the country and the economy, that immigrants (documented or undocumented) tend to fill jobs that most Americans don't want, and that immigrants of all stripes are not material contributors to rates of crime or violence. Data points don't just back up these claims; they demolish our preconceived ideas of them: Immigrants are 80 percent more likely to start a business than native-born Americans are, and their businesses range from mom-and-pop shops to giant firms. On average, immigrant-founded businesses hire more workers than the others. Immigrants, regardless of their status, are far less likely to commit crimes than native-born Americans, and, according to one thorough study, immigrants pay $1.38 in taxes for every dollar of government benefits they use. What's more, each year, undocumented Americans use Individual Taxpayer Identification Numbers (ITINs) to pay billions of dollars in taxes, with individuals regularly paying more to fund social programs and schools and public projects than loophole-savvy billionaires and presidents alike. And rather than seizing a finite piece of national resources, immigration has been proven to expand the economy and increase the demand for labor.

We're all familiar with this debate, but frequently missed beneath its superficial terms is how profoundly work factors into national attitudes about citizenship. New arrivals proving their worth through work visas and skilled-worker policies reflect American priorities in the same way that Catholicism as a prerequisite for citizenship reflects the priorities of Vatican City. In the United States, one of the few legal ways to jump the line toward permanent residency is if you start a business that will hire at least ten people for full-time work. It's not exactly Liechtenstein, the European country that requires some aspiring immigrants to live there thirty years before becoming a citizen, but it's not exactly the open arms of Canada, either.

For those arriving, the whispering about the United States as a modern land of milk, honey, or easy prosperity has never quite matched the reality. Ben Franklin was mostly right about that. Painted on the wall of the Ellis Island National Museum of Immigration is one poignant testimonial by an Italian immigrant from 1903: "I came to America because I heard the streets were paved with gold," it reads. "When I got here, I found out three things: First, the streets were not paved with gold. Second, they weren't paved at all. Third, I was expected to pave them."

Yea Ji Sea is well acquainted with the modern agitations of the immigration and acculturation process. She arrived in California from Korea in the late 1990s, when she was nine, along with her little sister and her parents. For most of her life, she was undocumented, living without status before eventually submitting to the process to legally affirm what she already knew: that she is an American. When she agreed to tell me her story, I asked if we could meet somewhere that carried particular meaning for her. She knew just the spot.

If we're lucky, there's a place out there that doubles as biography or inspires an ease that disarms us a little. Having been conditioned to conceal herself out of necessity, Sea had collected a few of them: a local Burger King where childhood birthday parties were made, complete with honorary paper crowns; the apartment complex where she'd grown up, which was, by intention, a secluded, self-contained universe of mostly Korean émigrés and Korean Americans, with a pool and a playground and neighborhood cats to chase around. She told me that when she was young, "maybe because we siloed ourselves by moving into one concentrated area—but I thought this was America." For Sea, what was more elusive than celebrations or more fortifying than the confines of home were instances of seeming normalcy. Those moments took the form of dinners out on the weekends with her mom. And that was how we ended up at a Sizzler in the heart of Los Angeles' Koreatown on a spring afternoon.

There are roughly 11 million people without legal status in the United States, according to the most recent data. Contrary to popular belief, the government maintains a firm grasp on this number. To be one of those millions made Sea reluctant to obsess about the particulars that made her story unique. It felt gratuitous to her. After all, so many others had it so much worse. But with an assist from Sizzler's will-weakening cheese toast, Sea allowed me to pry. "I dealt with feeling like a second-class citizen for a while," she told me. "You live a normal life, but in the back of your head, you know you're different." She described growing into the sense of danger about her status. When she was a teen living in Southern California, cross-border outings to Mexico became a popular pastime among friends—and obviously an activity that was forbidden to her. (Worse yet, when Sea's paternal grandmother died, her father couldn't travel to Korea to attend the funeral. Sea believes that broke him. "After that point," she said, "he was gone. Very depressed.")

As she grew up, the isolation begot an aimlessness, especially as her opportunities seemed to narrow. "To live like that for many, many years, you start losing a lot of yourself." Service jobs in restaurants offered a way to earn money and granted access to an ingathering of others in similar predicaments. "You find yourself with the people that understand, too, and there's always a group of them, undocumented," she said. "I was able to find those groups of people because I was at the right places. I was getting paid under the table, I was working in restaurants, and obviously a lot of us were in the same shoes." She applied and got into a few colleges, but having to apply as an international student supercharged the cost of tuition by three or four times and put them out of reach. "I was like, I don't know what to do with my life. Might as well just make money and party."

Somewhere between tradition and caricature, children of immigrant parents are yoked to an unwieldy expectation of success, especially—*especially*—in the land of opportunity. Ruminating on the pressure to become a doctor as a kid in an immigrant family, the Malaysia-born comedian Ronny Chieng once joked that "helping people is on the bottom of the list of reasons [why] . . . if it's even on the list." Even as Sea was bound by the restrictions of her status, she wasn't exempt from that burden. "My mom always says, 'I still pray for you to become something, I'm praying every day,'" Sea confided. "And I'm all, 'Okaaaay. Thanks.'"

And then an opportunity presented itself. In the wartime fog of the post-9/11 years, noncitizens who had what Liam Neeson once described in the movie *Taken* as a "very particular set of skills" became eligible for a pilot program called Military Accessions Vital to the National Interest (MAVNI). In exchange for service in the U.S. military, a path to citizenship would open for recruits with unique abilities, in order to make up for certain shortfalls in the armed forces. It was a new riff on the theme of jobs that other Americans didn't want or couldn't do. Sea's willingness and her fluency in Korean made her eligible. "I didn't think twice," she said.

The concept of having noncitizens or recent arrivals serve in the military—often to earn citizenship—isn't anything new in the United States. "It's been a tradition in America since 1775," explained Margaret Stock, a former army lieutenant colonel and MAVNI's former project officer. "I think something like half the Continental Army at Valley Forge was made up of immigrants." Stock went on, without pausing, to list everything from immigrant casualty rates in the Revolutionary War to the classic Steve Earle song "Dixieland" about the Irish nationalists who escaped to the United States to flee the British and were immediately sent south to fight for the Union in the Civil War. Then there was World War I, in which immigrants made up "close to a fifth of the army . . . A lot of those people were folks who had literally just gotten off the boat."

Though the arrangement of earning a spot through military service continued through the Vietnam War, the high-water mark of those contributions came in World War II, when 300,000-plus foreign-born people served in the U.S. Army. More than 100,000 servicepeople would be naturalized, including a number of German Jewish refugees who fled Hitler, were awarded citizenship during basic training, joined an intelligence unit, and "were responsible for about sixty percent of all actionable intelligence on the western front."

After signing on, Sea was first shipped off to Oklahoma for three months of basic training, a detour she remembered for its unexpected cold. "It's a flat area and so windy!" she explained with some exasperation. "And short people, when they're in formation, they have to wait in the front. And that wind is just hit-ting your face." From there, she went on to Texas, where, based on the army's needs, she became a medic. Sea loved it. "What the army did," she said of her training, "it motivates you to keep going." She was on her way.

———————

While Sea and tens of thousands of other noncitizens were training and serving, a new tempest was brewing behind the scenes. One irony of the decade that followed 9/11 is that even as it catalyzed a new spell of domestic xenophobia and spawned the Global War on Terror, it also steered one of the last comprehensive national pushes to overhaul America's immigration system. "There was a brief, bright moment, which is how Yea Ji Sea got into the MAVNI program," Stock explained. Ultimately, those efforts would fail, and bipartisan collaboration would fall out of favor. In lieu of big action on immigration, states would begin to act unilaterally, pursuing tactics of differing punitive levels, especially during the gloom of the Great Recession. The harshest action happened in Arizona, where, almost sixty years after the state's Hispanic communities were targeted for sweeps under a federal program called Operation Wetback, the state instituted what became known as its "Papers, Please" law, which allowed authorities to check the status of anyone deemed "suspicious" and forbade the hiring of undocumented workers, starting in 2010.

Amid those intensifying complications, Sea forged ahead with her service, as she always had, while the unsettling developments played out in the background. In a dreamlike turn, she was deployed to South Korea, returning for the first time since childhood. "It felt foreign," she said of her first leave off base. "It was so weird. I remember it being just so packed with everything. There were signs for everything, anything, anywhere. And nothing closes. I was shocked."

In Korea, Sea served as an ambulance aid driver and pharmacy technician at a base not far from the DMZ and North Korea. In her free time, she took care of injured soldiers and served as a translator for doctors. After several months, she returned to Texas, where she earned two medals and a promotion to the rank of specialist. Everything had clicked. With newly allotted reserves of safety, order, and control steadying her, Sea thrived. She now planned to become a career army doctor and had become eager to make up for lost time. "When I came [back] to San Antonio, I thought, *I have to do something to prove that . . . I can be this badass person.*" She changed her hospital schedule to evenings, working twelve-hour overnight shifts at her base and then going straight through a full day of classes to knock out her prerequisites for medical school. She did that for three years, starting around age twenty-five, working through two full days at a time and then sleeping through her day off. To net a few bonus minutes of rest, she would nap in her car before class instead of going home after work. "Maybe I was possessed."

All that urgency turned out to be warranted. The MAVNI program, which had been met with ambivalence by the Obama administration's Defense Department, would be gutted by President Trump's. By 2018, the army had already begun quietly discharging foreign recruits, often without explanation and often without letting them fulfill the requirements for naturalization. The lives of those without status immediately went into limbo. Though already vetted and serving, by the simple fact of having living parents in other countries, some of the MAVNI recruits were belatedly deemed suspicious for their foreign ties. Worse yet, by enlisting in the U.S. military, many had placed themselves in irrevocable danger. If deported, they would instantly become targets for interrogation, jail, torture, or execution, depending on where they ended up. "They killed this recruiting program that was giving the U.S. hundreds of valuable, loyal Chinese Mandarin speakers," Stock explained by way of example. "The Chinese government didn't want them to join the U.S. military through the MAVNI program. . . . And I'm sure they were celebrating in Beijing [when MAVNI was canceled]."

Sea, who aspired to devote her entire career to the military, soon became one of the program's exiles. She was thirty, without official status, suddenly vulnerable to deportation once again, and scared. "I really thought the military was going to protect me. So the political landscape . . ." She trailed off. "I didn't think it would matter."

In the second-ever episode of CNN's hit culinary travelogue *Parts Unknown*, the late chef and secular saint Anthony Bourdain arrives with some bemusement at a now-defunct Sizzler in Los Angeles' Koreatown, not far from the one where Sea and I met for lunch. It's there that his host, the artist and actor David Choe, introduces Bourdain to the wild and haphazard possibilities of culinary fusion at Sizzler's legendary all-you-can-eat salad bar.* As Choe fills a corn taco shell with meatballs marinara and tops it with guacamole, nacho cheese, and sour cream, he brandishes it as an edible metaphor of America's wonder, pluralism, and unexpected bounties. "There's nowhere else in the world where you can have this."

The U.S. military has also served as a similar symbol of unlikely integration, where the distinctive strands of a disparate citizenship fuse into one column. Its recruitment slogans ("An Army of One" and "Be All You Can Be") have long tapped into the individualistic soil first tilled by the Pilgrims, but the army has also exemplified the collective potential of America's demographic variety. The concept of cohesion was a rationale for keeping the military racially segregated until 1948 and for silencing gay and lesbian service members about their sexual orientation until 2011; however, on those two fronts, the army was actually ahead of the curve—neither racial integration nor same-sex marriage, for example, was a protected facet of civilian life until years after the armed forces acted first.

If the army's lead is prologue, it makes Yea Ji Sea's saga that much more unnerving. "There are a lot of reasons why Rome

---

* The son of Korean immigrants, Choe is well known in part for painting murals at the first two offices of Facebook in Silicon Valley. He chose to be paid for his work in the form of company stock in lieu of cash, a gamble that would net him hundreds of millions of dollars.

fell, but when we're talking about the military, the Roman military was really, really successful when it allowed people to earn their citizenship through military service," Stock told me. "They were drawing on all kinds of diverse people, and they had a superstrong military, and when they started to become afraid of foreigners and wouldn't let them get benefits of Roman citizenship, that contributed a lot to the fall." Stock pointed out that immigrants currently make up 14 percent of the population and only 4 percent of the military, a result of what she contended are "deliberate policies of the Pentagon."

Even before roughly two dozen active and retired service members were found to be among the ranks of those who stormed the U.S. Capitol on January 6, 2021, the hazards of having an armed services blanched of its demographic variety were becoming apparent. For decades, government bodies and national watchdogs alike have worried aloud about the rise of far-right extremism in the armed forces. In 2018, a *Military Times* poll found that the number of active nonwhite service members who reported witnessing incidents of racism or racist ideology in their ranks had grown to half. And with the military failing to meet its recruiting goals, Stock argued that it has loosened its requirements and vetting processes to make up for a shortfall that could be remedied by looking outward. "The reality right now is that they're increasing the numbers of white supremacists in the ranks to make up for the lack of immigrants."

Much like the tedium of Ben Franklin's life hacks or the rosiest version of the Pilgrim Thanksgiving story, the history of the MAVNI program reveals something bigger: it tells us what happens when an insular obsession with self-reliance limits our ability to be imaginative and generous—individually, communally, or nationally.

Following her release from the army, Yea Ji Sea returned to an uncertainty she had hoped never to revisit again. "I was very lost after I got out," she said. "It was very hard, not just because I got out, but because my life centered around being the model citizen, trying to prove to be American actually on paper." For Sea, what has since hit home is a deeper understanding of what draws her to working in public health and treating others. "I find it hard to relate to people that are not stressed. Or I feel that I can't relate to people who don't know or who have to deal with pain for a long time," she said. "But I'm trying to break that cycle."

A series of terrifying delays, legal processes, and red tape later, Sea managed to secure her citizenship with the help of advocates and glowing referrals from former commanders. "As a model citizen going through the hurdles, you're supposed to be happy about it," she told me. "So that means you have to act like you're okay. But none of this was an open process, for anyone in general. I know it's not just me." Officially an American for nearly five years when we met, Sea said that the depth of true believerism that tends to accompany new citizenship had faded a bit. I asked how holidays like the Fourth of July resonate after her long road to legal status. "Do I feel a sense of pride when I see those fireworks and the flags?" she said. "No. Because that's not how I envision America." When I asked her how she envisions America, she made a circle of the Sizzler dining room with her hand, gesturing around at the loose confederation of families, unfussy work lunchers, seniors, and all-you-can-eat warriors. "This is a real version here. Where people are hustling to have a little bit of a better life." Like them, Sea had hustled. She had fully absorbed the American ethic; of course, it had stung when none of that mattered.

Sea is finally making it down to Mexico these days, albeit rarely to relax. She visits to volunteer with groups serving immigrants with medical needs near the border in Tijuana. Among the communities amassed there are fellow foreign-born Americans. A growing number of them are deported U.S. veterans, numbering in the hundreds, their names painted by muralists on the planks of the border fence. Back at home, she has taken up lobbying for the Veteran Service Recognition Act, a bipartisan bill introduced in Congress that would create a process to track and review the deportations of foreign veterans and jump-start the process for them to obtain their hard-won citizenship.

Sea skated a fork across her plate as she described them; it's an endless buffet, but she'd barely made a dent. "Their native language is English, the majority of their life is here," she said. "They went to war. They came back, probably fucked up, went back to their neighborhoods and probably got in trouble and got deported. There are a lot of cases like that. But they're getting older. They're dying. And they're dying alone. . . . No one's keeping track of them."

CHAPTER FIVE

FORDING THE RIVER

BIG BUSINESS AND THE FRONTIER MIRAGE

THUS WAVE AFTER WAVE IS ROLLING WESTWARD;
THE REAL ELDORADO IS STILL FARTHER ON.

—JOHN MASON PECK

Grover Cleveland stood in the Chicago rain and, after basking for a few minutes in the roar of the gathered crowd and the mass waving of their handkerchiefs, launched the 1893 World's Fair. The newly inaugurated president started with a short speech, blessing the grandeur of the scene as well as the inborn democratic ambition that had summoned it into being. "We have made and here gathered together objects of use and beauty, the products of American skill and invention," he stated, "but we have also made men who rule themselves." Those grandiose stakes now set, Cleveland moved to a table decked out with an American flag—forty-four stars and still growing—and leaned toward the ceremonial pyramid at the center. He pressed the gold button on its top, and a generator fired up the fair's attractions: the fountains, the rides, the whole glorious spectacle to life. More than a hundred thousand Westinghouse Electric incandescent lamps lit up, marking the debut of the first-ever World's Fair powered entirely by electricity. Next came cannon fire as an orchestra-backed choir belted out the "Hallelujah Chorus" from Handel's

Messiah, later followed by "The Star-Spangled Banner" and "Hail, Columbia." Of the two hundred thousand or so visitors present, many reportedly wept.

Somewhat lost to history and overshadowed by the exploits of the fair's resident serial killer is the fact that the World's Columbian Exposition, as it was more formally known, was meant to belatedly honor the four hundredth anniversary of Columbus' discovery of America. But really, it was a showcase of the Gilded Age zeitgeist, a dizzying groove of patriotism and marketplace gimmickry, over-the-top opulence, industrial and technological wonder, all on the grandest scale. In public memory, the Chicago World's Fair symbolizes many things, including the moment when the rustic, preindustrial United States formally gave way to the commercial, bulb-lit, factory-floor America, raucous and recognizable to many of us today, and when American ambition materialized into physical form with all its wares and wows.

In the spirit of its namesake honoree, the Columbian Exposition had a defiant intensity about it, a chip on its oversized shoulder. Only twenty-eight years since the end of the horrors of the Civil War, the United States was in the midst of a period of settlement, mass migration, racist pogroms, robber-baron monopoly, and income inequality with few parallels in U.S. history. Moreover, the United States had recently been humbled by the 1889 Exposition Universelle in France, where the Eiffel Tower had made a stunning debut four years earlier.* Paris' new marvel hadn't just eclipsed the Washington Monument as the world's tallest structure but had done so using steel, a growing pillar of America's industrial swagger. Like a newly divorced dad at Coachella, the fair offered prospects of a badly needed rebrand.

Befitting the era and the ante, the organizers got a little carried away. That inaugural flood of electric light at the fair's opening ceremony was the first of many dumb-striking wonders in a six-month run featuring sixty-five thousand displays and exhibits. There were Venetian gondolas in man-made canals, donkey races,

---

* In a top-tier historical "what if," France, which was using the fair to commemorate the hundredth anniversary of its 1789 revolution, chose the Eiffel Tower over another imposing structure: a colossal guillotine a thousand feet in height.

and a 1,500-pound Venus de Milo made of chocolate. Programs and artifacts were put on view from every state as well as forty-six nations and housed in sparkling white palatial halls with classical porticos, an aesthetic decision that influenced American architecture for generations. Alongside the fine art, faithfully reproduced foreign blocks and villages, grand statuary, patriotic lectures, and expansive displays of high-tech novelties (with an enormous emphasis on electricity), the fair offered something that the others around the world hadn't: accessible, unstuffy entertainment in the form of cowboy-themed carnival games, amusement rides, feats of strength, and exotic animals. Attractions like the World's Congress of Beauty ("40 Women from 40 Nations") and a belly-dancing show drew well, with attendance at the latter goosed by a marketer's invention of the suggestive phrase "belly dance" and a local minister's denunciation of it. (If this doesn't adequately convey the fanfare, imagine a six-week residency of live military marches led by maestro John Philip Sousa. That also happened at the fair.)

Then, of course, there was the debut of the titanic Ferris wheel—America's response to Gustave Eiffel—that could withstand Chicago's notorious winds and hold two thousand passengers at once. The wheel lit up the ether with three thousand lights as it revolved on a forty-six-ton Bethlehem Iron Company axle, the largest piece of steel ever forged in the United States. And unlike the Eiffel Tower, which had been partially financed by the French government, it was a point of pride that the funds for George Washington Gale Ferris, Jr.'s, leviathan had come from private investors.*

The Columbian Exposition would go on to host roughly 27 million fairgoers, equivalent to over 40 percent of the U.S. population, a serious deed considering that the Panic of 1893 had been the worst economic depression in the United States

---

* Despite its success at the fair and in a nod to the hard-luck American way, Ferris ultimately lost his shirt and died penniless of typhoid three years later. His ashes would be kept for more than a year by an undertaker demanding that his unpaid funeral expenses be met.

until that point. To this day, legends persist about hard-hit citizens selling their stoves or spending their burial money just to see the fair with their own eyes. The hype paid off; sweeping hardship aside, it would become the first American exposition to turn a profit.

A feat is a feat. The Columbian Exposition wasn't some static landscape like the high-desert New Mexico wilderness. Nor was it some futuristic rendering of a faraway utopia like Disney's Tomorrowland. In an urgent tone and familiar spirit, the exposition telegraphed that ordinary Americans could invert the deep depths of the tough times and the reigning economic disparity with a barrel roll of self-correcting moxie. "Its exhibits displayed achievements already available in America—provided, like Horatio Alger, you put your shoulder to the wheel," the great Stephen M. Silverman wrote in *The Amusement Park*. "Its location provided a harbinger for what was still available to those with fortitude—it stood on the Eastern edge of the American frontier."

And when depression-battered Americans did transcend their circumstances and fulfill the supposedly simple terms of the abracadabra, a shimmering marketplace would be waiting for them. Inside the exposition's great halls, fairgoers witnessed the debut of iconic American brands and commercial inventions, including Cracker Jack, Cream of Wheat, Juicy Fruit gum, Shredded Wheat cereal, the first fully electric kitchen, the first moving walkway, and the zipper. The familiar blue ribbon displayed on every can of Pabst lager crushed at tailgates, hipster parties, and lunch bucket dives originated with its first-place prize at the 1893 World's Fair. The company Vienna Beef links the global ascendance of the Chicago hot dog to its stand at the fair's Old Vienna section, where, despite a tragic lack of ketchup, the celebrated sandwich took off. As part of a broader social phenomenon, the vast array of goods at the fair and the status they seemed to bestow would inspire Thorstein Veblen, an American economist with a needlessly cool name, to coin the term *conspicuous consumption* in his book *The Theory of the Leisure Class* a few years later.

One common moniker attached to the Columbian Exposition— "The Fair That Changed America"—wins an overstuffed bear for its accuracy. One of the many millions to pass through the Chicago fair that year was Milton Hershey, who was a caramel maker at the time. After seeing a demonstration by a European chocolate maker, he purchased the exhibitor's equipment and, within years, sold his caramel concern and fully transitioned into the chocolate business. The writer Katharine Lee Bates, another visitor, found inspiration enough at the exposition to include its alabaster imagery in a poem that became the patriotic hymn "America the Beautiful." During a visit, Helen Keller climbed upon a German Krupp gun and apparently scandalized crowds when she met Braille innovator Frank Haven Hall and kissed him on the cheek in gratitude. Henry Ford also passed through and was captivated by the sight of an internal combustion engine at the fair; he would set out on the road to build his first car within three years. The writer L. Frank Baum modeled the Emerald City in *The Wonderful Wizard of Oz* on the fair's ornate "White City," while Elias Disney, a local carpenter who worked construction on the fair, would later regale his son Walt with stories about its magnificence.

Looking back on the fair's legacy, one historian christened it "a dry run for the mass marketing, packaging, and advertising of the twentieth century." One of the most highly trafficked displays adopted America's first living advertising trademark, Aunt Jemima, a character whose origins stemmed from a popular minstrel show. To inhabit the role, Nancy Green, a formerly enslaved woman, posed in a Mammy costume beside "the world's largest flour barrel." There, she sang, told inoffensive, magnolia-scented tales about forced servitude in antebellum America, and demoed the first-ever ready-made pancake mix for passersby. (Though the pancake's modern associations often lean toward hangovers or childhood breakfasts, early Aunt Jemima campaigns promoted pancakes as the perfect fuel for getting down to brass tacks. One ad appearing in a newspaper in 1893 shows a man standing at a worktable full of tools with the caption "He evidently feels like working. Everyone does who has enjoyed that kind of breakfast.")*

The hustle suffusing the fair didn't stop at the gates. Not wanting to pay 50 percent of his admission fee to the fair organizers, the legendary impresario Buffalo Bill Cody decided to open his famous traveling show Buffalo Bill's Wild West and Congress of Rough Riders of the World in an arena next to the fairground. With the help of the fabled sharpshooter Annie Oakley, some heavy-handed pioneer worship, and several dozen equestrians in Indian garb, Cody's show netted a swell million-dollar profit. Similarly impressive were the efforts of Bertha Palmer, a Chicago socialite and the matron of the deluxe hotel the Palmer House. Palmer used her sway to have women's achievements incorporated at the expositions and also directed her chefs to concoct a portable dessert for her hotel's fair-going guests. Consisting of butter, flour, eggs, sugar, chocolate, and walnuts, the pastry would eventually become known as the brownie.

Still, even in that atmosphere of high art, go-go gadgetry, and ostensible progress, the Columbian Exposition delivered a pinhole view of who the country was leaving behind. Sophia Hayden, the first female graduate of the architecture program at MIT, won the right to build the eighty-thousand-square-foot Women's Building at the fair and was paid 10 percent of what her male counterparts made for similar work there. (Hayden apparently never worked as an architect again.) During the construction and execution of the fair, several dozen workers died or were injured on the job, leaving behind families in need and without many options. Outside the grounds, the scope of the poverty and neglect were evidenced by the vast efforts made by Daniel Burnham, the exposition's head architect and one of the United States' most prolific builders, to pipe in clean spring water from nearby Wisconsin rather than draw from the cholera-infested neighborhoods nearby.† And in a tragic grace note, Chicago mayor Carter

* In the summer of 2020, Quaker Oats conceded "that Aunt Jemima's origins are based on a racial stereotype" and renamed its products under the Pearl Milling Company banner.
† It's darkly fitting that Burnham married into the family who supervised the powerful Chicago animal stockyards, the filth and smoke and stench of which covered urban

Harrison III, a relative of the recently defeated president Benjamin Harrison, was murdered at his home after giving the fair's closing address. His assassin, Patrick Eugene Prendergast, was a delusional job seeker who believed he had been denied a city job.[*]

Not all of the fair's shortcomings went unaddressed. In a standout moment of confrontation, the abolitionist Frederick Douglass and the journalist and activist Ida B. Wells, along with other writers, created a pamphlet titled *The Reason Why the American Negro Is Not in the World's Columbian Exposition* and distributed it to attendees in several languages. They sought to draw attention to the lack of opportunities for Black Americans in the exhibition's workforce and planning committees and, broadly, to the lack of documented Black contributions to national life on display in its tens of thousands of exhibits. "Theoretically open to all Americans," pamphlet contributor Ferdinand Lee Barnett wrote, "the Exposition practically is, literally and figuratively, a 'White City,' in the building of which the Colored American was allowed no helping hand, and in its glorious success he has no share."

In response, the fair's planners added a Colored American Day to the calendar, supplying two thousand free watermelons for attendees as a promotion. Needless to say, the idea did not win wide acclaim. While Wells boycotted the themed day, Douglass essentially headlined it. As he spoke to a crowd of thousands, a heckler interrupted, demanding that Douglass address the country's "Negro problem." Douglass replied, "The real problem has been given a false name. . . . The true problem is a national problem." Further, "the problem is whether the American people have honesty enough, loyalty enough, honor enough, patriotism enough to live up to their own Constitution." Thirty years after the Emancipation Proclamation, Douglass implored the group assembled there in the Land of Lincoln to celebrate American achievement to also consider the position of those who had faced

---

areas of Chicago. The low wages and deadly working conditions of workers in the yards would be thoroughly cataloged later in Upton Sinclair's influential novel *The Jungle*.

[*] Though newly invented electric chairs were part of a popular display at the Columbian Exposition, Prendergast was later executed by hanging.

such basic denials: "Bend down and measure him—measure him from the depths out of which he has risen."

It was one of his last campaigns; in 1895, Douglass died, and in 1896, the U.S. Supreme Court would uphold the *Plessy v. Ferguson* decision, the history-making "separate but equal" case that provided legal cover for states to impose Jim Crow laws and racial segregation for decades to follow. The next World's Fair, in Nashville, Tennessee, would be the first with separate facilities for the races of its attendees, followed by its 1898 counterpart in Omaha, where the exposition's opening address was titled "Destiny of the Anglo-Saxon."

———————————

As much as the Columbian Exposition dazzled millions with its shiny instruments and orgiastic force field of commerce and self-congratulation, it also held fast to an evergreen kernel of national identity: the boundlessness of the land, ranges open and ready to be put to use by diligent hands. Unlike the Paris fair, the grounds of the Chicago exposition were purposefully built away from the center of the city, allowing it to stretch across nearly seven hundred acres. The total spread of sights and sounds measured roughly a square mile.

In addition to its physical abundance, the confines of the fairgrounds had metaphorical dimensions to spare. That the Chicago World's Fair was four times larger than Paris' was a flex. America didn't just have space; it had a frontier. And during that summer of 1893, the concept of the frontier would transform from a geographical commodity into a cultural lodestar.

A few days after the fair's rowdy Independence Day program, which brought in a record 275,000 visitors and in which enough saltpeter was detonated to make a pyromaniac faint, a historian named Frederick Jackson Turner delivered a little-noticed speech during a meeting of the American Historical Association in Chicago. And as unlikely as it sounds, that speech, later dubbed "The Frontier Thesis," would become one of the most influential in American life. In it Turner argued that the true character of the United States—a rugged, heroic, industrious one, to be sure—had been forged by the waves of movement west across the continent by settlers. "Since the days when the fleet of Columbus sailed into the waters of the New World, America has been another name for opportunity," he asserted, "and the people of the United States have taken their tone from the incessant expansion which has not only been open but has even been forced upon them."

Turner didn't elaborate on which expansion had been forced upon the United States, but his synthesis of the American character struck a nerve as the country stretched to grasp the moment. In 1890s America, demography was fast changing, economic disparities were sweeping and destabilizing, corruption and patronage were rampant, and politics were radicalizing. Turner argued that some of that tension and uncertainty had to do with America's having reached the limits of the frontier. There were no more unseen horizons to master. "And now," he lamented, "four centuries from the discovery of America, at the end of a hundred years of life under the Constitution, the frontier has gone, and with its going has closed the first period of American history."

Whether he meant it to or not, Turner's nostalgic eulogy for the frontier would help cement the yeoman farmers, cowboys, outlaws, rustlers, hustlers, rangers, trailblazers, pioneers, homesteaders, scallywags, and speculators into caretakers of national values that, if not imperiled, were already vanishing faster than a tumbleweed in a Wichita dust storm.

The virtues that Turner credited with "winning a wilderness" will ring flowery, but familiar: "that restless, nervous energy; that dominant individualism, working for good and for evil, and withal that buoyancy and exuberance which comes with freedom." Away from the crusty norms and elitist culture and institutions of the East Coast and the feudal histories and class warfare of Europe and the psychic legacy of slavery, Americans could be their truest selves: frontier folk, no-nonsense and practical, driven and efficient. His pioneers wore their "coarseness and strength" firmly, like church neckties and corsets. They were on their own, and they didn't need help.

Moreover, if the World's Fair had presented a record of America's growing technological progress and expanding power, Turner implied that it was because the trials of the frontier spurred the very traditions of ambition and expedition that had brought those triumphs to life. His stout, romantic, self-justifying mixture of tall tales, fiction, legends, and history would settle over the nation like a layer of ozone. As the historian Colin Woodard noted, the frontier myth would quickly stand out, becoming "prevalent in political speech, in the way high schools taught history, in patriotic paintings—in short, everywhere."

Of course, *frontier* is a deficient term. First, it suggests that nothing and no one of value existed in those wide territorial expanses before American settlers arrived with their taming plows, rifles, and broadaxes to cultivate it. In especially ugly code, Turner marked the boundary of the frontier as "the meeting point between savagery and civilization."

Notably, his narrative came smack within a series of grim, pivotal moments that undercut the frontier's beefy themes of independence and bold self-construction. In 1890, hundreds of Lakota people (mostly women and children) were killed by U.S. troops in the massacre at Wounded Knee in South Dakota, in what's considered by some to have been the final confrontation over expansion between Native American communities and American forces and settlers. A few weeks after Turner spoke, the largest land rush in history took place in present-day Oklahoma on land that the Cherokee Nation had been forced to sell to the government for a song, only for it to be given away for free. Those were just two dents of many in the lore about the West being won solely by an unaffiliated tangle of brawny pioneers instead of by direct government force, policies, and incentives.

With the help of outside capital, the frontier also turned out to be big business. The longhorns herded up the legendary cattle trails by intrepid drovers ultimately ended up in the Chicago stockyards, a link in the same hardened production chain.* "The American cowboy is often seen as this independent, lonely individual, and they may have been that," explained historian Olivia Mahoney, "but they were also working for a giant food company headquartered in Chicago."

And from Chicago, settlers and troops went west while goods and frontier fables went east. This arrangement was made efficient, profitable, and possible by the railroads, which had largely been built with exploited foreign labor.† The railroads also expanded through an innovative new form of financing that would become enormously popular: government-funded capitalism. Counting up the sins of California's famous "Big Four" merchant tycoons who had profited mightily from the transcontinental railroad, the historian Richard White once explained, "They put little of their own money in it—they didn't have much. It was built on land grants, government loans, and government-guaranteed bonds. When their loans came due, they refused to pay and the government had to sue. In effect, they stumbled into a business model where the public takes the risk and those taking the subsidies reap the gain."

Just as the railroad companies had created time zones to help keep trains running on schedule, which eventually became the national standard for keeping time, so, too, did railroad boosters change the way that many defining American industries came into being: with a leg up from Washington, D.C., and taxpayers like you.

———————

Outside of Turner's Frontier Thesis, America's long-enduring cultural obsession with ten-gallon hats and range life has another essential link to the 1893 World's Fair. One more invention to

* Henry Ford, usually credited with inventing the assembly line, took a large loin of inspiration from the operations at the Chicago stockyards, where animals went in whole and came out packaged in pieces.

† In lieu of basic pleasantries, an English-Chinese phrase book for sale in 1867 contained translations for everyday sentences such as "Come at 7 every morning. Go home at 8 every night" and "I want to cut his wages."

make a public debut in Chicago was Thomas Edison's Kineto-scope, which delivered what's now considered to be the first-ever commercial movie. It wasn't much, a lo-fi batch of photographs, including galloping horses, shown in fast succession to paying crowds. Still, all these years later, from *The Great Train Robbery* through *Yellowstone*, the fascination with the West abides on-screen, reinforcing the national story with a set of epic themes like an American *Gilgamesh* or *Iliad*. In a calculated nod to the allure of individualistic frontier grit, presidents Dwight D. Eisenhower, Ronald Reagan, and Bill Clinton all claimed that their favorite movie was *High Noon*, the dusty, low-budget Cold War classic featuring Gary Cooper. In it, Cooper plays a duty-bound town marshal in prestate New Mexico who does battle with an evil gang of outlaws all by himself instead of running away with his new bride, a Quaker pacificist (Grace Kelly), who begs him to flee.

For the truest of believers in the exceptional American way, the frontier also implied a certain endlessness, as if it were pre-ordained to expand beyond the borders of the American West like the universe into the outer reaches. "Movement has been [American life's] dominant fact," Turner warned, "and, unless this training has no effect upon a people, the American energy will continually demand a wide field for its exercise." By this logic, which became popular logic, once the Pacific Ocean came into view, America as a nation of habitual line steppers was destined to keep going from there. It didn't take long for that to happen.

On July 7, 1893, a few days before Turner spoke, three ships appeared on the Chicago lakefront. They were caravels—replicas of the *Niña*, *Pinta*, and *Santa Maria*—built by Spain in honor of its adoptive son Columbus and towed across the Atlantic Ocean for the celebrations at the fairgrounds. Despite the diplomatic chumminess of the gesture, within five years, the United States and Spain would be at war over Spanish control of Cuba. It was a surefire sign of America's growing regional clout and imperial ambitions, the new frontiers that Turner had envisaged. By the end of the war and the start of the twentieth century, the United States had lassoed control of Cuba, Guam, Puerto Rico, the Philippines, and Hawaii, the first jewels of its profitable intercontinental empire. As for the three Columbus-themed ships, they remained docked in Chicago for the next twenty years before being dispatched for symbolic duty again. In 1914, they were commissioned to sail south for the opening of the Panama Canal, another foothold in the expansion of the American frontier. Fittingly, the power behind the canal was President Theodore Roosevelt, both a fabled former frontier lawman and a fellow historian who knew Turner personally and admired his work. The Panama Canal opened with great ceremonial pomp despite the absence of all three ships; only the *Santa Maria* made it past Milwaukee.

Yet another uniquely American way in which the frontier fascination manifests is in the nation's long legacy of mobility. Turner was right when he singled out movement as an American rite, a custom both kinetic and frenetic in its need for new wildernesses to conquer. More than all other Western industrialized nations, there has been a tradition (and usually a need) in America to uproot for opportunity, be it during the Gold Rush, the Dust Bowl, the Great Migration, Reconstruction, recessions, depressions, harvests, or pandemics.

Passage remains an ever-present theme as well as a national point of pride. Visiting the United States in the early 1800s, the French engineer Michel Chevalier was taken by the ubiquity of America's "wandering" laborers. Of Americans, Chevalier wrote quite beautifully, "No one assimilates a new method more rapidly; he is always ready to change his tools, his system, or his profession. He is a mechanic in his soul." Movement remains a fact of national life. In the 1950s, roughly 20 percent of the U.S. population still moved house each year. By one account, nearly a third of American job seekers relocated their lives for new positions between 1986 and 1997. Even as an aging workforce, the internet, remote work, and dual-income households have dampened the rate of mobility, the United States maintains one of the highest fevers for itinerancy in the world.

Not all these voyages have been instigated by good vibes, economic dynamism, and warm prospects, and not all movement is created equal. Even just in recent years, millions of Americans have remained either stationary or in constant motion by virtue of the high costs of housing and childcare or the general precarity of everyday life.* Those traditionalists who criticize late millennial and Gen Z workers for changing jobs every few years do so without grasping that the heady gold-watch-and-pension days are long dead. Ultimately, though, there's an irony in this pattern of American movement that goes root deep: even as the land demands sweat and blood and devotion, when the well dries up or another frontier opens, you gotta go for it.

To catch a glance at the modern frontier, I found myself in an unmarked warehouse in Tulsa, Oklahoma. There, like a visitor to the Chicago World's Fair some 130 years earlier, I stood marveling at an array of products, shelves upon shelves of high-tech offerings and evidence of breakneck innovations in material form, all in the service of a new way of life. But instead of electricity as the market's guiding current, the force here was weed.

Among the warehouse's provisions were contraptions so sophisticated in their construction that many of their uses baffled me. There were smell-proof backpacks, precision scales, tank-shaped bongs, pipes in every size and color, bulk packs of strawberry shortcake–flavored blunt wrappers, and inexplicably, at least to my soft, wet brain, mouse pads with designs of a stoned Homer Simpson dressed up like Hunter S. Thompson traipsing through a desert. Had I ever anticipated the need for a cleaning liquid that rids your bong of pot resin *while* you pull rips from it? I hadn't, but there was an entire endcap devoted to it. Over by the front, I passed a large stand of Randy's brand vaporizers embossed with a perfectly calibrated tagline: "Alt. Culture Pioneers."

I was there to meet Arshad Lasi, a twenty-four-year-old entrepreneur who had built up this empire in the green rush that accompanied Oklahoma's unlikely embrace of medical marijuana. Owing to the demands of his budding business and no other possible factors, Lasi had completely forgotten that we

---

* Nearly 75 percent of American adults live within thirty miles of their nearest parent or adult child, one study noted in 2020, while higher levels of wealth and education were associated with greater distance from family.

were supposed to meet at eleven that morning. Over the phone, he apologized and told me he'd be there in an hour, at the highest of high noons.

Rather than skulk around the parking lot like some narc, I spent the hour wandering Tulsa, a town loaded with remnants of frontiers past. Lasi's warehouse sat on the original Route 66, known to many dads as either "America's Main Street" or "the Mother Road." Across the street sat the Black Gold tattoo shop, a nod to Tulsa's bygone fixture as "The Oil Capital of the World," and an old defunct Spanish-style Sinclair gas station from 1929 that had since been listed on the National Registry of Historic Places. Next to the warehouse, in another unmistakable spliff of genius and opportunity, there was a taco shop.

The story of compulsive movement in America without Route 66 is like a blunt without strawberry shortcake flavoring—it lacks the saccharine quality that Americans love, even if the essence is mostly artificial. Indeed, nostalgia, schmaltz, and romance for our most legendary highway set off many of the same trills as the frontier: destiny, independence, and discovery. Starting on Michigan Avenue in downtown Chicago and spilling out some 2,200 miles later onto Ocean Avenue in Santa Monica, the Mother Road and the frontier occupy the same cerebral space.

In particular, Route 66 has a complicated significance in Oklahoma, where sections of the road trace parts of both the old Osage Indian Trail and the Trail of Tears. Later, in the Dust Bowl years, John Steinbeck dubbed Route 66 "the road of flight" in depicting the westward exodus of thousands of Okies during the Depression. Like many of their real-life migrant counterparts, the fictional Joads in *The Grapes of Wrath* arrived to find that the orange-scented Eden of dignity and jobs in California didn't exist for most, especially desperate new arrivals. Of California, the Okie folk legend and Dust Bowl balladeer Woody Guthrie similarly crooned, "Believe it or not, you won't find it so hot / if you ain't got the do-re-mi." That disenchantment was also no doubt familiar to readers of Victor H. Green's *The Negro Motorist Green Book*, the annual guidebook that steered Black travelers away from dangerous stops around the country, including the sundown towns along Route 66.

I drove a few miles west down 66 to see the city's statue of
Cyrus Avery, the Tulsa oilman and national highway commissioner known by the honorific "The Father of Route 66." Avery,
who lobbied Congress to make the highway national and elbowed
its trail to go through Tulsa, appears in bronze heading west on
Route 66 in his Model T with his wife, daughter, and the family cat. In the rendering, the Avery family car is about to collide
with another object: a horse-drawn wagon driven by a roughneck
heading east from the oil fields with his dog. Titled *East Meets
West*, the statue isn't subtle; the horses are afraid of the car, rear-
ing up onto their hind legs. Nevertheless, they're all sharing the
same road: horses and cars, industry and progress, work and wan-
derlust. Harkening back to the "pioneer days," Avery described
the bounty of Route 66 similarly: "I challenge anyone to show a
road of equal length that traverses more scenery, more agricul-
tural wealth, and more mineral wealth than does U.S. 66."

Beyond the Cyrus Avery statue sits the Cyrus Avery Bridge,
the first bridge in the United States built west of the Mississippi,
extending over the Arkansas River. No longer fit for use by either
cars or pedestrians, it's too expensive to repair and too prized to
tear down. In this way, the bridge is a battered emblem of all of
Route 66. When the Interstate Highway System came along, it
bypassed the old cut-throughs, small towns, and quirky pit stops
that had made the road iconic. Like the old, prosperous canal
towns whose demise was hastened by the railroad, the spread of
superhighways reduced sections of Route 66 to artifact, another
decertified frontier that had outlived popular use. Much like
Turner's frontier, the prose that accompanied Route 66's down-
grade was as purple as the thistles on the roadside. On the eve
of its decommission in 1985, one TV correspondent from *Today*
eulogized Route 66 on-air as "a thoroughfare for freedom, beat
across the wilderness, a time-warped ark upon which so many of
us determined the dimensions of our American dream."

Back at Lasi's warehouse, there was no time for that brand of senti-
mentality; a new frontier was alive and in bloom. Although several

states had legalized cannabis, either recreationally or medically, its emergence in deep-red Oklahoma in 2018 sent would-be tycoons scrambling to capitalize. "Oklahoma got this title of the Wild West," Lasi told me. "Licenses were really easy to come by, and regulation was not really there. There was no checking by the government or seed-to-sale tracking. It was very laissez-faire." (Today, given the state's conservative bona fides, the sudden appearance of dispensaries in Oklahoma feels like a hallucination.)

For entrepreneurs like Lasi, legalization was a chance they'd been waiting for. Arshad's parents, Imran and Gulzar, had immigrated from India when Arshad was young and had spent years managing convenience stores and gas stations. By 2011, they'd opened Nirvana, a smoke shop in Tulsa that sold tobacco and marijuana paraphernalia in the industry's gray zone. "My upbringing was always seeing my parents take a chance. They would move from Atlanta to Missouri if they could make an extra thousand dollars when they first got there. It didn't matter if they had to live in Joplin, Missouri, or even had to leave Atlanta and their community and their families. It was all about opportunity."

By his late teens, Arshad, who'd come up filling ice bags in the back of his parents' gas stations, had grown into a bigger role. Word of a dispensary for sale in Michigan led the family to consider uprooting their lives once again. "It was in this small township with about nine thousand people, so a big change for us," Lasi said. "But we thought, *No, this is gonna be good. We'll make good money.*" By the time they arrived, the property had already been sold at a price way above asking. "We left really disappointed, but we're like 'No, this is what we're gonna do. We're gonna sell weed.' We looked at a bunch of other opportunities across the country, but nothing seemed to click for us." When the medical marijuana ballot measure passed in Oklahoma, the Lasis pounced. "A month later, they opened up the application process for licenses, and we started applying." They already had the smoke shop, so extending the business seemed like a natural next step. Arshad helped first with the launch of Nirvana's dispensary and then with a wholesale distribution business, which sends thousands of products, including the family's own in-house creations, across the state.

Lasi's office in the back of the Nirvana warehouse is a white, windowless room that he shares with his parents. Minus the computers and stray jars of cannabis concentrate, it looks more like a teacher break room than an industrial nerve center. Along the walls are hand-lettered inspirational quotes. One behind Arshad's desk comes from the organizational psychologist Adam Grant: "The greatest originals," it reads, "are the ones who fail most because they're the ones who try the most."

It only took a few minutes with Lasi to sense that his ascendence in the family business had been inevitable. After starting a T-shirt company and running a digital advertising side hustle in high school, he had interned at a wealth management firm and then started studying business at the University of Houston. But after the family dispensary opened, he stacked his classes from Monday through Wednesday, taking the last flight to Tulsa on Wednesday, working Thursday through Sunday, and arriving back in Houston in time for class on Monday. When the pandemic hit, everything changed. Across the country, cannabis sales surged and classes went online. Lasi moved to Tulsa full-time as the family worked to keep up with the demand.

When I asked him at what point the reality of Nirvana's success had hit him, he admitted that the moment hadn't been obvious. The family had started a search for a new lawyer who understood the specifics of the cannabis business, and while most of the exchanges had been duds, one candidate took a deep dive into their books. "The meeting finished, and he's like, 'I don't think you guys realize this, but you're probably one of the biggest operators in the state of Oklahoma,'" Lasi explained. "And we were like, 'No. No, we're not. We're this mom, dad, and kid running around sometimes like a chicken with no head.'" For once, a lawyer was right; they were the biggest operator in the state by revenue, bigger than the multistate cannabis conglomerates that had wormed their way in with preexisting infrastructure and heavy backers.

Sketching out the basic requirements for a fulfilling existence, the Danish fairytale writer Hans Christian Andersen once wrote,

"Just living is not enough. . . . One must have sunshine, freedom, and a little flower." Beyond the sunshine and flower, Nirvana's growth had yielded Lasi some freedom to be creative. When I asked him if there was a product that he was most excited about, he brought over two bottles of Sauz, the company's homemade cannabis-infused sauces. "We made this [cannabis] infusion with a water-emulsified base," he explained. "And we were like, 'Well, what else can we put this in?' You can put it in beverages. You can put it in sodas, you can put it in lotion. And then we asked ourselves, 'Well, what if we just put it in barbecue sauce? What happens? Will it mesh? Will it taste good? Will it be shelf stable?' And we just did it and then decided, 'Let's bottle it and see if it sells. We can do small-batch productions, so let's make a thousand bottles.' And then we thought, 'Well, why stop at barbecue sauce? Let's make a whole line.' So we did chipotle, ketchup, sriracha, hot sauce, and steak sauce. It just happened."

Lasi raised an eyebrow when I suggested that it had been bold to introduce his own barbecue sauce in Oklahoma, a state known for being just north of the world's best barbecue. "You can't treat it like regular barbecue sauce," he said with a laugh. "You need to use very little, or you're gonna be *real stoned*. You mix it with your current sauce so you don't even taste it." Even in pursuit of a mainstream category, the Lasis had found a special niche.

Like the Wild West or the old retro landscapes of Route 66, the low-stakes, imaginative tinkering on display at Nirvana seemed like a scene from another time. In the past few decades, the mechanics of modern business in the United States, so unforgivingly focused on growth at all costs, have surrendered something fundamental in a quest to attract deep-pocketed speculators, extract profits, and enhance shareholder value. "The only essential thing is growth," the tech entrepreneur and investor Paul Graham once wrote, adding, "The good news is, if you get growth, everything else tends to fall into place. Which means you can use growth like a compass to make almost every decision you face." Unfortunately, not every compass points to true north, especially in a marketplace progressively creased by monopolies and corporate concentration. The Lasis themselves had found their way into the cannabis business in part because the built-up world of gas stations and convenience stores undercut even the hardest-working operators. "Oklahoma has QuikTrip and OnCue, these really big competitors," he explained. "It's very tough as a mom-and-pop to beat them in the gas station business."

Not even big businesses are safe from this environment of constant shakeout. One mind-boggling recent study found that over half of Fortune 500 companies doing business in 2003 (52 percent) had ceased to exist by 2023, lost to mergers, acquisitions, and bankruptcies. As the average life span of businesses has gotten dramatically shorter, the once-foolproof metrics of success and growth have come to defy earthly logic. In more and more cases, a company hasn't needed to turn a profit (see: Uber), serve its immediate community (see: Airbnb), improve its service (see: airlines), or safeguard its consumers from harm (see: social media platforms) to navigate successfully.

Sadly, nonsense tends to be contagious. In the past, I had interviewed business school students who had described a pressure to scheme up a buzzy, *disruptive* billion-dollar moon shot idea, ready-made for acquisition, instead of plotting out a business that would scale slowly and grow sustainably. "There are very real things—black-and-white, pen-and-paper things—that a business needs that, as a business student, you're not exposed to," Lasi explained when asked what he had learned in the field that he hadn't learned in class. "How to balance a checkbook," he added. "That was the first thing that slapped me in the face because they don't teach you that in school."

With such screwy incentive models, much of the durability and dynamism that did exist in the economy has been sacrificed for shortsighted, short-term wins. "The evidence of a growing short-term orientation among American public companies isn't hard to find," Stanford's Ryan Beck and Amit Seru noted, pointing out some terrifying recent examples. "Boeing's corner-cutting on the Max 737, Wells Fargo's fraudulent customer accounts and Johnson & Johnson's opioid scandal are all examples of short-term behavior with disastrous long-term consequences." Consider one bellwether survey in which four hundred of America's most prominent CFOs were asked if they'd trade their company's long-term economic value for a good quarterly report that met earnings expectations; 78 percent said they would.

The quirks of this modern ethic seem exceptional in many ways—and they are—but they also reflect the wide berth that business has long enjoyed in American life. From the early settler outposts and the railroads to the Interstate Highway System and Silicon Valley, the cultivating of American commercial frontiers has rarely taken into account how growth wreaks havoc on the broader ecosystem. In Oklahoma, for example, the consequences of the nineteenth-century land rushes and government-spurred settlement are a glossed-over part of the Dust Bowl story. More than a simple force of nature or an act of God, the epic dust storms that laid the plains low were partially the result of wicked droughts as well as a sudden drop in grain prices, inferior lands becoming overproduced by farmers who needed to make ends meet, and the mass abandonment of soil conservation methods. The resulting damage still defies description or a full accounting.

———————

After parting ways with Lasi, I headed to the Greenwood District, a historically Black section of the city that developed and thrived during Tulsa's boomtown days in the early 1900s. The legacy of Black Wall Street—the name bestowed upon Greenwood's wonder of interdependence and community-driven growth by the Black educator and advocate Booker T. Washington—is now overshadowed by the resentment and white-hot hatred that led to the razing of nearly all thirty-five blocks of Greenwood in the 1921 Tulsa race massacre. One of many racist spasms in the aftermath of World War I, the Tulsa attack was also the biggest act of domestic terrorism in U.S. history. (Ultimately, the attack would be downplayed in the media; none of the perpetrators in the death and destruction would ever be held to account; and most, if not all, insurance claims filed in good faith by Black home and business owners would be rejected.)

What the story of Greenwood's birth offers, however, is a corrective to many of the cautionary tales of wild, wanton, unequal, and uneven growth in America. One irony of Greenwood's success is that its self-sustaining framework was supercharged by Black exclusion from white businesses during Jim Crow.* Facing commercial isolation from white Tulsa, the district created its own economy. The first business established was a grocery store; local leaders went on to build transportation infrastructure, centers for care, community meeting places, and landmarks such as the grand Stradford Hotel, thought to be the nicest in Tulsa and the largest Black-owned hotel in the country. "The 1920 census recorded a multitude of African American–owned businesses in the community, including billiard halls, clothing stores, music shops, furniture stores, confectionaries, meat markets, hotels, restaurants, and a movie theatre," noted a 2018 report in the *American Journal of Economics and Sociology*. "According to the 1921 city directory, Greenwood comprised 191 businesses. It was also home to a library, two schools, a hospital, and two newspapers."

Greenwood wasn't perfect or uniformly prosperous, but it had demonstrated what tough-worn aspiration could produce with community support. With Black residents often excluded from banks and lines of credit, local investors bought in, funding the efforts of young entrepreneurs to get businesses off the ground. Alliances paid off. By one account, every dollar that entered the neighborhood changed hands twenty-six times before leaving. One of Greenwood's first residents, John Williams, started an auto repair shop and garage that became popular among all Tulsans, while his wife, Loula, not content with domestic work, opened a soda fountain and confection shop that became a popular spot for marriage proposals. The two then opened Dreamland, a lavish 750-person landmark theater in the heart of the town. The theater was in the middle of a film screening as word spread about an attack under way on the community; the Dream-

---

* After Oklahoma was admitted as a U.S. state in 1907, the very first law its legislature passed—quite literally Senate bill number one—was a measure to codify segregation on railways.

land would be burned to the ground. Greenwood, which rose in large part in a dogged embrace of the abracadabra, wouldn't be saved by it.

What I saw in modern Greenwood felt like an antidote to the frontier. One sentiment found on the walls and in the museums and shops of the district today as well as in the testimonies of its survivors and their descendants is the desire for rebirth; a contradiction to all those discarded landscapes that are forgotten, become obsolete, or diminish into passing scenery on the road to somewhere else. "This store had been a shoe-shine parlor back in 1921," Angela Robinson, who opened the Black Wall Street Corner Store & More in 2021, told me when I passed through. "It was important to have something the neighborhood needed and to pay homage to my forefathers."

Greenwood, like many historically Black areas of the country, is now physically split by an interstate highway. Leaving the main commercial stretch of Greenwood, I crossed under the highway, where a large mural spelling out "Black Wall St." had been painted on the interstate wall; fitted within each letter were images paying tribute to the wealth, grandeur, faith, culture, destruction, and ultimately the renewal of Greenwood. Across the street stood the historic Vernon African Methodist Episcopal Church, its stained-glass windows painted with the names of those who had helped rebuild the church after it had been burned down to its basement in 1921. As I ventured over, a group of Black teens from nearby Booker T. Washington High School gathered at the base of the highway mural. It was late May, and they were in their caps and gowns. They'd come to take graduation pictures there.

CHAPTER SIX

RIGHT OF WAY

THE TALL MYTH OF THE MAVERICK

**I WOULD RATHER NOT SPEAK WITH HISTORY
BUT HISTORY CAME TO ME.**

—JOY HARJO

The next morning, I left Tulsa for Pawhuska, forging through a landscape of small oil derricks, beefy livestock, deep green pastures, and stray armadillo roadkill. I'd come north to visit Circle Time, a weekly tradition where a group of schoolchildren and their families gather to sing songs and socialize on Friday mornings.

There was nothing outwardly remarkable about that activity. Nor was there anything unique about the way the students either stood up straighter or hammed up their antics more than usual in front of their parents. But all that quickly changed when a projector fired up, music began to play, and the kids began to sing.

Even at that early hour, I recognized the first song right away; it was an instrumental version of the 1970s psychedelic jam "Come and Get Your Love." Written by the Native American band Redbone, the song had been a Top 5 *Billboard* hit in its heyday and then enjoyed a generational resurgence in 2014 when the actor Chris Pratt danced an extended jig to it in the opening scene of the Marvel flick *Guardians of the Galaxy*. The key difference was that everyone in the small assembly room in Pawhuska was singing the song in Osage and reading from lyrics written in the Osage alphabet. As scenes go, this one felt momentous because there were maybe six Osage speakers left in the world. And now the chorus was growing.

Like most other scholars, linguists tend to be a persnickety, contentious lot, but generally, they seem to agree that an endangered language is close to its end when there's only one generation of older speakers left. Osage, like many Indigenous languages, lies treacherously between this moribund stage and extinction.

Listening to the students sing at Daposka Ahnkodapi (Our School in Osage), it was hard not to think about how the language hadn't fallen away because of globalization or depopulation or the other modern pressures that tend to imperil world languages. It hadn't been weakened by the natural biases against languages or dialects in multilingual societies. Instead, it had been deliberately targeted, lost in the way that an expanse of natural life is lost when a river is forcibly diverted.

Countless languages have been squeezed out of existence since the Tower of Babel fell, but only a fraction of those have been sidelined in an individualistic society founded in defense of free expression. By foisting English upon Native American groups, the U.S. government had betrayed its own proclaimed democratic keynotes with a familiar ruthlessness. And embedded within the effort to revive Osage, there lives a model to lead us all somewhere new and better.

After the song session wrapped, my host, a soft-spoken language whiz and administrator named Patrick Martin, explained that I'd arrived in the midst of some excitement. One day earlier, the official trailer for Martin Scorsese's true-crime drama *Killers of the Flower Moon* had dropped. The big-budget movie, which takes place largely in Pawhuska and stars Leonardo DiCaprio, Lily Gladstone, and Robert De Niro, had been long in the making. "A lot of us participated in it; some of us were in the background," Martin told me. He turned to ask the room if anyone had seen the trailer yet, and little hands shot up in the air. "Dude, it looks good!" one shouted. Earlier that week, a local delegation that included the current Osage Nation leader, Chief Geoffrey M. Standing Bear, had been flown to France ahead of the movie premiere at the Cannes Film Festival. The making of the blockbuster had also functioned as a welcome distraction and an economic boon for the area during the pandemic. "I was driving this taxi [in the film], and that was fun," Martin said, mimicking a gearshift. "I learned how to drive a Model T!"

Based on the gripping book of the same name by David Grann, *Killers of the Flower Moon* covers the Oklahoma oil boom in the early 1900s, during which a confederation of villains exploited and murdered several members of the Osage tribe for their wealth and for annual mineral payments known as headrights. The story also casts new attention on the federal government's paternalistic efforts to exert itself over the Osages by deputizing white guardians to control and allocate their own money for them. Worse yet, the murders continued for several years, with many left unsolved and the culprits more or less acting with impunity. Throughout the ordeal, and long afterward, the Osage community remained riven by fear and shattered by death. The idea of this grim, little-known epic reaching a mass audience held the promise of a disinfecting light. Much like Black Wall Street's destruction, it was a chapter of violence and resentment that had been suppressed or minimized in classrooms and public histories until quite recently.*

With Circle Time nearly up, Martin turned to the weekly assembly's pièce de résistance. "The Osages—the Wahzhazhe—are divided into three districts: Pah-soo-oleen, Zhahn-tsee-oleen, and Wah-xah-oleen," Martin said, using the traditional names for the Osage Nation and its local districts of Gray Horse, Hominy, and Pawhuska. "We have families from all three districts here today. And so we're going to end with a circle dance."

The children quickly fell into three circles around a drum in the center of the room and waited. With the regularly scheduled drummer out, a little imagination would be required. As a recording of a drumbeat and a chant sounded, the children of the

---

* Later, the buzz around the film would reportedly lead to a soft ban on Grann's book by teachers wary of Oklahoma's "divisive concepts" bill, which passed in 2021.

three districts sidestepped in a circle around the drum, a ritual act undertaken with a precision, austerity, and focus generally not associated with children of that age (or most adults, for that matter). At the end, the children dispersed and returned to their classrooms while their parents chatted briefly.

Martin introduced me around the room and then kindly offered to take me around the area. On the way out, he pointed to a garden in the playground where the children were learning to grow their own vegetables. "There's lettuce and spinach and broccoli," he said. "There's a chicken coop over there. So we have chickens, and we raise eggs."

We hopped into a van and took off for a stop not far from the school—an empty field set off by a granite marker. We idled for a minute before Martin cut the engine. The site had been home to the St. Louis School, an Indian boarding school for Osage girls that operated from 1887 until 1949. The marker noted that the school had been operated by a succession of missionary groups. Martin hesitated a little bit before he spoke. "My great-grandmother lived there. There was a Catholic school," he explained. "That's where she said the Osage was beaten out of her. That's the only thing she ever said. That was the boarding school experience for so many of the Indians. She never spoke Osage at home."

In a moment like this, you can't help but fumble around for something reasonable to say, no matter how dumb or obvious. All I came up with was that I had to believe that with trauma like that, there must be a reluctance to speak. "That's what trauma is," Martin replied. "Reluctance to speak about it. Nobody wants to talk about something like that . . . how they've been beaten or abused, had their hair cut. They had to take their clothes off, and they would shave all the boys' hair and cut their braids off. It was a big deal. It was deculturation instead of inculturation."

Indian boarding schools had once been a source of national pride. In fact, back at the Chicago World's Fair, one exhibit set among the modern wonders had been a working model of one such boarding school. Designed by the U.S. Bureau of Indian Affairs, the interactive schoolhouse set out to dazzle fairgoers with the spectacle of young Native American children assimilating into *American* culture. The participant-performers were real students shipped in from Indian boarding schools around the country, schools that most had been forced to attend, having been wrenched from their homes, families, and communities by federal authorities.

The schoolhouse display in Chicago had aimed to drive home the greater ideals of what exemplary American citizenship looked like to reformers at the time. Although the guiding policies, curricula, and philosophies of the boarding schools shifted slightly over their 150 years of operation, they generally led back to a few timeless themes: work and utility, individual-mindedness, and (more often than not) religion. "The boarding schools hoped to produce students that were economically self-sufficient by teaching work skills and instilling values and beliefs of possessive individualism, meaning you care about yourself and what you as a person own," one Native American advocacy group noted. "This opposed the basic Indian belief of communal ownership, which held that the land was for all people."

As fairgoers passed through the mock schoolhouse, the students were taught English and split off for menial tasks by gender. The girls sewed, and the boys did carpentry and made harnesses and shoes. The students were products making products; Daniel M. Browning, the commissioner of Indian affairs, who oversaw the fair's mock boarding school, rhapsodized in a government report about how the exhibit heroically contradicted American assumptions about the abilities of Native Americans to conform, achieve, and yield. "It shows concretely and unmistakably [the Indian's] readiness and ability for the new conditions of civilized life and American citizenship upon which he is entering," he boasted. "Indian youth actually at the school-room desk, the work bench, the kitchen stove, and the sewing machine, and surrounded by the most creditable displays of the products of their own handiwork, are plain facts not to be disputed, even though they fail to fit the cherished theories as to what the race is or is not capable of."

Of the hundreds established, the best-known Indian boarding school operated out of a former army barracks in Pennsylvania under an ominous name: the Carlisle Indian Industrial
School. Viewed as a model for other schools, Carlisle was run
by the country's most influential Indian educator, Richard Henry
Pratt, an army veteran who had traded frontier battles against
Native Americans for culture wars against them in the classroom.
He had adapted the Carlisle curriculum from a prison education
project and originated the stark, well-known motto of the mission of reeducation: "Kill the Indian in him and save the man."*
As at many boarding schools, including the one Martin showed
me, part of the intake process at Carlisle involved stripping the
students of their traditional dress and burning the clothes, cutting off the students' braids and long hair, and forbidding the use
of Native American tongues (with brutal punishments for any
deviation). Then there came a rechristening. "Almost immediately our names were changed to those in common use in the
English language," a Sioux man named Luther Standing Bear
later wrote of an early moment at Carlisle. "I was told to take a
pointer and select a name for myself from the list written on the
blackboard. I did, and since one was just as good as another, as I
could not distinguish any difference in them, I placed the pointer
on the name Luther." In the classroom, the students would learn
to venerate Columbus; in the mess halls, they'd eat completely
unfamiliar foods; and in the summer, they'd often be farmed out
to work field or menial jobs or perform domestic labor in the
homes of strangers.

Indian boarding schools weren't just a racist flash in a racist
pan. The heart of the boarding school era lasted about 120 years,
overlapping with the last years of slavery and reforming moder-
ately during the Depression. Boarding schools outlasted World
War II—even as Native American–language code talkers saved
the lives of thousands of American troops and shortened the

---

* One chilling quote from Pratt's autobiography, *Battlefield and Classroom*, reads, "In
Indian civilization I am a Baptist, because I believe in immersing the Indians in our
civilization and when we get them under, holding them there until they are thoroughly soaked."

war by creating near-unbreakable codes—and went through the moon landing, truly changing focus only in the late 1970s after Native American parents were guaranteed autonomy over their own children again by an act of Congress. Zooming out, the crusade to convert Native Americans goes all the way back to early European settlement in North America. When Harvard, for example, nearly went bankrupt during its early years in the 1600s, it secured funds for its survival by promising that it would "Christianize" Native American students. Indeed, the very first Bible ever printed in North America came from Harvard's printing press; it was written in Algonquian.

As we drove around, Martin told me he had taken over as the superintendent of Daposka Ahnkodapi after spending several years in Europe teaching various languages. He'd been drawn to return home, though, and found himself working as the principal of a bilingual school in Tulsa before the opportunity in Pawhuska came calling. "I was fluent in Spanish and French, and others helped me come here and learn Osage, which I'm still in progress," he said. "But I knew how to run a school, which is what they wanted. The language was a bonus." The school now had over fifty students across two small campuses, one for infants through kindergarten and another for first through seventh grades.

Learning Osage isn't like picking up another language with an existing infrastructure; it is more like restoring a bridge out of scattered materials without a blueprint. "The language was oral, it was never written," Martin said of Osage. "Whereas the Cherokee language, another tribe in Oklahoma that's here now from the Trail of Tears, they had a leader named Sequoia, and he invented this alphabet. And so the Cherokee language has been written down and they are more advanced. There are a lot more native speakers because of this Sequoia, because he made a language." The Osage alphabet, he went on, had since been built out and looked a bit like Greek, but without any of the familiar roots. It wasn't easy or intuitive. "I studied Chinese when I was in high school," he added. "So really, to me, this is more like Chinese, just as far as your brain learning it. Because there's nothing to grasp on to, no Latin or Greek, no romance languages."

As we continued our ride, I asked Martin if his students had absorbed the context of why they were learning Osage or the importance of knowing the language. "They're very aware of the reason for the school, the mission," he said. "And the parents have to buy into it. And they're very aware, too, because, if not, the kids go to the public school." To affirm their commitment, the parents were required to take Osage-language classes once a week in the evening. "Everybody buying into this makes it work."

As a waning language becomes arid, so, too, do the sacred traditions, histories, and knowledge that inform it. In addition to the language, the songs and the rituals were finding new life. On our drive, we passed the town cultural center, which facilitates workshops for Osage members to learn to make their own moccasins and drumsticks, two more fragments in the mosaic. "It's to start with language and build out from there."

The mission brought back to mind his great-grandmother. "I was about fourteen when she died, so I knew her pretty well," Martin said. "I never heard her speak Osage, but I knew she did when she was little. I mean, it was understood. But it wasn't like right now, where we're really promoting it. I wish she were alive so we could talk about it."

———

Our next stop was downtown Pawhuska. First, Martin showed me around Kihekah Avenue, the town's main street, meaning "chief" in Osage. It was where the 1920s had been re-created for *Killers of the Flower Moon*. The street had a lived-in quality that spoke to ongoing economic distress. Amid some old brick facades were antique storefronts that had been left up from the movie shoot along with some vacant buildings. For the film, the entire road had been shut down and covered in dirt. "I remember when they started, they came out and took soil samples from us because they were trying to find the right dirt," Leah Jenkins, an Osage Nation member who works with Martin at Daposka Ahnkodapi, had told me earlier. A century-old steam engine hauled into town from a Nevada museum had been the source of some delight. "When my son was having baseball practice one day up here," she said, "they could hear the train making a sound."

As we walked south, the vibe of the town began to change, with a mass of cars and the sound of people. Martin told me to take notice of the out-of-state license plates. I spotted a minivan from Colorado and a sedan from Arkansas, but also visitors from as far away as Illinois and Michigan. He showed me into a bright, airy lobby that was jam-packed with tourists, mostly middle-aged women. Off a small-town street, we were now suddenly inside a massive, intensely designed home goods store flaunting an obscene number of decorative pillows, animal-themed dishware and crafts, and faux-wood decorative signs stenciled with messages like "I love you like biscuits and gravy." Beyond a tall entryway, a restaurant bustled with a lunch-hour rush. Martin led me upstairs to the bakery, which had a display case full of sticky buns and cinnamon rolls.

Martin and I had entered the high-fructose domain of Ree Drummond, a local blogger turned cookbook and children's book author turned Food Network star. Drummond, who is white and better known as "The Pioneer Woman," had built an empire here on the vastness of the reservation. In addition to the bakery, restaurant, and home goods trifecta known as the Mercantile, she had opened an ice cream shop, a pizzeria, and a hotel branded as a boardinghouse in recent years, all within a block or two of one another. Drummond devotees from all corners of the country go there by the busload. Describing the deep appeal of her brand of glamorized range life, the journalist Amanda Fortini wrote, "The Pioneer Woman is like an artifact from a more wholesome era: Ozzie and Harriet on a ranch."[*]

It was surreal to observe two different sections of the same small town of a few thousand people undergoing two massive and dissimilar cultural moments. I asked Martin if there was a prevailing opinion about the Pioneer Woman franchise in Pawhuska.

---

[*] Driving the aesthetic home, the actor Reese Witherspoon had once been attached to play Drummond in a film adaptation of Drummond's memoir *Black Heels to Tractor Wheels*, but the project ultimately stalled in production.

He told me that the local perception was that Drummond was good for business. But of course, feelings went deeper than that. "The town is divided and it always has been between whites and Osages," he explained. "And so there is some animosity throughout, which stems from this movie." The Pioneer Woman origin story began after Ree Drummond married into the locally famous (and comically powerful) Drummond family, who have ranched cattle in Oklahoma for generations and whose holdings now include a chunk of land thirty times the size of Manhattan. Today, the Drummonds rank among the twenty-five biggest landowners in America.* Historically, they were purported to have preyed on the Osages, gouging them at their old trading stores. "You go to a store, and you have one price; then an Osage comes in, and they have a higher price," Martin said. "There's a lot of ill will."

These tensions run at least a century old, going back to the days of the oil boom and the Osage murders. "They were put in charge of Osage families' finances, borrowed from Osage estates, probated Osage wills, and collected on debts that they claimed as owners of a government-licensed store," the journalist Rachel Adams-Heard wrote of the Drummonds in Bloomberg in 2022. "They bought headright fractions, even as they lobbied for the headright system to be abolished."

Still, Martin joked that they hadn't brought up bad blood with the Drummonds "because the bakery is good." And it was. As we sat down over some sausage rolls, he explained how outsiders like the Drummonds had amassed the rights to annual payments that had been earmarked for the Osage community. (In a 2023 statement about the premiere of *Killers of the Flower Moon*, the Osage Nation made a special point of noting that 26 percent of oil headrights were still controlled by "non-Osage individuals, churches, universities, and other non-Osage institutions.") I asked if the Drummonds had since made an effort to smooth things over. "No," he said, "and they could. The Drummonds

---

* One of their tenants is the U.S. government, which has reportedly paid the family $20 million–plus over the past few decades to host wild animals on their property in the name of animal protection.

have several headrights, and they shouldn't. They could just give 'em back. It's just one of those things people won't forget."*

———————

"History is a merciless judge," David Grann wrote in *Killers of the Flower Moon*. "It lays bare our tragic blunders and foolish missteps and exposes our most intimate secrets, wielding the power of hindsight like an arrogant detective who seems to know the end of the mystery from the outset." This is as true across those three square miles of northeastern Oklahoma as it is across the expanses of the entire United States.

Before Martin and I parted ways, he told me a story. "We're accredited as a private school, so we don't get state funds," he started, "but we're accredited by the state. And we have an accreditation visitor come once a year; she was here about a month ago. We go through this whole checklist of questions, and then she says, 'Now, this is new: I have to ask you this: Do you teach history in a way that would make anybody uncomfortable?' And I looked at her and said, 'I don't know how to answer that.'" At that point, he explained that the visitor had kind of smiled, seemingly as if she understood that she was asking the question at a Native American school. "I said, 'Yeah. It really is uncomfortable,'" Martin went on. "'It makes me uncomfortable to teach American history *and* Native American history. So the answer is yes.' It could be a tick against us, but it doesn't matter since we're private. But if we were public, I could get fired."

It might have been the aftereffects of the sausage roll, but I suddenly felt tired. I thought about the depth of delusion thrumming through the story and the level of collective dysfunction that had made it possible. And I wondered how things could be different.

Wending my way through Pawhuska earlier that morning, I'd taken notes about what I'd seen. The shiny new Osage Nation government campus with stop signs in English and Osage, a free health clinic for tribal members, special parking spaces for elders,

* Ree Drummond's press team declined to respond to a request for comment.

the offices of a local newspaper, a newly dedicated memorial for Osage veterans of the U.S. military. Next door to Daposka Ahn-kodapi, a low-cost childcare center hummed with activity. Both of the facilities operated with tribal funds that were poured back into the community; purpose enabling more purpose. "None of the tribes had any money before casinos," Martin explained. "This is all the result of the casino operations and how successful they've been."

When I looked at my notes later, I knew I hadn't been in a utopia; there wasn't such a thing. But I had been in a community that was seemingly doing its best to equip its members with support and imbue civic life with meaning. Osage high school graduates were automatically eligible for tribal resources for college or vocational training. And on our way back to the school, Martin detoured us to a newly built pavilion where members of the Nation, even far-flung and scattered ones, would be returning for the annual ceremonial dances in June. On the way there, we passed a spray-painted mural created by an arts collective for Native American youths; it featured an Osage dancer in traditional attire. Below it in Osage, it read, "It is time for the dances for the Osage people. All people are coming like a welcome song."

I couldn't help but envy the shape of such a community—a place with inbuilt support where successes were designed to flow directly back to its members in visible, affirming ways. Oddly enough, seeing Pawhuska also helped clarify the draw of Ree Drummond and the world of the Pioneer Woman, but for different reasons. Given what it takes to muscle through an American culture so suffused with obstacles and self-reliance, how could anybody resist the escapist pull of Drummond's make-believe life, where, as one writer put it, "Whole continents of contemporary worry go unmentioned . . . a universe free from credit-card debt, toxins, 'work-life balance,' and marital strife."

As important as they are, these individual stresses aren't the only costs of America's lonesome code. Across a few days in Tulsa and Pawhuska, I'd seen how our totalizing way of life had cut off entire inventories of meaning. By way of the Trail of Tears and frontier paths, the old Santa Fe Railway and Route 66, willingly or by force, people had arrived here to build a life or just salvage one, only to scatter again once the droughts and busts and infernos stoked by human hands made it impossible for them to stay.

On the way back to Tulsa, I passed a few more disused Indian boarding schools on unremarkable roads and felt, beneath the sense of horror, a dark irony in the idea of forcing entire communities to conform to an ethos of individuality. Hundreds of these schools were raised around the country, and, as the law professor Maggie Blackhawk noted in 2024, they were also "replicated in the Philippines, Hawaii and other sites of American colonization." These schools may have been shuttered or changed course, but the belief behind them is still detectable in our modern-day, individualistic, business-obsessed culture, where ambition and personal attainment outstrip the collective good.

One way to think about this is to step back and look at how the singular genius-mavericks, mold-breaking entrepreneurs, and "self-made" successes have been elevated to celebrity in America, often at the expense of the communities and structures as well as the unseen and often uncompensated helpers who made their triumphs possible. Thomas Edison, the avatar of excessive perspiration, is almost certainly America's most famous inventor. But he wouldn't be such an object of fascination were it not for the work of the rivals and employees whom Edison bought out, leaned on, pilfered from, or deliberately overshadowed over the years. Granville Woods and Lewis Latimer, two unsung, self-taught Black inventors, offer up two clear examples. After Woods invented the multiplex telegraph, which enabled train station personnel to communicate with moving trains, Edison unsuccessfully sued him, claiming that Woods hadn't actually invented it first.[*] (After losing the suit, Edison offered Woods a job; he declined.) Likewise, it was Latimer's invention of the carbon filament that made Edison's world-changing lightbulbs efficient enough to be affordable for the masses.

To this day, Edison personifies the conventions upheld in American life. Though descended from ancestors who had fled

---

[*] Woods also built a complex telephone transmitter that was deemed a superior invention to Alexander Graham Bell's telephone—and a sufficient enough commercial threat that Bell bought it.

to Nova Scotia during the American Revolution out of loyalty to the British Crown and fought against the United States in the War of 1812, Edison would secure more than a thousand patents in his lifetime, averaging one every eleven days. The youngest of seven children in Ohio (only four of whom would survive to adulthood), he was a bad student who would be taught telegraphy and Morse code by a grateful railroad worker whose son Edison had saved from being hit by a train. He hustled newspapers as a teen, printing his own broadsheets on a portable letterpress and selling them on trains. During a fifteen-year period of his career, he also claimed to average twenty hours of work per day and generally slept only about three or four hours a night, regarding sleep as a "criminal" and wasteful "heritage from our cave days." It's fitting that his most celebrated invention was the lightbulb, which would change humanity's relationship with sleep and work and also serve as a primordial emoji symbolizing new ideas, enlightenment, and American progress all at once.

Wyn Wachhorst, one of Edison's many biographers, defined this archetype as the Edison symbol. "The Edison symbol has been a vehicle for every major American theme: the gospel of technological progress, the rural Protestant virtues (hard work, initiative, perseverance, prudence, honesty, frugality, etc.), the success mythology of the self-made man, individualism, optimism, practicality, anti-intellectualism, the American Adam and the New World Eden (America as a new beginning for mankind), the sense of world mission, democracy, egalitarianism, the idealization of youth, and others." With those symbolic tailwinds (along with Edison's predilection for self-promotion), it was inevitable that he'd become one of the most famous and admired Americans during his lifetime.[*]

Whether it's Edison, Edsel, Elon Musk, or Einstein, the American affinity for fixing a spotlight on individuals turns up in wild, wide-ranging ways. Historians may split wires over the true creator of the lightbulb, but without Edison, we probably

---

[*] Sadly, Granville Woods didn't have that luxury. Though dubbed "the Black Edison" by many for his prolificacy, he would often tell people he was from Australia instead of Ohio because he believed it would garner him more respect in his business dealings.

wouldn't have another critical American invention: the lightbulb joke, which generally twists on the idea that something's wrong if it takes more than one person to do a job.

One analysis of early twenty-first-century start-ups found that among tech companies that raised at least $10 million in funding, the biggest segment of them by far (45.9 percent) were start-ups created by solo entrepreneurs instead of founder groups of two, three, four, or more. Similar research also found that more than half of start-ups (52.3 percent) that were successfully acquired, absorbed, or otherwise bought out in the early 2010s were companies with single founders.

In her book *The Act of Choosing*, the social psychologist Sheena Iyengar looked at how the individualistic bent in America compares to the ethos of various national cultures. Citing one fascinating study of Olympic athletes, she points out that speeches given by American medalists disproportionately focused on their own achievements or personal stories, while Japanese winners "were more likely to attribute their success to the people who supported them." She also highlighted media coverage of major financial scandals in which American newspapers focused on the specific characters and wayward actors involved, while Japanese papers "referred more to institutional factors, such as poor oversight by managers."

The spirit behind our single-minded attention to individuals has never existed in a vacuum; it's always in the service of something else. Take the federal government's effort to socially engineer whole Native American generations into a force of assimilated, English-speaking laborers.* Or the steel railroad lines that ran through Chicago and artificially carved up the West, which blossomed not out of organic national demand but as by-products

---

* In his 1885 memoir, *Hunting Trips of a Ranchman*, here's how Theodore Roosevelt articulated his telltale prescription for Native American groups who lived off the land instead of turning land into productive farms and homesteads: "let him, like these whites, who will not work, perish from the face of the earth which he cumbers."

of furious, ego-driven competition among robber barons using public funds. Only in America do these two cases fit within the same operating philosophy of prioritizing industry ahead of the public good.

Contemporary evidence of this imbalance is easy to see in the ways that communities have handed over responsibility for the basic features and utilities of society to major companies. During the pandemic, large retailers like Target simply declared themselves part of the country's "essential" infrastructure to keep their stores and warehouses open—no matter the potential hazards for their employees. In recent years, ride-sharing apps like Uber and Lyft have all but replaced public transportation in certain markets and for certain travelers, while McDonald's is where lonely seniors and kids who need internet to do their homework often go in underserved areas without libraries, public Wi-Fi, or community centers. And regardless of the fact that it peddles a powerful diarrhetic, it's kind of weird that Starbucks holds the unofficial title of America's default public bathroom.

Much like a Starbucks bathroom, Americans' pact with business has considerable spillover. There are few places in the democratic world where businesses actively veer into politics and public discourse with more energy and presumption than the United States—whether it's apparel businesses making toothless statements about gun control and reproductive rights, a Lockheed Martin–branded rainbow float rolling through a pride parade, or industry lobbying groups such as the American Petroleum Institute, the American Dehydrated Onion and Garlic Association, and the Balloon Council, which have been oddly silent on the country's recent struggles with inflation.

In the place of meaningful social change, American businesses serve as the face of cosmetic inertia. Following the killing of George Floyd by Minneapolis police in 2020, several companies began rebranding their historically insensitive wares and trademarks. That summer, Disney's amusement parks dropped the plantation-themed "Song of the South" from their Splash Mountain rides in Florida and California. Cream of Wheat, the storied 130-year-old kitchen staple, phased out its longtime icon, a smiling Black chef named Rastus, a derogatory term for a Black man. Over the ensuing months, a chain reaction followed as Land O'Lakes, the Minnesota dairy brand, removed the long-standing image of a Native American woman from its packaging. Eskimo Pie became Edy's Pie, and Uncle Ben's became Ben's Original. NASCAR banned fans at its venues from toting Confederate flags. The Cleveland Indians became the Cleveland Guardians, and the Washington Redskins became the Washington Commanders.

As big business seemed to tilt to the moment, observers applauded the moves while also noting their obvious limitations. "Taking the stereotypical image of a Black servant off the Cream of Wheat boxes isn't going to end systemic racism tomorrow," said Professor Todd Boyd, who chairs a program on race and popular culture at USC, "but it's part of a larger series of myths, thoughts and ideas that combined have the ability to change perceptions." For now, the gulf between public relations and private action remains enormous. In the place of wage transparency or boardroom representation, American workers watched a thousand Diversity, Equity, and Inclusion (DEI) initiatives bloom and then disappear. After expressing solidarity with racial justice projects around the country, JPMorgan Chase CEO Jamie Dimon was pictured taking a symbolic knee with employees while visiting a local bank branch near his country home in 2020. The following year, hours after publishing Dimon's passionate shareholder letter about the corporate duty to battle racism and income inequality, the bank giant urged its shareholders to reject a proposal for a racial equity audit of the company and its practices.

The privileging of business in America is ubiquitous, detectable even in the strangest of places. Speaking at a health forum in June 2023, Robin Vos, the speaker of the Wisconsin State Assembly, who built his fortune as a landlord, explained that "it saddens me . . . to think about how many Americans would be alive in our workforce doing all the things that helped make America great if we hadn't had easy abortion access."

At bottom, this is what the primacy of American business looks and sounds like. By one estimate, the existence of a single Walmart Supercenter store costs American taxpayers an average of over a million dollars each year in public assistance money received by its underpaid workers for food, housing, and health-care. (There are 3,500-plus of these stores in the United States, by the way.) Meanwhile, a 2023 study found that over 25 percent of all food stamps used in the United States are spent at Walmart stores. Under this arrangement, the company and its sharehold-ers make out twice while the tax-hating public foots the bill for it and then blames the workers for needing help or not trying hard enough. (And this isn't even getting into the popular gripe that Walmart's initial rise from regional player into the world's big-gest retailer and the United States' largest private employer was powered in part by the billions of dollars it received in tax breaks, free land, cash grants, and more.)

As we shift from the foundations of American work to our modern rough-and-tumble arrangement, I can't help but think about what so many have given (or have been forced to give) for this all-consuming, at-all-costs faith in individual destiny; what we're missing by devoting our best efforts in the provision of work; and whether it wouldn't be wise for us to try for something better. This dilemma brings to mind the classic lightbulb joke: How many psychotherapists does it take to change a lightbulb? Only one, but the lightbulb really has to want to change.

PART II

THE PERSPIRATION

CHAPTER SEVEN

BUSTLE

WORK THEATER AND THE DEATH OF LEISURE

IF WORKING HARD MADE YOU RICH,
DONKEYS WOULD BE COVERED IN GOLD.

—FRENCH PROVERB

Throughout the centuries, Paris has been an axis around which big ideas have revolved. Its intellectual movements, salons, science labs, and studios have influenced thought, culture, and philosophy the world over, while the clatter of French defiance has poured out of Paris and into caricature. It's telling that Georges-Eugène Haussmann, the controversial nineteenth-century functionary who destroyed much of the ancient city and then rebuilt it into its grand and now-familiar form, did so in part with the hope of making Paris physically resistant to the barricades regularly built by French revolutionaries. (It's also telling that this plan didn't work out.)

With that legacy in mind, I was hardly surprised that within hours of arriving there, I was presented with a question that cut right to the heart of the moment: Are you Team Alfie or are you Team Gabriel? Like Jean-Paul Sartre and Albert Camus before them, Alfie and Gabriel were two cultural figures who had become fabled rivals in France—not in the pursuit of letters but as competing love interests in the hit Netflix sitcom *Emily in Paris*. This urgent debate had been instigated by a Parisian named Fabien, who is the host of a popular *Emily in Paris* tour that I had signed up for shortly after coughing up plane fare to France.

For the tragically uninitiated, *Emily in Paris* follows the exploits of Emily Cooper, a twentysomething marketing inge-nue from Chicago played by Lily Collins. And her story, however unintentionally, offers a snapshot of how the American relation-ship with work is out of step with that of much of the world. The saga begins when Emily's company acquires a French marketing firm, and her boss, who is tasked with aiding the transition, finds out she's pregnant and declines the posting in Paris. And so the mission inexplicably falls to Emily, who is promised a promotion if she makes it through a year. Armed with nothing but can-do American moxie and a French translation app, Emily parachutes into La Ville Lumière, where she is immediately reviled by her new French coworkers for her irrepressible midwestern enthusi-asm, provincialism, and bright-eyed naiveté. Within hours of her arrival, the entire Paris office dubs her *le plouc* (the hick).

Naturally, Emily does what any American corporate careerist would do and strives to make herself indispensable. She obsesses over her job, ingratiates herself with clients, engineers bizarre but successful brand campaigns on social media, and fends off work-place hostilities potent enough to make a mime shriek. Over the mess of the first few seasons, Emily also finds herself torn pro-fessionally between two jobs and torn romantically between two men, Alfie (a hunky British finance exec) and Gabriel (a hunky Norman chef and Emily's downstairs neighbor).

The in-person deliberation over Alfie and Gabriel that I was now witnessing in Paris served as a testament to the show's suc-cess; I was one of a dozen tourgoers from six different countries to gather in the Latin Quarter and sink a spring afternoon in trib-ute to the show. (For those wondering, the overwhelming major-ity of the group preferred the Frenchman Gabriel, although two friends visiting Paris from Belgium were Team Alfie. Playing the role of Switzerland was a bemused German father on holiday with his wife and teenage daughter, who hadn't seen the show and abstained.) Notably missing was my fiancée—also named

Emily, also in Paris—who politely but firmly declined an invitation to join me on the tour.

Anyone with a passing awareness of *Emily in Paris* likely knows that the show has proven to be a tiny bit divisive. First released during the early days of the pandemic, its gauzy, sweeping shots of Paris and parade of fashionable and telegenic characters served as a frivolous reprieve for couch-bound streamers. Similarly soothing were its Seine-deep gaps in reality, perspective, and narrative logic, all of which assisted in the provision of low-stakes, good old-fashioned, uncomplicated TV. *"Emily in Paris* Is like Happy Hour for the Brain," read the headline of an approving piece by Sangeeta Singh-Kurtz for The Cut, which one commenter echoed with "Watching this show was like popping a bunch of Xanax." In its presentation of Paris, the show mostly vanishes from view the city's myriad troubles: traffic, riots, strikes, class conflicts, crime, and poverty. As Emily dashes off to countryside chateaux, Provence, or Saint-Tropez, the often sluggish regional trains operate without a hiccup and Paris' tension-wrought *banlieues* elude the sight lines. In Emily's universe, even McDonald's is delicious, while the biggest hazard is either Paris' lack of air-conditioning or the occasional finger being severed while sabering open a bottle of champagne.* "Emily's story is about living an anxiety-free existence without any negative consequences," the culture writer Alex Abed-Santos explained in a screed against the show, a screed in which he also allowed that he was "fine with letting *Emily in Paris* eat my brain." Much like the Pioneer Woman, the popularity of the show seems to speak to the escapism that many of us require to stay sane amid the stressors and obscene demands of the real world.

Nevertheless, *Emily in Paris* has drawn its share of unforgiving detractors. "At times, I wondered what the French had done to deserve *Emily in Paris*," wrote Rebecca Nicholson in *The Guardian*. "Beneath the Bambi-like visage and the sweet ebullience lies a stark void of nothingness," Iva Dixit wrote of the Emily char-

---

* With the help of some quick action and socialized medicine, the finger is sewn back on, and everyone laughs about it.

acter in *The New York Times Magazine*. Even our group's intrepid host, Fabien, was willing to concede that "French people think the show is cliché. They love to hate the show."

As a middle-aged American man in New Balance sneakers attending an *Emily in Paris* tour by himself, I try to reserve comment on the stylistic merits of anything. But as a document of American work culture colliding absurdly with French life, I find it useful. *Emily in Paris* is a show that can exist only because there's a built-in familiarity with Americans as a relentlessly career-obsessed people and France as a place that's generally suspicious of The Grind.

Of course, it's dangerous or at least troublesome to make typecasts of two entire countries. (Yes, there are plenty of hard workers in France and no shortage of *flaneurs* in America.) Still, as a thought exercise in making clarifying contrasts, the show offers fertile terroir. As Philippe Thureau-Dangin, the owner of a French publishing firm, generously wondered aloud, "Maybe the creators of the series are trying to mimic Molière. Molière also exaggerated and created impossible situations for comedic effect." (Right on, Philippe.)

Entire arrondissements of opinion havers have lambasted the show for its alleged vapid writing and lazy stereotyping, but I'd argue that *Emily in Paris* still packs some wormwood into the absinthe. In the show's pilot, when a friend asks Emily how she plans to navigate an entire new life and job in Paris without any knowledge of French, she replies with the long-sanctioned American cri de coeur "Fake it till you make it." On her first full day of work in Paris, she arrives early at 8:30 a.m., only to wait outside in a panic before learning that the office doesn't open until 10:30. ("We sometimes don't start work until eleven!" Fabien told our group.) Then the entire office—antagonistic to her every breath—takes a long, boozy lunch together without her. And finally, after hours, Emily runs into her coworker Luc, who comes clean about the collective nerves that her arrival in Paris has stirred up.

LUC: Now you are here and maybe we feel we have to
      work harder, make more money.

EMILY: It's a balance.

LUC: Exactly. A balance. And I think the Americans have
      the wrong balance. You live to work. We work to
      live! It's good to make money, but what you say [is]
      "success," I say is punishment.

EMILY: But I enjoy work. And accomplishment. It makes
       me happy.

LUC: Work makes you happy?

EMILY: Yes! It's why I'm here—for work. And look where
       it's brought me—to this beautiful city.

LUC: Maybe you don't know what it is to be happy.

So it's not exactly the acid bite of Molière. However, for
an entry of mass culture that's been accused by various critics
of being "a sugary soufflé" "with the emotional complexity of a
hair bobble" that succeeds in "deactivating the thinking part of
your brain until you're gazing at your screen like it's a dentist
who gassed you 20 minutes ago," the show still manages to stuff
absurd American careerism through the lunette of a guillotine in
the very first episode.

In thinking about the suffocating, all-engulfing nature of modern American work culture, the real-life French way presents
some approaches that are worthy of evaluation. In 2016, the
French Parliament established "the right to disconnect" with a
law that's designed to give employees the right to not respond
to work-related communication after business hours. "Employees physically leave the office, but they do not leave their work,"
one member of Parliament argued with characteristic Gallic flair.
"They remain attached by a kind of electronic leash—like a dog.
The texts, the messages, the emails—they colonize the life of the
individual to the point where he or she eventually breaks down."
    At the time, plenty of jabs were taken at the right to dis-

connect, even as future events and technology would prove the law prescient. Once the pandemic hit, whatever separation still existed between work and life would be annihilated for many, whether it was after-hours Slack messages, Zoom meetings taken from closet floors and bedrooms, or last-minute texts from shift leaders about covering for sick employees. Since the inception of the right to disconnect, a number of countries from Canada to Kenya have introduced their own versions of the legislation. (In April 2024, California became the first U.S. state to propose a version of the law; the bill stalled in committee.)

The right to disconnect derives from France's thirty-five-hour workweek, another legislative work boundary that caused even more preoccupation and global hyperventilation. Initiated in the late 1990s, it created a cherished standard for blue-collar employees in France. It also created a transatlantic punch line that's been in use ever since. During a 2015 presidential primary debate, former Florida governor Jeb Bush used it to accuse his rival, Senator Marco Rubio, of having a lackluster work ethic. "I mean . . . the Senate, what is it, like a French workweek? You get like three days where you have to show up?"*

My favorite of the storied French workplace novelties, however, is *la pause déjeuner*, the lunch break, a fascinating mandate that was codified in the late 1800s. The rule requires that employees physically vacate their desks or work areas for lunch. The midday break initially grew out of a concern for worker safety during the Industrial Revolution, when factory chemicals and tuberculosis spread easily in workplaces. It was literally a breather etched into the French labor code. "Article 8 said that work sites had to be ventilated during eating breaks," the French historian Martin Bruegel explained. "And Article 9 said worksites had to be evacuated during eating breaks." After an early adjustment period, the lunch break developed into a prized national ritual during which workers leave their jobs for at least one hour and often two (!),

---

* As presidential politics go, the French often serve as inspiration for negs, like when Mitt Romney was criticized for his ability to speak French in a 2012 attack ad by Newt Gingrich, and John Kerry was regularly mocked for the sin of looking French in 2004.

traditionally to eat, drink wine, and grab a coffee. Like a Sunday in small-town America, a significant number of businesses in France close their doors during the lunch break.

In theme, the lunch break custom is designed to improve workers' lives, building rapport among coworkers for creative collaboration later or, barring that, to allow workers to take some time for themselves. (The historian Bruegel and his wife actually met-cute during a lunch break.) It's viewed as enough of a social positive that the lunch break is now a subsidized benefit in France: Companies are obliged by law to provide their employees with amenities such as a kitchen or cafeteria (usually with cheaper food than can be bought outside) or meal bonuses on top of employee salaries. Beyond the generous allotment of time, the lunch break's wildest feature may be the employer-provided meal voucher, which millions of workers apply in restaurants, bakeries, and supermarkets against the bill for lunch. (Employers are required to cover at least half of the cost.)

Let's compare this to the American lunch culture, where spending more than ten minutes luxuriating in a meal built on a fast-casual assembly line and served in a disposable clamshell might get you reported to HR. In her book *Trick Mirror,* Jia Tolentino depicted the vibe at Sweetgreen, one trendsetting chain that serves $15 grain bowls, as "less like a place to eat and more like a refueling station," designed for people whose "purpose in life [is] to send emails for 16 hours a day with a brief break to snort down a bowl of nutrients that ward off the unhealthfulness of urban professional living." In a related flourish, Chipotle's onetime in-house music curator Chris Golub once revealed that the chain intentionally plays faster-paced songs because doing so has been proven to make diners eat quicker and leave. "The lunch and dinner rush have songs with higher BPMs [beats per minute] because they need to keep the customers moving," he told Bloomberg.

This assumes that employees can get out of the office at all. In 2015, around the time that a whopping 62 percent of Americans confessed to typically eating lunch at their desks, the New York–based culinary font Food52 launched a column called "Not Sad Desk Lunch." The long-running feature offered recipe-driven correctives for the grim-looking lunches, sometimes known as #SadDeskLunch, notoriously eaten by American office workers hunched over their laptops. Instead of settling for soggy leftovers or slapped-together sandwiches, Food52 argued with great enthusiasm that basic salads could be zhuzhed up by using leftover stale bread from the office kitchen as croutons and that better lunches could quickly be made fresh by storing certain ingredients in the office fridge. The feature proved popular enough to grow into a full-blown video campaign featuring the site's staff delivering well-assembled lunches to the offices of various companies, whose employees would marvel at them. "We believe desk lunches can and should be happier," a defiant voice announced in the opening salvos of Food52's video *The Not Sad Desk Revolution*. It wasn't alone in the crusade. One of the earliest uses of the term "Lunch al Desko," a clever but unsettling workplace adaptation of "lunch al fresco," can be traced to the food magazine *Bon Appétit*, which, despite its name, is distinctly not French.

To even suggest that we import some of France's workplace customs is enough to make a U.S. Chamber of Commerce policy officer stab someone with their ceremonial ribbon-cutting scissors. After all, as Gordon Gekko declared in *Wall Street*, "Lunch is for wimps." The U.S. Department of Labor seems to agree: in addition to not mandating lunch or coffee breaks, as many retail workers will tell you, paid lunch is rarely a given, either. "Meal periods (typically lasting at least 30 minutes), serve a different purpose than coffee or snack breaks and, thus, are not work time and are not compensable," our federal guidelines read.

Still, I'm not suggesting that America turn itself into France, only that legislative initiatives like the right to disconnect, the thirty-five-hour workweek, and even the lunch break aren't the productivity-stomping, socialist conspiracies that they're sometimes made out to be. The right to disconnect applies only to companies with fifty or more employees, and even then, it stipulates that management and unions must hash out the best policy for work communications together. In France, there are no gendarmes waiting to haul a worker away to jail for housing a *jambon beurre* at their desk during lunch hour. Much like its thirty-five-hour workweek law (which has plenty of loopholes), French regulations create guardrails that are meant to protect against extreme or predatory behavior more than to prevent employees from getting things done.

Moreover, French workplace laws alone certainly haven't remedied the messy, slow-simmering cassoulet of slow economic growth there, and in some cases, they have made problems worse. As opposed to America's AFL-CIO, France has (at least) five different major trade union federations competing chaotically for political clout. The growing inaccessibility of France's sacred vacation culture has spurred national protests among some workers, best embodied by the Yellow Vest movement, a recent protest movement centered on addressing the country's slipping living standards.

So it's better to think of these practices as norms that reflect cultural priorities.* "Of course your boss shouldn't send you emails on a Sunday when you're at lunch, enjoying a leg of lamb and a good Bordeaux," said Bernard Vivier, an obviously French workplace consultant, about the right to disconnect. Protections like these can be seen as a way to cultivate a basic awareness about the ways in which work intersects with life. "I work Saturday, Sunday, and Monday," Patty Lurie, an American expat who works in a Paris wine shop, told me. "My coworker is French, and every time I write him on a weekend, I know that he doesn't have to answer me. I do think about it more [when I email him]." For American companies doing battle with employees who don't want to be in the office, encouraging a culture that presents workers with more time, more life, and stronger social ties would help their cause.

The benefits of the French approach go beyond digital peace and quiet or the ability to get a little tipsy in the middle of the

---

* For example, as I learned in France, most major museums and institutions offer discounted or free admission to citizens who are currently looking for work, something much harder to imagine in the United States.

workday. In fact, when new parties sweep into power in France, the arguments frequently made in favor of maintaining these policies revolve around data—backed by a lot of scientific research—suggesting that French workers are happier, healthier, and less prone to burnout when there are built-in breaks in the workday and when stronger barriers exist between work and everything else. Indeed, even though France has a shorter workweek than either the EU or U.S. average, it enjoys levels of productivity that are 25 percent higher than both averages of the European Union and the thirty-eight member countries of the Organisation for Economic Co-operation and Development (OECD) and are almost on par with the United States in terms of gross domestic product (GDP) per hour worked.

It hasn't always been this way. Back in the 1960s, French and American workers logged about the same number of hours each year, according to the International Monetary Fund. "The French chose time and the Americans money because they preferred it," the economist Eduardo Porter argued about the two countries' divergence in his 2011 book *The Price of Everything*. He added, "Their choices should make them both happy. But there is another possible reading: Americans chose an unhappier path."

Porter presents his evidence using metrics such as annual hours worked and reported levels of happiness of French and American workers. And the data from 2011 still hold true today: French levels of happiness are higher than American ones; the average French person works more than two hundred hours less than their American counterpart each year and also gets more sleep than the average American, roughly a third of whom are sleep-deprived. Compared to Americans, the French devote around an hour more each day to their meals as well as an hour more each day to the pursuit of leisure activities. That's not even including France's longer life expectancy (5.5 years longer than the United States'), its better health outcomes, or its healthcare spending per person (less than half that of the United States).[*]

---

* Believe it or not, the particulars of healthcare spending between the United States and Europe are a fascinating ball of wax. While European doctors tend to make less

Additionally, labor force participation and general satisfaction in France are no doubt boosted by the existence of universal paid parental leave and affordable, government-subsidized daycare that looks after infants from two months of age until they are three years old, when they go off to free universal preschool. (Infamously, the United States remains the only developed country in the world without some required form of paid family leave; as of March 2023, only about 25 percent of the private sector workforce had access to it.)

———

In recent years, some U.S. companies, particularly in white-collar industries such as tech, law, management consulting, and finance, have sought to boost employee loyalty and productivity by taking pages from the European work manual and translating them into American. Perhaps with French lunch breaks in mind, Google cofounder Sergey Brin issued a specific directive when specifying the design of Google's company offices: "No one should be more than 200 feet away from food." The idea being that (like France) communal access to food fosters collegiality, but (unlike France) food also turns a casual snack break into a potential ideation session for the company. "Maybe they'll hit on an idea for our users that hasn't been thought of yet," wrote Laszlo Bock, whose unnerving onetime title, senior vice president of people operations, at Google, would have made George Orwell blush.

Unfortunately for its employees, the endless search results for free food at Google's well-stocked minikitchens, snack stations, and sprawling cafeterias (often serving breakfast, lunch, *and* dinner) led to a weight gain phenomenon known—with a small measure of pride—as the "Google 15." ("The Google 15 is very real," one current employee told me on the condition of anonymity. "It's something that a lot of people mention or know

———

money, their medical training is usually heavily subsidized by the state, which means they often enter the workforce without gobsmacking levels of student debt or the crushing need to make money as fast as medically possible. This almost certainly has an impact on patient care and its cost.

about before you even start.") In response, Google didn't exactly encourage workers to go for walks outside, dine off-site, or leave the office earlier. Instead, it turned the problem into a workplace experiment by color-coding food offerings in its cafeterias by relative healthiness and squirreling away offending snacks like M&M's into opaque bins. Google being Google, it later gloated about the outcome of the trial with a data-driven flex (and seemingly little awareness of the privacy implications). "In seven weeks, New York Googlers consumed 3.1 million fewer calories from M&M's," Jennifer Kurkoski, a former head of Google's People Analytics (!) department told ABC. "We're busy," she added. "Everyone has work that they are trying to get done, and so you don't want to think a lot about what they are going to grab as a snack. So let's make the thing that people default to the healthiest one possible."

It's these kinds of statements that inspire a wee bit of cynicism about the battery of perks that some well-funded companies offer. In addition to endless food, some modern white-collar offices have entered an arms race of benefits that suspiciously gesture at keeping employees at work, whether by offering onsite laundry, haircuts, healthcare clinics, and gyms or, say, by offering to cover the cost of egg-freezing treatments to delay employees' family planning. Of course, one alternative to this would be to create policies and culture that empower people to take the time they need to maintain their lives.

Finally, and most important of all, there's time off. In the years before the pandemic, Americans already avoided using their existing days off before unlimited vacation days or unlimited personal time off (PTO) became a popular perk at several companies such as Netflix, Oracle, General Electric, and Microsoft. "It is used to attract and retain talent," an adviser from the Society for Human Resource Management explained of unlimited PTO in 2023. "Conceivably, there is a little bit less of administrative burden in terms of tracking vacation or PTO. And it also has been known to help with limiting the liability that's on an employer's balance sheet." (Also, when an employee with unlimited PTO leaves, they're generally not owed for days not taken off.) But while Americans always avoided taking days off before the proliferation of these policies, surveys show that American workers take *even fewer days off* when given an endless allotment of them. "One problem with unlimited PTO is that it seems to only exist in theory," the journalist Anne Helen Petersen, who studies the various miseries of work culture in America, told me. "When it's only in theory, then it's not actually yours to take."

Still, the riddle over unused PTO raises another question: If Americans have truly chosen money over time, what does it mean for them to willingly ignore their paid time off?

In 1670, some 350 years before Emily arrived in Paris, the French playwright Molière debuted his celebrated satire *The Bourgeois Gentleman*. In it, the action follows a hapless character named Monsieur Jourdain as he tries to ascend into Paris' aristocracy from his middle-class station. Although he's acquired the money to do it, in order to truly enter the nobility, he believes that he must learn the codes and rituals of the wealthy. And so he hires teachers and befriends aristocrats, all of whom happily separate him from his cash while instructing him in the dark art of being a fancy-pants nobleman. Jourdain tries to learn about music and how to dance and fence; he studies philosophy and orders his clothing from the finest tailors. All the while, he generally makes an idiot of himself in the eyes of everyone profiting off him. "What a dupe!" a servant breaks the fourth wall to tell the crowd. "If he had learned his role by heart, he could not have played it better."

Paris of the late 1600s syncs nicely with present-day American life, where the ambitious still strive to learn the secret codes of the elite. (Also universal is the built-in resentment between the entrenched elite and determined would-be up-and-comers.) But what's different about the modern version of this dynamic is that the prevailing image of the well-to-do in America isn't one of leisure or philosophy. Instead, members of the modern American noblesse—who still very much dress in expensive clothes and learn fencing and dressage to gain entry to elite colleges and social clubs—often go to extreme lengths to show themselves wearing a badge of busyness through long hours, dealmaking, and excessive work commitments. In this paradigm, to be successful isn't enough; it's success in the exhausting service of more success that has become the much more aspirational thing.

In his influential "workism" theory, the journalist Derek Thompson asked why economists who had believed that we would work significantly less in the twenty-first century had turned out to be so wrong. Back in 1930, for example, John Maynard Keynes predicted that a fifteen-hour workweek would exist by now and suggested that the average person would be so thoroughly relaxed that they would struggle with "how to use his freedom from pressing economic cares."* Keynes' reasoning was fair. The right mix of scientific progress, compound interest, and technology should inevitably have made work much easier, less necessary, and less time consuming, right? But then something happened. "The economists of the early 20th century did not foresee that work might evolve from a means of material production to a means of identity production," Thompson argued. "They failed to anticipate that, for the poor and middle class, work would remain a necessity; but for the college-educated elite, it would morph into a kind of religion, promising identity, transcendence, and community."

The obsession with work among wealthy Americans hasn't just broken with the forward-looking predictions of yore; it's broken with many long-standing conventions of what success was traditionally meant to afford the successful. Thorstein Veblen, who coined the term *conspicuous consumption* in 1899, a few years after the gadget-filled Chicago World's Fair, also critiqued the wealthy of the Gilded Age for flaunting their elite status through leisure. "Conspicuous abstention from labor therefore becomes the conventional mark of superior pecuniary achievement and the conventional index of reputability," he wrote baroquely. Not all that long ago, the good life in America closely resembled what it meant centuries ago in France, even if the classics had been replaced by the market's shiniest newest products as the hobbies of leisure.

---

* Whoops.

More recently, economists, academics, and voyagers of social study have set out to understand why the elite life of leisure in the United States didn't last. The reasons are involved. First, experts connect the shift toward overwork to social trends like the steady decline in religious observance and the demise of places to mingle outside work and home. Other factors include the tech-powered encroachment of work into off-duty time (facilitated through a problematic ménage à trois involving email, phones, and a cultural expectation to be available) as well as the general pressure to keep up socially and financially with successful peers. In his book *The Meritocracy Trap*, Daniel Markovits partially homed in on uber-wealthy Americans who, by working excessively, essentially guarantee that elite advantages carry from one generation to the next. In a 2023 survey that focused primarily on wealthy Americans, one global insurer found that 83 percent of respondents claimed to work while 68 percent did not consider themselves wealthy, despite having a minimum of $500,000 in investable assets.

To be wealthy or successful in a deeply unequal society is not without its complications. And so others have suggested that the wealthy often work harder (or make an effort to appear to) out of a sense of self-consciousness about income inequality, the popularity of the idea of social mobility in America, or the reality that wealth has so often been amassed through inheritance or other wide-ranging forms of exclusive financial chicanery rather than work itself. In *Uneasy Street*, her ethnography of New York City's wealthiest in the late 2010s, the sociologist Rachel Sherman describes how those she interviewed cast themselves as hard workers to mitigate their worries about their affluence. "They valued self-sufficiency and productivity, and rejected self-indulgence and dependence," she wrote. "Those who had earned their wealth wore their paid employment proudly. Those who had inherited wealth or did not currently work for pay resisted stereotypes of laziness or dilettantism, and offered alternate narratives of themselves as productive workers."

In 2016, three professors—Silvia Bellezza, Neeru Paharia, and Anat Keinan—added fuel to the fire when they published the results of their research on the rise of busyness as a status symbol in America. A major theme of their findings focuses on how work has changed as the primacy of manufacturing has given way to what they call a "knowledge-intensive" economy.* In this brave new workplace, the concept of staying superlate in the office and being too consumed with tasks takes the place of, say, clocking out from the plant at five and knocking back postwork boilermakers and stale peanuts with coworkers over some Dire Straits at a local bar.

With the diminishing supply of good, solid, steady jobs in the United States, the supposed need for this diligent bustle turns into a sadistic bragging right. As Bellezza, Paharia, and Keinan argued, "By telling others that we are busy and working all the time, we are implicitly suggesting that we are sought after, which enhances our perceived status." (Nevertheless, for anyone with a reasonable work-life setup, this is kind of like boasting that you lost ten pounds by cutting off your arm.)

––––––––

Whatever the cause or exact combination of factors, this American fever of busyness and overwork has some truly bizarre symptoms, the first being that many people in the best position to work less appear to choose to work more than nearly everyone else does. According to census data, the top 10 percent of income earners in the United States work an average of 4.4 hours a week more than the bottom 10 percent, a dynamic unlike that of most other industrialized nations, where the opposite tends to be true.[†]

The busyness fever also lives and breathes, for example, in the zealous revival of life hacks, the Franklin-esque self-help

––––––––

* Usually lumped together in the "knowledge economy," many of these hard-to-land, well-paying, and allegedly specialized jobs were characterized by the late economic anthropologist David Graeber as "bullshit jobs," in part for their lack of benefits to society at large.
† It's worth mentioning that census data are self-reported. With a nod to our busyness experts, it may be possible that top earners, who are more likely to have jobs where they don't clock in or out, may feel compelled to say they work harder than they actually do.

practices designed to free up time and mental space by making us more efficient and productive instead of having us wonder why we need to compulsively optimize all of life's basic tasks in the first place. Back in Tulsa, I asked the cannabis entrepreneur Arshad Lasi about the recent rise of THC-infused products that are specifically marketed for use in the workplace or for creative and professional pursuits. Pass through a few marijuana dispensaries, and you'll likely stumble over edibles, beverages, or canisters of pot with labels hazily promising to lead a user toward focus or clarity instead of a pantry full of Cool Ranch Doritos. "That functional aspect of it is just coming forward," he told me, "and people are really looking for not just being stoned on the couch but enjoying an elevated feeling and also getting some good out of it."

Like a psychic Loch Ness monster, you can sense the thrum of the bustle lurking below the surface in those popular media features about the daily routines of successful public figures. Their regimens basically involve waking up at 4:00 a.m., crushing a five-mile run at a 6 percent incline followed by seven hundred burpees, casually breezing through all their emails, setting intentions for the next eight years of life, and then reading nine hundred pages of Proust, all in time to watch the sunrise, somehow without mention of coffee or childcare. Even a commute becomes an occasion to be seized for squeezing more out of a day, whether by creating a killer to-do list or reaching transcendence faster by listening to meditation exercises at a sped-up rate.

Another example of tedious American busymaking can be seen in the ceaseless commercial diversions of our celebrities. In another era, actors, athletes, luminaries, and pop stars might have been happy to while away spare months sunning themselves in St. Barts instead of using their status as influencers to start lifestyle websites, apps, and restaurant chains. Or shill for cryptocurrency exchanges. Or launch their own lines of tequila, gin, hard seltzer, upmarket snacks, shapewear, activewear, footwear, and cosmetics. Enterprise making has come to hold the same sway in the world of modern celebrities as artistic or athletic merit; why else would the rapper Post Malone have a rosé label, an esports gaming company, or collaborations with Crocs, Bud Light, and Doritos?*

Though we're accustomed to the exhibition of success in the service of more success when it comes to brands—the billions of people served by McDonald's, for instance—it's an odd practice for individuals to take on. Way before ticket prices for her Eras Tour caused irreparable rifts among American families, friends, and children, Taylor Swift released her indisputably brilliant album *1989*. In an Instagram post at the time, she celebrated her album sales by gloating that "industry experts predicted *1989* would sell 650k first week. You went and bought 1.287 million albums." In an accompanying video, Swift sits behind the wheel of her car, lip-syncing along to a verse from the rapper Kendrick Lamar's hit "Backseat Freestyle" about feeling the euphoria of winning and at the same time the compulsion to never let up: "Goddamn I feel amazing, damn I'm in the matrix / My mind is living on cloud nine and this nine is never on vacation."

Dear readers and fellow Swifties, this is *not* a critique of Taylor Swift. With or without her, business and boardroom triumphs have been fascinations of pop culture since at least the lean days of the Great Recession. From the private jets of *Succession* and *Billions* to the cobwebbed confines of abandoned lockers in *Storage Wars*, a tenacious focus on the ciphers of work and the mechanics of success and moneymaking has fueled prestige dramas, reality TV franchises, and wave after wave of documentaries about the inspiring rise and scandalous fall of various companies, commercial fads, hucksters, and founders. Each and every hour, we can find ourselves, selectively edited and out there in the world, restoring kitchens and flipping houses, courting and signing clients, gaming out how to bring troubled businesses back to life, doing an endless and relentless soft shoe.

Glomming off the popularity of *Shark Tank*, the long-running

---

* Indeed, one of my first bleary sights after getting off the overnight flight to Paris was a Cartier ad in Charles de Gaulle airport featuring the *Emily in Paris* actress Lily Collins. Later, when I asked Fabien whether it was controversial that an actress who plays a vilified American who can't speak French had landed a high-profile deal with an iconic French jewelry house, he didn't shrug. "Oh, no!" he explained. "It's no problem. Every brand wants her. Even every French brand."

show where desperate small-time inventors beg celebrity investors to help bring their products to market, Apple launched its first original television programming in 2017, a reality show called *Planet of the Apps* (ha-ha). In it, software engineers were given exactly one minute to deliver an elevator pitch for their apps . . . while standing on a moving walkway. Part of what seemed new and unique about the show was how brazenly self-promotional and self-serving it was for Apple. Assuming that a contestant succeeded in pairing with one of the show's celebrity "advisers"— a group made up of serial entrepreneur Gary Vaynerchuk and stars turned magnates Jessica Alba, Gwyneth Paltrow, and will.i.am— they would eventually owe Apple a "creator fee," 30 percent of their revenue, just to have their products appear in the company's all-powerful App Store.

Although, thankfully, *Planet of the Apps* lasted only one season, it represented the ever-deepening blur between entertainment and commerce. In 2023, the star-studded movie *Air* garnered wide acclaim, despite being little more than a big-budget dramatization of how Nike executives had made a historic sneaker deal with Michael Jordan. Later that year, the buzz around *Air* would be thoroughly eclipsed by *Barbie*, a film that smartly brought existential and social dread to a universe of plastic dolls while also being approved by Barbie's parent company, Mattel, and even produced by Mattel Films. (As *Barbie* hurtled toward the billion-dollar mark in ticket sales, news outlets reported on a list of more than forty potential new film adaptations featuring other Mattel toys including Barney, Hot Wheels, Magic 8 Ball, and more.)

Naturally, *Emily in Paris*, with its marketing gambits and work culture misunderstandings, is at home as a sitcom variation of this category. And as the seasons go on, Emily's unerring ambition spills over into everything else. By the end of season three (spoiler alert), her chef crush, Gabriel, is pursuing a Michelin star while her best friend, Mindy, goes from striving street busker to Eurovision contestant. During a very brief, one-episode bout of unemployment, Emily declines a vacation and becomes a waitress before redoubling her efforts to spend her free time building her follower count on Instagram. (Along the way, she accidentally lands a spot on a coveted list of Paris' most influential people.)

As for those of us who binged the show for some mindless Parisian escapism, we somehow ended up watching people work all the time.

As the economists of olden days suggested, it didn't have to be this way. Over the past few generations, several open, advanced economies such as France, Germany, and Denmark have shifted away from manufacturing toward service and technology jobs without turning excessive busyness into high pathological fashion.

Try to imagine, if you can, the U.S. State Department crafting an entry about the work-life balance in the United States that sounds anything like the one written by the Ministry of Foreign Affairs of Denmark: "Stop by a Danish office at 5pm and nearly every desk will be empty," it begins. "While the Danes are hard workers, they prefer to do their jobs within Denmark's 37 hour official work week. Staying extra hours is discouraged, and most employees leave at around 4pm to pick up their children and begin preparing the evening meal." (Åh, Gud!) And, as if this didn't already sound like some surreal Nordic fairyscape, the Danes go on to brag that they actually have a higher productivity rate than the United States and nearly all of the rest of Europe without feeling "the need to demonstrate their dedication by working long hours"—labor that Danish companies would likely have a hard time demanding anyway, given that nearly two-thirds of Danes are in unions. (By contrast, the only easily found mention of work-life balance on the State Department website is an archived page from the Obama years with a list of instructive articles and books about how to improve your own work-life balance; on it, the first resource is a link to the site WebMD, which advises workers who feel burned out to try ordering their groceries online or outsourcing their lawn care to "a kid down the street.")

Indeed, in most other Western industrialized countries, the idea of someone cranking out an eleven-hour day at the office isn't typically construed as a sign of loyalty to boss or company; if anything, it's seen as a sign of inefficiency. "The tendency in other countries is not to see working late as a personal failure, but actually as a structural failure," Anne Helen Petersen explained. "It's as if something's wrong with that company." To be sure, not every employer in the Scandinavian utopias acts perfectly. But like the French lunch break, widely adopted customs create a common baseline.

We don't need to read another round of missives and trend pieces about burnout, quiet quitting, and bed rotting (don't ask), or to endure yet another round of research detailing how overwork is linked to sleeplessness, stress, depression, loneliness, and a host of chronic health conditions, or to learn more about how a lack of time away from work weakens family bonds, community engagement, and even democracy to know that we have a problem that's in need of solutions.

As I brilliantly chronicled in the first half of this book, much of our current anguish stems from the ideals embedded in the Protestant work ethic, our neurotic exceptionalism, and the shimmery promise of social mobility (along with the cold, zero-sum calculus of the American abracadabra). To resist (or even just redefine) those treasured bits of the national ethic is the first step in creating a more durable foundation for life—a country that's better, more equitable, and stronger at the roots. "Our very idea of productivity is premised on the idea of producing something new," Jenny Odell wrote in her book *How to Do Nothing*, "whereas we do not tend to see maintenance and care as productive in the same way."

In addition to adjusting the basic perception of what hard work is, what it means, and whom it benefits, we owe it to our miserable selves to redirect our energies away from the diminishing returns of the work-obsessed way of being. Or, as Rainesford Stauffer put it in her book *All the Gold Stars*, "When we can, saying no to something at work can mean saying yes to so many other things." That includes a more expansive definition of ambition, one in which engaging with friends, family, and community, as well as resting and having hobbies,* are seen not as impediments to ambition but as worthy forms of ambition in their own right.

---

* Please, no more sketch comedy, though.

Unfortunately, the margin for personal life isn't something that is readily yielded by employers, particularly in a society where devotion to work is equated with transcendence. The well-documented and growing unionization efforts across the United States over the past few years signal the emerging demand for stricter boundaries between work and life as well as better pay and benefits (like paid leave and secure scheduling) that will make it possible to take and enjoy personal time. These things will never be given without a fight or culture shift, which is why it's helpful to look at other models and see how they improve life for workers *and* the bottom line. Denmark, again as an example, has created legal standards under which employees must have representation on a company's board of directors and pay disparities between genders must be reviewed and corrected. (Research shows that neither measure affects a firm's profitability.)[*]

In the case of employers, there are also clear ways for businesses to reappraise the value of what their workers do, *especially* as the ongoing experiment with remote and hybrid work continues. Even before the pandemic, Professor Silvia Bellezza, one of the busyness experts, proposed this simple adjustment for the managerial set to adopt: "Shift as much as possible their attention to what people are producing, rather than how long they're in the office." In addition to resisting the theater of overwork, employers would also be wise to embrace flexibility regarding how their employees live and work best.

Most important, for a culture so deeply fixated on productivity and profit, there's an ironclad business case to be made by employees (as well as managers, CFOs, CEOs, HR reps, efficiency hawks, bottom-liners, political leaders, union reps, marriage counselors, gender equity champions, family and community advocates, health and medical professionals, kids, and household pets) to have steady, regular, nonnegotiable time carved out for workers to be away from their work—whether it's built flexibly

---

[*] In 2018, Senator Elizabeth Warren introduced a bill that would require larger companies to have workers elect a significant portion of a company's board members; it never came up for a vote.

into each day, set aside across entire weeks, or, better yet, both. Not that anyone needs evidence to prove this, but a desiccated forest's worth of studies shows that workers who take adequate time off are fitter, happier, and more productive as employees (and as humans, I'd imagine) as well as more loyal, more creative, and better motivated.

Though again, this idea may seem achingly obvious, most employers haven't bothered to read the memo yet. Take a recent survey by the American Psychological Association, which found that "only 41 percent of U.S. workers reported that their organization's culture encourages employees to take time off, and just 38 percent said their supervisor encourages the same." A solution to this problem is also achingly obvious: employers, who have already become so keen to foment productivity-themed paranoia by tracking the hours, movements, and even keystrokes of their employees, should instead track their employees' time off and enact policies that require workers to actually take time away for the collective good.*

Precedents for this approach already exist, and not just among those degenerates in Europe lazing away perfectly good work hours on their socialist fjords. In 2022, the financial services titan Goldman Sachs—not exactly a progressive operation—instituted a requirement that its overspent workforce must take at least fifteen days off work each year, including one set of at least five consecutive days off. It's pretty telling that even Goldman Sachs, which once doled out bonuses of $1 million or more to nearly a thousand employees less than a year after receiving billions of dollars in taxpayer bailout money, has grasped that it can't partner with oppressive regimes or sell subprime mortgage–backed securities as effectively with a staff that's overextended into exhaustion.

Whether it's fast food or finance, social work or sex work, there is virtually no business model that wouldn't benefit from placing a higher premium on employee health and well-being.

* Given the current state of the office, it's truly baffling that employers seem surprised that they have to bribe, cajole, or threaten their employees to return there.

After all, the opposite of a fulfilled, well-rested workforce isn't just one that's burned out; it's one that's rife with turnover and costly instability.

Using data from the Bureau of Labor Statistics in 2019, Gallup put a *conservative* price tag of $1 *trillion* on the replacement cost of employees who leave their jobs in the United States each year. Including factors such as low morale and lost worker knowledge, lower productivity, and recruitment and training expenses, it estimated that "the cost of replacing an individual employee can range from one-half to two times the employee's annual salary." (Other sources place the replacement cost of an employee at three or four times the employee's annual salary.) Gallup also found that over half of those who had left their jobs might have been convinced to stay had their companies been better in sync with their needs.

All of this brings us back to Paris, where my tour group was making its way toward Emily's apartment. The building, now listed as a local attraction on Google Maps, sits at the southeast end of a small, picturesque park with flowers, a fountain, and green benches. There we were met by an unallied scrum of *Emily in Paris* enthusiasts, tourists who had made a special pilgrimage to see the apartment building. While Fabien dished more insider details about the making of the show, they took selfies in berets and jokingly (at least I think) called out for the character Gabriel to come down and cook them dinner.

After shooing away onlookers who hadn't signed up for the tour, Fabien fielded a tantalizing question posed by another American in the group: What were the odds we would run into a cast member or even an *Emily in Paris* film shoot while we were gallivanting around town? Fabien quickly burst our bubble. In addition to a calendar full of paid federal holidays, French workers are also (technically) required by law to take at least two to four consecutive weeks of vacation between the months of May and October. This annual custom, part of the guaranteed five weeks of annual vacation, is part of what makes *Emily in Paris* easier to film.

"If you come back this summer, you will see the filming of season four," Fabien promised the group. "It's always summertime [for filming] because we leave Paris. It's empty in August, and there is no one here. We go to the south, we swim, and that's why they can film a lot here." Everybody nodded at this explanation, but it was clear that not everybody could fathom it.

CHAPTER EIGHT

HUSTLE

THE IMPOSSIBLE ACT OF KEEPING UP

**THE PEOPLE WITH CAREERS NEED TO LEARN
TO SHUT THE FUCK UP AROUND PEOPLE WITH JOBS.**

—CHRIS ROCK

By now we know that the problems of white-collar workplaces spill over in destructive ways. Prestige aside, the reality that salaried employees work too much has far-reaching effects on society writ large, from nuts-and-bolts problems with community engagement, public health, and gender equity to perceptions of what hard work means, what jobs are deemed valuable, and who is deserving of good compensation and time off. But irritations like organizational red tape, idiotic hierarchies, untaken paid leave, and after-hours communiqués inspire a bit less sympathy when we're talking about white-collar workers. Generally speaking, these are still the workers who have the security of knowing when their next check will hit their bank account, how much they're bringing in, and what their working hours will generally be. Hardships and soul suck aside, it was much of this lucky group who got to work from home during the pandemic, who have luxuries like professional boredom or benefits like employer-sponsored retirement plans, and who, by and large, aren't unionized, often because they haven't felt a need to be.

Although being part of the W-2 set in America hardly guarantees security anymore, there's also a whole other body of American workers who scrap so hard for a much simpler reason: they have to. While the cost of necessities has gone up, real wages have mostly remained flat over the past fifty years. Solid, steady middle-income jobs (and shoddy, unsteady ones) have given way to contract work, automation, part-time employment, and the gig economy. (According to the consultancy firm McKinsey & Company, which no doubt advises many companies to reduce their full-time head counts, 36 percent of American workers classified themselves as independent workers in 2022, up from 27 percent in 2016.) Also, setting aside some slight improvements, we're still not far from levels of income inequality that rival the peaks of the 1920s, back when some economists were theorizing rapturously about Americans' prosperous and leisure-rich future.

These are serious problems with the power to destabilize our society and unknit our democratic character. Plenty of smart people argue, not unconvincingly, that they already have. But in America, the answer is always more America. Rather than address how obstacles have become insurmountable, we've trained much of our collective focus on the power of individuals to overcome them. Speaking at a town hall forum in Nebraska in 2005, President George W. Bush, who was packaged as America's first president with an MBA, met a divorced mother of three who told him that she worked three jobs to get by. "You work three jobs? Uniquely American, isn't it?" he said to applause. "I mean, that is fantastic that you're doing that. . . . Get any sleep?" In the years since, the tougher the requirements for success and stability have become, the more high-flying and absurd the language about sacrifice, hard work, and grit has seemingly become. All of this is best summed up by American hustle culture.

The word *hustle* has taken an odd and expansive journey in the United States, moving from a verb to a noun to a doctrine of basic endurance. As Isabella Rosario explained on *Code Switch*, the meaning of "hustle" started as "to shake or toss" (from the Dutch *husselen*) and grew into "hurry" and "obtain by begging." She noted, "By the late 19th and early 20th century, hustle started being used to mean 'gumption' or 'hard work,'" an interpretation with which we're all familiar. But around the same time, *hustle* also acquired a subversive connotation, evolving to mean "to scheme" or "a scheme." Initially narrowed to Black vernacular and culture, this version of hustle identified a way to survive, implicitly against the long odds imposed by external forces like oppression and economic exclusion. Relaying his life story to Alex Haley, Malcolm X characterized his youth as one of a survival-bent hustler without good options: "forever frustrated, restless, and anxious for some 'action.'"

Then, as often happens, *hustle* got adopted and motto-ized into a mainstream mantra. Hustle now appears everywhere and for everyone. As a call to be resilient or self-reliant; as a commodity that fetishizes overwork and infuses it with good cheer and New Age self-actualization. On the platform Etsy, countless side hustlers sell everything from framed posters to cheap key chains to journals tagged with phrases like "Good things come to those who hustle." Fitness start-ups like Yoga Hustle peddle $145 fitness mats while Lingua Franca, a fashion brand whose well-heeled, politically liberal target audience has been dubbed "resistance socialites" by The Cut, features a $380 cashmere sweater hand embroidered with "everyday i'm hustlin'" in cursive script. Decrying the popularity of working from home, JPMorgan Chase CEO Jamie Dimon declared, "It doesn't work for those who want to hustle." And when Dunkin' introduced a line of summer drinks in 2022, including its Cake Batter Signature Latte, it did so by dubbing the drinks "Ice Cold Liquid Hustle."

Along with a proliferation of aspirational branding and consumer swag, the hustle morphed into a career-driven lifestyle, born in the nervous aftershocks of the Great Recession. Founded in 2010, the coworking space company WeWork aligned itself with the catchword by branding itself as the official address of the scrappy, tech-adjacent set. In hundreds of cities, WeWork offices attracted freelancers, bespoke advertising agencies, media outfits, and early-stage start-ups angling to bootstrap, with the lure of beer-stocked kitchens, endless networking events, and coffee mugs emblazoned with "Always Do What You Love." Stenciled on the walls and plastered on bathroom mirrors were motivational aphorisms like "Thank God It's Monday."* Though marketed as an incubator of collaboration and creativity, the "we" part of the WeWork equation always crosshatched with something a little less high-minded and quintessentially individualistic. "On the one hand, community," its cofounder and former CEO, Adam Neumann, once explained of his vision for the company. "On the other hand, you eat what you kill." (Yikes.)

Despite its starring role in the glamorizing of modern striving, WeWork's business model eventually represented a slightly less virtuous definition of hustle. Inflated by the easy cash that accompanies unhinged investor hype, WeWork expanded rapidly and acted recklessly, with little regard for profitability. The Red Hot Chili Peppers and Deepak Chopra appeared at all-expenses-paid company summits in faraway locales, tequila shots were dispensed at meetings (and even job interviews), janitor strikes were crushed, a private jet was purchased and subsequently filled with so much weed smoke that its crew apparently had to wear oxygen masks. Along the way, company operating losses blew close to the $2 billion mark. As trouble became evident, the company withdrew a planned IPO in the fall of 2019. Its value then collapsed from its dizzying $47 billion valuation in 2019 to $361 million in 2023. Even before the pandemic forced many WeWork offices to close in 2020, thousands of its employees had been laid off, while Neumann, in classic CEO form, had already parachuted out of the mess by agreeing to step down in exchange for a deal worth up to $1.7 billion. That comeuppance aside, WeWork still hangs on for now, with several locations still bearing huge vinyl window clings that urge passersby to "HUSTLE Harder."

———————

Elsewhere, for those shut out of fast-evaporating full-time work or otherwise unable to gain admittance to the modern laptop-and-kombucha class embodied by WeWork, the gig economy

* Timely little disclosure number one: one of the many things I did when journalism work didn't pay enough was moonlight for *Creator*, WeWork's short-lived online magazine.

supplies another chaotic facet of hustle. Facilitated through digital platforms such as Uber, Lyft, TaskRabbit, DoorDash, and others, gig work takes part-time work with no protections, no benefits, and diminished wages, marinates it in gallant-sounding autonomy, and then broils it up as the ultimate way to "find the right work for you" (Upwork), "be your own boss" (Uber), and "offer any service you wish as long as it's legal and complies with our terms" (Fiverr).

The most famous of these platforms is Uber, which by some accounts was the most valuable start-up in history until TikTok melded goofy dance trends with harvesting private user data for profit.* Like WeWork, it was founded in the early days of the Great Recession and quickly became shorthand for the variety of apps that pecked at the hollow knotholes of various industries and called it disruption.

Whether it's food delivery, home repair, IT work, psychotherapy, legal services, caregiving, or dogsitting, there's a version of Uber for each.† There are sites to facilitate the renting out of spare bedrooms, yards, garages, cars, pools, bikes, instruments, tools, clothes, internet bandwidth, and baby gear to strangers, helping people turn virtually anything into a source of income. (In 2019, the writer Jean-Luc Bouchard described using Rent-AFriend, a platform where users pay hourly rates to rent friends for platonic companionship, as an experience that made him feel both "creepy" and "like a ruder person.")

The American treasure Dolly Parton has given us another way to understand how this era's scramble is different. In 1980, just as a fundamental economic breakage got under way in the United States, she released "9 to 5," her defiant anthem of office workers striving in the face of exploitation and the hassles of "barely gettin' by." In 2021, she reinterpreted the classic in a Super Bowl commercial for the website builder Squarespace. Titled "5 to 9," the modern jingle paid tribute to all the extra

* Timely disclosure number two: while reporting a story, I spent several weeks as a driver for Uber's food delivery arm, Uber Eats.
† Timely disclosure number three: I am and remain (as of this writing) an extremely well-reviewed dogsitter on the Rover app.

hours that people work *after* finishing a full day on the job somewhere else in the hopes of achieving their real dreams: "Workin' five to nine, you've got passion and a vision / 'Cause it's hustlin' time, a whole new way to make a livin'." (For obvious reasons, the ad was met with a fair share of eye rolls.)

The stats tend to lag, but at least 16 percent of Americans are thought to have worked for gig platforms as of 2021. During the pandemic, gig work grew by 150 percent, with 3 million new workers joining. That growth was led largely by younger women in their twenties, whose work mainly involved ferrying passengers around or delivering food and groceries. In 2021, nearly a third of recent or current gig workers said that the platforms had been their main source of income in the previous year—even as these companies filed lawsuits and funded ballot initiatives to make sure gig workers are not formally or legally acknowledged as their employees.

As a result, there's also little in the way of a safety net when it comes to gig work. Many Uber drivers, for example, use their personal cars, pay for their own gas, handle their own repairs, make their own shifts, and settle their own lawsuits. Like an astonishing 29 percent of other gig workers, many drivers don't make their state's hourly minimum wage, even before expenses are taken into account. This free-for-all approach is in harmony with the hectic-sounding principle that Uber's cofounder and former CEO, Travis Kalanick, etched into the company platform: "Always be hustlin' (Get more done with less, working longer, harder, and smarter, not just two out of three.)."

Not surprisingly, Kalanick's leadership style didn't win hearts, minds, or bottom lines. He was forced to resign as Uber's chief executive officer after being accused of fostering a toxic workplace culture for corporate employees, along with creating unsafe conditions for passengers and drivers. In a telling incident captured on a dashcam shortly before his resignation in 2017, Kalanick was recognized by an Uber driver named Fawzi Kamel during a ride on Super Bowl Sunday. Upon reaching the destination, Kamel turned to plead with Kalanick to address the company's falling wages of its drivers. Kamel claimed that the company had bankrupted him and that some drivers weren't even making minimum wage. After dismissing Kamel's concerns as "bullshit," Kalanick ended the feedback session by invoking a timeless American rebuke: "Some people don't like to take responsibility for their own shit. They blame everything in their life on somebody else." With that, Kalanick wished him "Good luck," got out, and slammed the door. Kamel, otherwise powerless, gave Kalanick a one-star passenger rating.[*]

There's nothing inherently wrong with hustle. The problem is that the need for it speaks to the growing precarity and insecurity of American life.

Like a self-driving Uber drifting into a highway pylon, troublesome realities keep obstructing the value of the stock we place in hustle. Another mess born of an economy that rewards disruption and worker uncertainty is that there are not enough jobs that fulfill the basic needs of most workers. According to a 2022 report by Qualtrics, 57 percent of Americans who already have a full-time job said they want to work extra shifts or overtime to keep up with the cost of living. That same year, another broad-reaching survey by a small-business insurer found that 44 percent of employed Americans said they had already taken on an additional job or side hustle to make ends meet, averaging thirteen extra hours of work each week. Meanwhile, it's a relatively common practice of many employers to keep hourly, low-wage workers from working forty hours per week to avoid giving them full-time benefits or paying them overtime rates. This is a reversal from forty years ago, when the bottom 20 percent of earners were more likely to work fifty-plus hour weeks than the top 20 percent were. In other words, despite the sanctity of hustle—the core imperative of the American abracadabra—a majority of workers struggle to find good opportunities to do so.

----

[*] Later, after the video of the exchange went viral, Kalanick tracked down Kamel to apologize. The two ended up in another debate before Kalanick resolved the matter creatively enough—by giving Kamel $200,000. (Kalanick is now the CEO of another start-up currently valued at tens of billions of dollars.)

And so, the idea that Americans diverged from workers in countries like France by choosing work and money over time and leisure makes sense only when the arrangement pays off. It certainly did for employers. Between 1979 and 2021, the productivity of American workers increased by 64 percent and the U.S. economy more than doubled in size. But over that same stretch of time, the hourly pay of a typical American worker grew by only 17.3 percent.

These imbalances of time, money, and quality of life didn't ensnare everyone all at once. An older millennial, I was a teen during the 1990s, remembered by some as the halcyon days of middle-class prosperity and the greatest period of wealth creation in human history. The standards of a good American life seemed bundled like a cable TV package at your best friend's house. By the time you went back for a high school reunion, the offerings had gone à la carte. And then they became impossible to find. "Compared with the economy in 1999, millions fewer Americans today can afford the middle-class security blanket of a house, car, health insurance, college for their kids, and saving for retirement," Jim Tankersley wrote in *The Riches of This Land*, noting that if incomes had kept pace with the anticipated trajectory from the late 1990s, "a typical American household would have earned 50 percent more in 2018 than it actually did."

There are a lot of ways to metabolize how precarious life has become in the United States in the twenty-first century for everyone but the country's top earners. One stat never fails to stun me: in 2018, a few years before an emergency money hose showered Americans with temporary relief during the pandemic, the Bureau of Labor Statistics reported that the average U.S. household in the bottom 40 percent was spending 100 percent of its income on necessities such as housing, food, healthcare, and transportation. In other words, for years, tens of millions of Americans went into debt if their members did anything more than work and breathe. A wedding, a funeral, an emergency, a school expense, or a vacation had the power to drive a family into the red.

The pandemic only paused that financial distress. Once COVID relief ended, levels of financial insecurity shot right back up again. In August 2023, the New York Federal Reserve noted one particularly grim national milestone: following a dramatic drop during the first two years of the pandemic, credit card debt in the United States had breached the trillion-dollar mark for the first time ever. In another bleak postpandemic benchmark, a record share of 401(k) participants made hardship withdrawals from their retirement plans. As one Fidelity executive explained it bluntly in 2023, "They are jammed up, they are in a bind. This isn't something that people take lightly." Those who had spare savings to raid were lucky; even as corporate profits surged to historic new peaks from 2021 onward, the squeeze was coming for more and more Americans.

All of that misery was front of mind as I headed out in search of a template for better jobs. Or maybe even better careers.

By the time I got to Milwaukee in early September 2023, nearly every leader, pundit, and consultant had already come and gone. President Biden had appeared there three weeks earlier to tour factories ahead of the first anniversary of the Inflation Reduction Act, the sixth visit of his term. One week later, eight Republican presidential candidates, minus the front-runner, gathered in the city for the party's first debate—an evening in which the words *dream* and *decline* were in heavy rotation.

In addition to $3 cans of PBR, Wisconsin holds the distinction of being one of only three states to flip from Obama (2012) to Trump (2016) to Biden (2020), and by a narrower margin each nerve-racking time. (Ahead of 2024, four of the last six presidential elections were decided there by less than a percentage point.) Wisconsin, along with Michigan and Pennsylvania, also hadn't sided with a losing candidate since John Kerry won it by a measly eleven thousand votes in 2004. Analysts describe it as a purple state, but "bruised" may be a better way to think of it. Wisconsin has one senator from each party, a Democratic governor, a Republican-led state legislature, and tons of resulting internal conflict. Political hopefuls now court the Badger State with all the subtlety and restraint of a *Fast & Furious* movie. Before the pandemic forced it to go to virtual, the 2020 Democratic National Convention had been slated to take place in Milwaukee, and as soon as scheming for the 2024 cycle got under way, the Republican Party quickly locked in the city for its nominating convention.

Setting aside the significance of polls, voting trends, and the electoral horse race, there's plenty of symbolic firepower that makes Wisconsin such political catnip. The state's dairyland and manufacturing credentials (and the modern-day troubles that go along with them), the vestiges of its old company towns, its skylines of factories and silos and church steeples and breweries built by generations of immigrant craftsmen, not to mention all the recessionary busts, spare seasons, soy fields, cheese curds, casseroles, and thrift associated with the Midwest. In this romantic industrial setting, it's only right that two of the state's three pro sports teams, the Green Bay Packers and the Milwaukee Brewers, are named for the type of hardscrabble occupations that tend to bring to mind steel-toed shoes, work shirts, and hazardous labor. In short, even taking the laziest stab at describing Wisconsin's bounties can come out sounding pretty impressive. Fox News analyst Brit Hume's pretaped intro to the first Republican presidential debate delivered a good example: "Some call it the heartland. Others, flyover country. . . . A state known for its beer and cheese, gridiron and grit, and also its razor thin elections."*

One small part of what I was looking for in Milwaukee was evidence to counter the bleak clichés and funereal Rust Belt homilies uttered by candidates when they whip through the Midwest on whistle-stop tours.† It only took me a late-summer weekend to find the opposite to be true—first at a Friday fish fry with a live polka band on the Milwaukee River, in a long-standing nod to local Catholic customs. I found it over two nights at Wolski's Tavern, a dark-lit 115-year-old neighborhood tavern where

---

* Not for nothing, you can't really say that about Delaware.

† The origin of the term *Rust Belt* is thought to be a political one, frequently linked to midwesterner and former vice president Walter Mondale. During a campaign stop at a steel plant in Cleveland in 1984, the presidential candidate argued that President Reagan's lifting of quotas on imported steel was turning "our industrial Midwest into a rust bowl."

they give you a souvenir bumper sticker if you're still standing when the bar closes at 2:30 a.m. and where, among a crowd of regulars and familiars, there were older Schlitz drinkers mingling with younger microbrew drinkers and a few kids running around the place in the early evening. I found it in the concept of *Gemütlichkeit*, a sort of gentility and comradery that, adapted to Milwaukee's historically German population, means that people you meet will casually swear and then apologize excessively for cussing when they find out you're from somewhere else. On a Sunday morning, I stopped at the city's annual Italian Festival, where I ate oversized arancini, played a game of bocce with a family dressed up for Mass, and heard an orchestra of mandolins; an hour later, I was watching the Packers' first game of the season at one of the many dives that flout health regulations during football season by serving homemade food, in this case, cookies baked by the mother of the bar's owner. (Every time Green Bay scored a touchdown, the bartender dispensed free shots of Jameson, and, to much collective joy and detriment, the Pack scored five in a win against its archrival Chicago Bears.)

Armed with cigarettes, which I often bring when I'm hoping to talk to people in a new place, I stepped out onto Brady Street at halftime and met a woman named Reyna, who bummed one from me. "R-E-Y-N-A," she spelled it out for me. "It means *queen*." Reyna was in her early seventies and had moved back to the east side of Milwaukee after a few years on the west. She told me that she missed the hardware store and shops selling basic necessities that had been gradually replaced by restaurants and bars along the strip. "At my age, it helps to have those things around," she said. "But folks will bring them by if you ask them." The second half was getting under way, but she wasn't in a hurry to get back to the game. "I only care about football when I got money on the game," she said.

Elegies for places like Wisconsin are usually tinged with a longing for the more steadfast days when work seemed like a promise and getting by didn't require an illogical and manic hustle. That promise was never a genuine one for many people, but like Moses dying at Mount Nebo in sight of the promised land, the hope was that maybe you'd see your children get there. Much of what's unsettling us so profoundly now is the flimsiness of that promise.

More than proof of life or a bratwurst, what I wanted to find in Milwaukee was an ember of that old faith, proof of something banal and workaday and basically functional that could allow us to forget (just for a minute) that everything has hinged on the fickle biases of a tiny number of voters in a stray number of counties for decades running now. Or that we're primed by algorithms, media bubbles, entrenched interests, and cynical political leadership to believe that we're much more polarized than we really are. I found that, too, on the south side of the city.

In the most basic sense, Polonia is a straightforward place. Its name translates as "Poland," a nod to the community that, starting in the mid-1800s, built the neighborhood, founded its parish, and worked brutal jobs in foundries and mills and tanneries. Like most everyone else within the city and without, they'd arrived to escape oppression and seek prosperity. And as with most ethnic enclaves in America, many of Polonia's residents eventually dispersed to other places and other parts of the city. Today, the area's demography is increasingly Hispanic, part of an influx that's helped Milwaukee avoid the population decline suffered by so many other midwestern cities like Detroit, Pittsburgh, St. Louis, Toledo, Decatur, and Rockford.

On a rainy Monday morning, I made my way to a small, older two-story wood-frame house with vinyl siding on the north end of Polonia. The front entrance had two items on display: a construction work order and a small pale blue nylon rosary hanging from a plastic hook.

When I walk inside, the first person I hear behind a barrier of plastic sheeting is Tim, the site foreman. An orientation is under way, and he's holding court in the kitchen, explaining some basic processes and laying out the work ahead with the even tenor of a high school baseball coach with forty seasons under his belt. It's a lead abatement job; there's a child with elevated blood lead levels living in the house, and the work entails replacing windows, doors, and interior and exterior trim and stripping a common stairway to make it safe. Huddled around Tim are four trainees in hard hats who are getting eight weeks of on-the-job training.

What I'd intruded on was the first day of a small two-week project that gets bigger and more complex the closer you look at it. The construction was being done by a local firm called Green Homeowners United in partnership with the Social Development Commission, an antipoverty organization created by the state of Wisconsin. The project was being funded using a grant from a federal program to help low-income residents living in older homes with health hazards. Meanwhile, the work training being led by Tim in the kitchen was happening in concert with the Milwaukee Climate and Equity Plan, a city-county initiative that supports green jobs and green projects partially as a way to address historic racial wealth gaps and improve housing in the country's most segregated city. So within a few hundred square feet, a private local business, along with city, state, and federal entities, had come together in a complicated interchange of priorities like loose drill bits in a drawer.

Overlooking the myriad forces at play, what stood out to me about the scene was its simplicity. For Milwaukee, where a lot of steady and sustaining work has vaporized, the development of green jobs offers a way to build a coalition between those left behind by the economy and those who were never brought along. "The idea was 'We've got to do something,'" Erick Shambarger, Milwaukee's director of environmental sustainability, told me ahead of the visit. "Climate change is a crisis, but we've also got these persistent racial disparities, and we've got to address those and be cognizant of it as we make the new economy, so that we're not repeating the mistakes of the past."

I'm a sucker for this kind of model because it gets at where there is a need, a consensus, and an undeniable collective benefit. Milwaukee's climate and equity plan hits at least three areas of general agreement: that there aren't enough solid, well-paying jobs; that we're collectively making too little effort on climate change; and that we need to do more to correct racial and social imbalances in America.

The deficit of good American jobs is a no-brainer, so let's talk about the environment and social change. As recently as 2023, according to the Pew Research Center, a full two-thirds of U.S. adults said they support prioritizing renewable energy sources and for America to become fully carbon neutral by 2050. Furthermore, a significant majority of Americans believes that various institutions—be they big business and corporations, state and federal governments, down to communities and neighborhoods— are not doing enough to combat climate change. (All too fittingly, the one group that a majority of Americans *do* think is doing enough to battle climate change is "you, yourself, as an individual.") And despite the very loud opposition claiming otherwise, 70 percent of Americans believe that the country needs to improve on issues of social justice, however vague these calls might be.

When united into a single plan of action, these three crises— jobs, climate, and social inequality—offer a clear route to transforming the economy, the country, and every community in it. But there's more here than just solving pragmatic issues like wage gaps, economic opportunity, and climate goals. The prospects of a far-reaching green economy also present a critical antidote for our demoralized culture of work in which irregular gigs, short-term gains, and the deadening generation of profit have widely replaced permanence and purpose. The tasks a seasoned foreman can plot out in a small kitchen in Polonia can multiply outward in endless forms. "To get a sense of the number of green jobs that are possible, you have to first think about the extent to which fossil fuels are used throughout our entire economy: everything from the production of electricity and all the jobs that go with the production of electricity to how homes are built and consume electricity, vehicles, and how our transportation systems use and consume fuels," Shambarger explained. That means adapting basic infrastructure and improving complex utilities, reworking transmission lines and overhauling manufacturing, as well as defending cities and areas that are vulnerable to extreme weather—and creating an entire new workforce to carry it out. (Not only are there already more green jobs available than workers qualified to do them, but according to analysis by the Bureau of Labor Statistics, they pay well above the national mean.)

Now, I know what you're probably thinking. Adam, you seem like a reasonably smart, incredibly handsome guy, but the political obstacles to making a vibrant, long-term green model truly take hold from sea to shining sea are enormous. During the first Republican debate in Milwaukee, which took place on a one-hundred-degree day during one of the three hottest months on record to that point—June through August 2023—not a single candidate raised their hand when asked if human behavior is causing climate change. And across the aisle, as with dire issues like affordable housing, much of the forward movement on climate has been hamstrung in part by Democrats' irrational and characteristic love of bureaucracy, process, permitting, NIMBYism, and red tape.* Even as President Biden shuffled around Milwaukee to celebrate the first birthday of the Inflation Reduction Act, the various incentives and subsidies for many of its important climate provisions were still being hashed out by bureaucrats in nondescript government offices in Washington, D.C., at a pace far too glacial for glaciers.

Climate change isn't universally depicted as the clear and moral and mortal threat that it obviously is; nevertheless, there is another useful way to frame it in terms that Americans, in our enchantment with efficiency, industry, hard work, and self-reliance, are already predisposed to respond to: as an engine of the American future and in the aspirational imagery of moon shots and unmet frontiers. "Literally every segment of the economy that deals with electric or deals with power and fuel systems has a chance to become green," said Shambarger, noting that a green job can be anything from an HVAC technician to an arborist. "Electricians are, to me, the number one example of what could be a green job going forward," he added, "and that speaks to the need to get people back into the trades and all that we've

---

* It's meaningful (and more than a little irritating) that every single Democratic presidential nominee after the peanut-farming engineer Jimmy Carter went to law school.

lost over the last twenty or thirty years, when the trades were maybe an afterthought to some people."

There's also a place to affix this familiar, totemic American line of thinking to initiatives that would make the U.S. economy fairer and more inclusive. When institutions place a priority on bringing historically excluded or neglected groups of people into the fold, it exasperates people who feel that these objectives violate the basic parameters of the American ethic or imply that some ambitions and struggles are more important than others. But hard numbers show otherwise.

Over the decades, economists have visited and revisited what powered the enormous postwar growth in the United States and gave rise to the American middle class in those years. And while it's true that the country enjoyed a huge head start over economies that had been battered during the war, what helped separate the American boom from more tenuous and ordinary growth, what helped supercharge it, was its expedition of opportunity for previously excluded groups of workers. Data and modeling from "The Allocation of Talent and U.S. Economic Growth," an influential (and scintillatingly titled) study by four economists from Stanford University and the University of Chicago, conclude that over 40 percent of economic growth *per worker* in the United States since 1960 can be attributed to better incorporating the talents of women and people of color into the economy, even in the limited ways that they have been.

More simply put, when the abilities of individuals were put to better use and talent went where it fit best, every worker, family, and community benefited considerably. Wages grew, there were more jobs for everyone, and when the boom times finally ended, the damage done was less extensive because the economy was more resilient. Unpacking the study, the economics reporter Jim Tankersley noted that rather than point out the extensive and well-known evidence of inequality in the workplace, "what this paper did that others had not done was spell out how that discrimination hurt the American economy. It added up the costs."

When a certain brand of American nostalgist writes an encomium full of yearning for the old economy, it's often this logic and efficiency that they're grieving. And if you're lucky enough to catch a glimpse of the old soundness in the right light, you can't help but feel energized by it.

The huddle in the kitchen breaks, and Tim, the site foreman, looks over with reasonable suspicion at the rained-on, mildly hungover stranger standing in the living room of his work site. After I introduce myself and he double-checks with some delight to make sure I didn't say my name was Adam Sandler, he introduces me around.

Outside the house, I meet Saidirick Walker. Walker is fifty and soft-spoken, with lines of silver in his black beard. Despite years of movement, his southern accent hasn't been knocked loose. Walker tells me he grew up in Florida, and after serving in the military, he found work with a commercial builder in the Pacific Northwest during a housing boom. In addition to heavy construction, he'd managed inventories and even survived a harrowing stint doing inside sales. Basically, he knew every angle of the business from logistics to big tilt-up construction. "I worked with the Department of Defense in Washington State for a while, working on World War II buildings and structures that they're still using. We had to abate these major installations for lead, asbestos—the HVAC and diesel boiler systems," he says with a laugh that makes clear the sights he's seen. "But I actually started in the warehouse first, driving the forklift."

Walker next moved to Milwaukee, and when a contract for weatherizing low-income homes ended, he met Kevin Kane, an economist and community organizer, who was looking for a way to merge green jobs with the growing needs of blue-collar workers. "We realized the best way to do it was to spin off our own general contracting firm that did energy-efficiency work, which eventually included home improvements to address health concerns," Kane explained in a call. "We became one of the only residential union contractors here because we're so interested in creating living-wage careers in a sector that traditionally is pretty low wage and transitory." Walker made a perfect fit for the new venture.

Three years later, Walker manages teams of workers at job sites for the company, in addition to coordinating its projects with local organizations and finding ways to make homes and buildings more energy efficient. "One really good thing that happened is that the City of Milwaukee and the Public Service Commission are actually allowing us to do some energy efficiency work on the same homes that have lead abatement," Walker explains. The work includes insulating attics and sealing ductwork, windows, and doors, and it's work that's only growing in need as climate initiatives slowly ramp up around the country.

The expansion of this type of work seems like an unambiguous good, especially for working Americans without a college degree, whose real wages have decreased since the 1980s, current workers in the fossil fuel industry such as coal miners and offshore oil rig engineers, and a generation of younger workers probing their way into a labor market filled with unsteady gigs and irregular work. "They're getting experience and training, they're endeavoring to just find out 'Hey, is this something that I like doing?'" Walker says of the new trainees, adding, "They're going to work, and if they show the aptitude or the willingness to learn, we can bring them on full-time right away." With the number of projects in the hopper growing by the day, trainees can join after eight weeks and earn union wages in a union shop with benefits, pensions, and family health insurance. "All of those things that are like, 'Yeah, this is what we need for our economy.'"

Beyond these benefits, a wholesale embrace of the green economy offers the means to remake the way we work and live as well as restore a collective purpose that has been lost in post–Cold War America. Seeing this theory put into real-life, load-bearing practice felt like peering into a magical alternate future, where complex problems have basic solutions, the at-odds worlds (tech and analog, red and blue, private and public) fuse in symbiosis, estimated recipe prep times aren't total lies, and all your passwords autofill correctly. "Our friends in the Sierra Club and others have long argued that this just transition to green jobs will help a lot of people," Kane told me. "The hard part is that they've been saying that for so long that it's hard to prove; solar jobs don't necessarily pay the same as power plant jobs. We are trying to show that it is possible, and we're trying to personify it."

What's more, you don't have to be versed or even invested in the ideological complexities of decarbonization to experience the basic fulfillment of work that builds and preserves and rewards and then ends. Before he and the crew got back to it, Walker said it better than I ever could: "I can go home in the evening and say, 'Man, I've done something good. Worked. I did good work.' And then, to see that improvement in the end and say, 'Yep.' It's a good opportunity to do that."

CHAPTER NINE

WORTH

THE WAGES OF GOING IT ALONE

**A DECENT SOCIETY IS ONE WHOSE INSTITUTIONS
DO NOT HUMILIATE PEOPLE.**

—AVISHAI MARGALIT

For most of his career, Steve Tucker worked out of the cinderblock police station in Ranburne, a four-hundred-person town in an eastern Alabama county named for a Confederate major general. By all accounts, Tucker was beloved for his easy laugh and admired for his dedication to the town where he came up. When talk turned to work over a phone call in 2020, I got the sense of someone animated by a simple calculus: Tucker understood how his job mattered, which fed his drive to be good at it.

Nearly three decades into an open-ended run as police chief, Tucker had never fired his service revolver at anybody. Before images of pies cooling on windowsills pop up or a passing whiff of wisteria drifts in, know that Ranburne isn't that seductive idyll of TV-tray sitcoms. Even in a town where everybody knows each other, Tucker told me he'd seen a lot since he'd started policing, including many deaths from despair, although that wasn't the term he used for it. I'd reached out to him about one incident in particular.

In the summer of 2019, Tucker got a call from the wife of his friend John. She told Tucker that John had locked himself in the house with a weapon and she was worried that he was suicidal. Ranburne, like many places, is distant from facilities equipped to handle mental health crises. When a crisis arose, phone calls like these often went to Tucker. As in most cases, Tucker knew John well. They'd been good friends for most of their lives. He'd known him going back to before Tucker had started on the force at age twenty-four. He was fifty-nine when he got the call.

Arriving on the scene, Tucker walked through the front door to check on him, and John fired a shot at the door. And though he had pleaded for calm, Tucker couldn't get through to his old friend. "I always could talk to him when he was frustrated," Tucker later explained in his deep drawl. "That day he wasn't about to be talked to. He wasn't listening to nobody." After more police arrived and a long standoff turned violent, John, who later tested positive for meth, was killed by police fire. At the funeral, Tucker would serve as one of his pallbearers.

Stories like these get neatly folded up into increasingly familiar boxes. They're distanced by tropes and tokens: a rural community with easy access to guns, a poor and distressed area with limited job prospects in a state where more people die from suicide than homicide. But this isn't simply a small-town or a red-state story, or any other story so easily reduced. It's too familiar.

John's tragedy was partially about work, a much messier and broad-reaching aegis in American life. It's work that increasingly steers identity and meaning here, and John was a victim of the purchase that work holds. Prior to his breakdown, a disability had knocked him out of the workforce, and though he did what he could—fished for catfish and raised money for his church—he had been spending a lot of time at home. "His wife worked hard . . . long hours at Walmart," Tucker said. "I think it got to him."

———

Creating better, more widely accessible jobs that support families and sustain communities is a key salve for what ails us collectively, but it doesn't relieve us of the social weight of work.

We already know about the telltale American tendency to derive status and importance from clocking excessive hours at the office. We're also well acquainted with the travails of the many millions more who work hard to either barely get by or fall farther behind. But work, as something that defines us or subsumes our identities or clarifies our worth, is another problem entirely.

Though modern American work culture shares spiritual contours with the Puritan ideals of callings and vocations, the emergence of work as a font of secular meaning is a relatively recent phenomenon. In *The Protestant Ethic and the Spirit of Capitalism*, the influential social theorist Max Weber argued that even Benjamin Franklin hadn't thought that work was anything more than a means of gathering money and keeping a good name. "Man is dominated by the making of money, by acquisition as the ultimate purpose of his life," he wrote of Franklin's example, pointing out that it's Franklin who's credited with expressions like "Time is money."

Now take a haphazard scroll through the cheery hellscape of LinkedIn or peer at the bookshelves beyond the wet sandwiches at an airport kiosk, and you'll see the furious treasure of a society thoroughly convinced that infusing work with meaning or blurring the separation between personal and professional is the path to fulfillment. It wasn't always this way. In *The Good Enough Job*, Simone Stolzoff noted a poll from 1962 in which only 6 percent of American workers claimed that meaningful work was important to finding success in the office. "Twenty years later, the number was 49 percent," he added. "Today, nine out of ten people are willing to earn less money to do more meaningful work."

The reasons behind the elevation of work hit on some refrains similar to the white-collar trend of overwork: the steep decline in religious affiliation, the rise of the internet, and the demise of places to socialize outside work and home. Another is a broad social fragmentation that's been the cause of hand-wringing in America ever since the sociologist Robert Putnam published *Bowling Alone* in 2000. Others have suggested that the nonconformity of 1960s counterculture carried over into the office for workers who "simply do not imagine a career along the old vertical lines," as Charles A. Reich put it in *The Greening of America*.

To be a little cynical about it, it's easy to imagine that mining your work for meaning also helps justify those increasingly long days at the office, even if that time is spent marketing a new fin-tech product and not curing ringworm or teaching English to refugees.

In this widening eddy, jobs became identities and doing what you love became a form of self-expression. And unfortunately, while all this talk of passion and noble work deepened, the quality of jobs deteriorated, unions and their bargaining power disinte-grated, email bled into evenings and weekends, and wages flailed. It's almost as if professing your love of your career became a way to fend off despair about it, sort of like a dad who euphemizes his obnoxious new son-in-law as "larger than life" in a wedding toast. The labor reporter Sarah Jaffe summed up this dissonance nicely in *Work Won't Love You Back:* "If we recalled why we work in the first place—to pay the bills—we might wonder why we're working so much for so little."

Employers and managers have been all too happy to egg on this movement toward professional identification. Deploying what's often termed "positive psychology," companies have tried to cast work as fun with compensation or as some higher expres-sion of the self or as a shared mission with chosen family. Walt Disney coined a special name for his theme park employees (cast members), derivatives of which can be seen on job-listing clear-inghouses at companies including Starbucks (partners), Subway (sandwich artists), and Apple (geniuses). During an odd stretch of the 2010s, before several companies seemed to think better of it, it wasn't unusual to see listings for "gurus" and "ninjas" for retail or service jobs that tended not to entail spiritual teaching or stealth combat. This tactic of rebranding work as performance or some higher calling was backed by decades of research showing that employees who deeply identify with their jobs tend to work more hours, be more productive, and quit less. But just because some-thing is determined to be fun or empowering by corporate bosses or the *Harvard Business Review* doesn't necessarily mean that it is. Just ask the cast member scraping hardened gum off the floor of Space Mountain for too little pay.

Further proof of the messy entanglement of individuals and

their careers can be seen through a snowballing of social obligations at the office. With the help of overextended HR teams
and personnel specialists with titles such as "people operations
manager," many workplace calendars have filled up with activities
perhaps best described as mandatory fun. (We're way beyond the
sad supermarket sheet cake for Greg in accounting's birthday.)
When loosed upon the workplace, elements of this forced mirth
have more recently taken on the terrifying form of Zoom parties,
department text message chains, themed dress-up days, employee
icebreakers that encourage oversharing, and lunch seminars on
self-care (but never work boundaries). Let's also not forget those
off-site retreats and happy hours, many of which butt their way
into postwork hours and create a variety of unnerving predicaments for groups such as parents, women, teetotalers, workers
with disabilities, introverts, and simply people with personal lives
beyond the workplace.

In what Anne Helen Petersen described to me as a "benefits
arms race," company recruiters even market these dorm vibes
and integrated work-life friendships as perks of the job. And who
would dare object? Nobody likes the office scold.

Plus, in all fairness to the trend, work hangs can be a good
time! Having worked in a few places with the resources to throw
at excessive team cohesion, I've enjoyed mustering up the extro-
version required to booze on the company's dime or socialize
while chucking axes. I've cheered at the CTO's trance music
playlist at the weekly happy hour as half-heartedly as the next
guy. In fact, I've felt *lucky* to have gotten to do it. But because
it's usually plain as day to anyone who is paying attention, I also
know that not everyone feels the same way about it.

Pointing out the trouble with deploying hyperfriendly tactics such as mandatory fun and positive psychology in the office
for *Academy of Management Review*, Professor Stephen Fineman
suggested that it creates an environment that "deflects attention
away from any disadvantageous structural conditions at work." It
also makes the built-in hierarchies of an office tougher to navigate and adds another, more subjective element to what being
"good" at a job means that has very little to do with actual work
itself. "Most Incompetent Coworker Once Again Shines at Office

Halloween Party," reads a perfect headline on this topic by the Onion.

Yet another facet of this jaunty, all-enveloping office culture is that it kind of makes you feel like a jerk for not enjoying the mechanics of your work. "These hip, shiny workspaces do make it, in an odd way, less acceptable to dislike a job or a boss; they are supposed to make us *want* to give our hours away," Apoorva Tadepalli wrote in a lament for the old workplace crumminess and misanthropy found in the fiction of Charles Bukowski and Hunter S. Thompson. One of the great and few joys of being part of the working world is bonding with coworkers over mutual disdain for a job or a boss. Imposing a work environment in which hierarchies are intentionally obscured and natural disagreement is replaced by passive aggression feels like a cosmic felony.

Probably the most unsettling variation on this theme comes from employers who compare the company dynamic to family. "When I hear something like *We're like family here*," the journalist Joe Pinsker opined in 2022, "I silently complete the analogy: *We'll foist obligations upon you, expect your unconditional devotion, disrespect your boundaries, and be bitter if you prioritize something above us.*" Add some open bars and sharp axes to this equation, and you've got the makings of real mayhem. Here, the software company Salesforce provides an object lesson. Nestled in the top third of the Fortune 500, Salesforce is one of the largest tech firms in the world and almost certainly the only one to use the Hawaiian expression *ohana* (chosen family) as one of its guiding watchwords. In a 2017 blog post, the company describes its adoption of *ohana* in some wince-inducing terms:

> In the late '90s, our CEO Marc Benioff wanted a break. He decided to take a sabbatical, so he rented a beach house in Hawaii (doesn't get much more relaxing than that). On the islands, he connected with locals and learned about many of the Hawaiian's [sic] traditions and customs, including the concept of Ohana. In Hawaiian culture, Ohana represents the idea that families—blood-related, adopted, or intentional—are bound together, and that family members are responsible for one another. When

he created Salesforce in 1999, he made sure that "Ohana" was in the company's foundations.

Later in 2017, Salesforce went a little overboard with the theme and released "We Are Ohana," an original song about the company set to footage of Salesforce employees at various conferences and retreats where there are abundant high fives, a disconcerting number of hugs and head-back fits of laughter, and, naturally, a private performance by U2. Nearly as astonishing as the fact that the song "We Are Ohana" manages to go on for more than three minutes is the video's comments section, which adds some dismal context to the self-congratulation. "This reminds me of the time my family laid off 10% of its family members," one reads, referencing company layoffs in 2023 that slashed eight thousand jobs. "Is this a cult?" another commenter asks.

For many companies that tout their familial bonds or their embrace of progressive ideals, such as eschewing profits for the greater good of the world, it's often a different story when a downturn arrives or the shareholders revolt. As one former Salesforce employee told me, "[CEO Marc] Benioff talks about stakeholder capitalism and Ohana and employees being more important than shareholders . . . until you get an activist investor."

What the Salesforce story makes obvious is that no matter where it is or what it is, the consecration of work is dangerous for everyone. During the pandemic, the championing of essential workers as "heroes" created a blind spot whereby workers, whether they were trying to save lives without proper PPEs in emergency rooms or enforcing mask mandates at pharmacies, supermarkets, or takeout counters, were shunted into a nebulous sort of martyrdom without much choice in the matter. "It's nice to be thought of as Wonder Woman, and the assumption that the real heroes are wearing aprons, scrubs, and plastic nametags certainly comes from a kind place," Michelle Nugent, a caregiver in Philadelphia, wrote on Broad Street Review a year into the lockdowns. "But expecting ordinary people to continuously shrug off both ordinary stress and the effects of a yearlong pandemic to offer 24 hours of service with a smile is just a different flavor of dehumanization." She added that her long days of caregiving work during the pandemic had less to do with some vaguely defined and unrewarded valor than the cold fact that she had to do it to keep her own life together. "When I work for 15 hours [a day], it's because rent can't be paid with eight."

In 2021, four researchers dug into the trouble with this involuntary hero making. In studying how essential workers were held up as brave offerings for the sake of the greater good, the researchers found that the impulse to exalt those workers made it harder for people to generate sympathy for and anger about the danger that they were in. The extreme examples set during the pandemic also help clarify how when we impose values such as selflessness upon underappreciated and undercompensated workers, we make their work less fair, harder to do, and harder to recruit for. "At a broader level," they wrote, "we hope to provide a cautionary note regarding the cultural practice of normalizing individuals in certain occupations (e.g., teachers paying for equipment out of their own pocket) and roles (e.g., moms as superwomen) as heroes and expecting them to make personal sacrifices, as such subtle cultural perceptions may contribute to inequality and only add to their burden."

Yet another noteworthy offshoot of this work worship is the starry-eyed pursuers of dream jobs, the idealists who seek salvation in a company or a position. In an admittedly scattered career that's included freelancing, several years of bartending, gig work, and stints at a nonprofit, a federal agency, and a few tech start-ups, I've also worked in book publishing and media. These two industries—in addition to attracting stone-cold narcissists like me—have long relied on their prestige to compensate for their weak salaries and structural imbalances. The combination of lousy pay with long hours and work often requiring residence in some of America's most expensive cities isn't a recipe for a viable career. And though, understandably, you won't see many tears shed over the plight of editors or reporters who decamp to PR houses or graduate school to find a better living, the corrosive effects of this bargain extend way beyond those who leave the field with a deep feeling of disillusionment.

Like any trade that narrows its workforce to the few who can afford to ride out several years of low pay, reducing the talent pool in journalism or publishing ultimately reduces the quality of the output. We've all stumbled through a tone-deaf story or book lacking basic perspective. Similar to law or medicine or political office or nonprofit work, a lack of demographic range and perspective in an industry stymies innovation and erodes public trust.

All of this is to say that even if you love your work, even if it's a dream gig, at the end of the day, work is still a job. And jobs have key performance indicators to hit and jobs have bottom lines for which brutal calculations and budget cuts and disappointing compromises are regularly made. Jobs almost always have deeply entrenched problems as well as imbalances, inefficiencies, and biases that are magnified by ineffective leaders and exacerbated by impatient owners, donors, or investors. As the articulation of an identity or a linchpin to fix one's life into position, a job is a hell of a risky bet, now more than ever.

Many aspects of the professional identification and career obsession that I've described, whether internally driven or externally suggested, tilt toward higher-paying occupations. There's a good reason for that: only a solid job can provide the basics of a secure American life through a livable income, a retirement plan, and health insurance.[*] Sadly, paid time off—be it for vacation or parental leave or even just to not have to work while sick—is a luxury in an economy progressively built on gig, temp, and contract work.

The fact that it takes a decent job to cover over the tatters in the U.S. social safety net is so much of what makes a good job valuable, both materially and socially. In this unforgiving way, what you do says a lot about how steady your life is. Maybe, then, it's not surprising that 47 percent of upper-income workers say that their work is central to their identity, according to a 2023 Pew Research Center study. For workers with lower and middle incomes, that figure drops to 36 and 37 percent, respectively.

* That or a ton of inherited wealth, I suppose.

One way to think about this discrepancy is that work has twin shadows. If a job doesn't provide security, the absence of security comes to define a person's life experience instead. Experts on poverty and financial precarity have long shown the all-consuming impact of scarcity, linking it to poor health and impaired executive functioning or even likening the cognitive effects of poverty to a night without sleep. However, work's other shadow is that it is still much more than just a conduit of financial security. Accepting his party's nomination for president in August 2020, Joe Biden told a story that he often tells about his father, Joe Sr., an "honorable, decent man," who "worked hard and built a great middle-class life for our family." After losing his job, the elder Biden told his son, "Joey, a job is about a lot more than a paycheck. It's about your dignity. It's about respect. It's about your place in your community. It's about looking your kids in the eye and saying, 'Honey, it's going to be okay.'" The lesson was clear. Even as candidate Biden meant to convey empathy toward people struggling to find good work, he was reaffirming just how much baggage is tethered to a job and all the ways in which work and worth intersect in American life.

The crises wrought by our obsession with work and the burden of work's cultural grip have a dwarfing power. It rarely matters whether a person feels attached to what they do; real-world conditions typically require that work remains central to life. For poorer Americans, this can be seen in the rise of insecure scheduling, in which workers (mostly hourly employees) are given little advance notice of when they're slated to work, much to the detriment of their mental and physical health, stability, family life, and finances. Or the phenomenon of income volatility—the dramatic amount that workers' paychecks and family incomes tend to fluctuate from month to month. Income volatility has at least doubled since 1970 and now affects roughly a third of U.S. households. Set off in part by the rise of gig work and jobs without a set number of hours, the erratic nature of wages has all kinds of consequences beyond sending families scrambling to adjust when the bottom of their budget falls out. Beyond the financial stress, wage instability can make it impossible to save money, make long-term plans, and get access to credit. A family with unpredictable earnings, for example, might qualify for public assistance one month and then breach the income threshold and be disqualified another. "Families close to the eligibility threshold for food stamps who had more volatile incomes were less likely to utilize this benefit in the years that they qualified for it," a 2022 report from the Federal Reserve Bank of St. Louis found, adding that nearly one in five eligible families don't sign up for SNAP.

Long before insecure scheduling and wage volatility became prominent features of the workforce experience, the United States was already a country whose institutions were hostile toward people who need help. One emerging (and depressing) field of study focuses on the opaque, confounding, and inefficient numbskullery involved in enrolling in public aid programs or even just dealing with a screwy medical claim. Writing on the "time tax," the journalist Annie Lowrey described it as the "levy of paperwork, aggravation, and mental effort imposed on citizens in exchange for benefits that putatively exist to help them."

In ways that seem to be by design, these hassles harm those who often need support the most. "Historically, with welfare programs, you tend to see not just opposition to the existence of those programs . . . but that opposition also translates into support for administrative burdens in the delivery of those services," the political scientist Donald Moynihan explained in 2023. Responding to the revelation that Florida's unemployment system was the slowest in the nation in 2020, Governor Ron DeSantis speculated, "I think the goal was, for whoever designed it, was, 'Let's put as many kind of pointless roadblocks along the way, so people just say, oh, the hell with it, I'm not going to do that.'"

On the ground level, not having a fixed address, internet access, or a computer, much less the time for endless calls and hours-long waits at appointments, can be the difference between whether someone successfully navigates America's patchwork of bureaucracy or doesn't. Back in Winston-Salem, Nakitta Long, who considered herself lucky to have secured her unemployment benefits in less than a month during the early days of COVID, is a clear example of the tyranny of low expectations that govern the experience of the public benefits system.

In *Poverty, by America*, the sociologist Matthew Desmond tallied up the hundreds of billions of dollars in government assistance that goes unused by low-income American families each year, which includes $17.3 billion of Earned Income Tax Credit as well as "food stamps ($13.4 billion), government health insurance ($62.2 billion), unemployment insurance when between jobs ($9.9 billion), and Supplementary Security Income ($38.9 billion)." To that, he added that only about a quarter of eligible families apply for the federal program Temporary Assistance for Needy Families (TANF), and less than half of the elderly receive the food stamps for which they qualify. It's easy to chalk up these astonishingly low take-up rates to a lack of awareness about these programs or their logistical complexities, but the tragically low adoption rate is also almost certainly influenced by the stigmas that surround them—in national preoccupations with self-reliance or a forbidding notion of *real* citizenship. "I really think Medicaid is good, but I'm really having a problem with the people that don't want to work," a healthcare enrollment worker in Kentucky explained to the journalist Sarah Kliff. "Us middle-class people are really, really upset about having to work constantly, and then these people are not responsible." Herein lies another sad American irony.

Though political blowhards love to gnash their teeth over spending on social programs for poorer Americans, it's nothing compared to the free lunches enjoyed by those with more power and financial security, such as employer-sponsored health insurance, 401(k) retirement programs, and 529 savings plans for college, all of which the government subsidizes, and the capital gains tax, which favors the wealthy by taxing profits from assets like stocks or property at a lower rate than income earned by working a job. "In 2020 the federal government spent more than $193 billion on homeowner subsidies," Desmond noted, "a figure that far exceeded the amount spent on direct housing assistance for low-income families ($53 billion)." What's more, for American homeowners, the act of writing off billions of dollars in mortgage interest doesn't involve a journey quest around the unlit corners of U.S. bureaucracy. All you need to do is fill in a box during tax season and move right along with your life. As a perk, it hides in plain sight—practically undetectable to the recipient—which is why fewer of its beneficiaries seem to appreciate the break they've been handed.

———————————

The *decision*—there's no other word for it—to make the logistics of life so selectively kludgy is a lethal one. A recent audit by the Government Accountability Office, an investigative arm of Congress, found that roughly eight thousand Americans file for bankruptcy and another ten thousand people die every year while waiting for a disability benefit decision (or an appeal) to be decided by the Social Security Administration.* For Americans with debilitating conditions that are harder to substantiate, such as PTSD, migraines, or Long COVID, the chances that a claim will be met with rejection increase exponentially. All told, less than 40 percent of disability applications are initially approved, down from 50 percent in the 1990s.†

Once again, hovering around many of these figures is the specter of work as worth. In order to qualify for many major safety net programs, applicants have to prove (repeatedly) that they're actively seeking a job or holding one down, even if they're chronically ill or lack regular access to stable housing, a car, or public transportation. Proof of industriousness outstrips all other markers of deservingness. It doesn't matter that in any given

———

* That audit, by the way, took place in 2020. As of April 2023, the average wait time for a disability benefit decision had risen to a staggering seven months and thirteen days, nearly double the pre-COVID wait time.
† It's generally understood that the applicants who fare best in the disability application process are the ones who hire lawyers, who then take a significant chunk of the money secured.

number of situations, the combined costs of childcare and transportation alone can easily surpass the wages earned in certain job markets.

For the hard up in America, nothing is simple. In the early years of internet virality, a stunt called the Food Stamp Challenge became a popular way for public officials, nonprofits, and celebrity activists to showcase how tough it is to get by on the average weekly SNAP allotment. "I personally broke and had some chicken and fresh vegetables (and in full transparency, half a bag of black licorice)," the actor and lifestyle cultist Gwyneth Paltrow wrote about giving up on the challenge after four days in 2015. Though interesting and occasionally virtuous in its own weird way, the challenge mimicked only one part of the experience. A more telling feat of courage would have participants get by on $6.20 a day,[*] work a job with unsteady hours, and adhere to the Talmudic complexities of the SNAP guidelines without, well, snapping.

The process of qualifying for public assistance in the United States is so dense and convoluted, you'd think the American flag had stripes of red tape across it. Heather Hahn was in college when she learned that a family member—a single parent on public assistance—had received a "very small" raise at work. That token boost in income had apparently been enough to knock Hahn's family member off the rolls of programs offering cash assistance, along with food and medical aid. "I thought, *Wow, that's really messed up,*" Hahn told me. Hahn, now Dr. Hahn and an associate vice president at the nonpartisan think tank Urban Institute, has since become an expert in public benefits. She has worked at the U.S. Government Accountability Office and conducted extensive research into how public programs function (and often don't). "They're not just inadvertent and inevitable parts of making sure that you've got the paperwork in line and making sure that you're following the rules," she said of the bureaucratic irregularities that beset social insurance programs and make life hell for their applicants. "The administrative burdens themselves are, in some

---

[*] The estimated average benefit per person in 2024, according to the Center on Budget and Policy Priorities.

sense, a deliberate test of deservingness. It's this assumption that only someone truly, desperately needy, who really has no other options, is going to put up with all that is required. That adds to this deservingness."

In the case of SNAP, which is theoretically one of the simpler programs, there are certain exemptions, work requirements, and time limits that change from state to state or go into and out of effect, depending on the local unemployment rate. "It's confusing for people," Hahn explained. "I know we talked with people in Arkansas who were subject to the SNAP work requirement, and there was just a lot of confusion around, 'Does this apply to me?' But also, 'How do I report my work?' I remember people in the focus group saying, 'Well, they seem to know if I lose my job, so they must know that I'm working, right?' But they don't. You have to fill out the right paperwork and submit it and all of that." Likewise, when people lose their job and seek out aid from Temporary Assistance for Needy Families (TANF), the program tends to steer them back toward the same type of job by limiting what kinds of certifications or skills they can pursue while receiving aid. "Those kinds of very specific explicit restrictions in the legislation serve to perpetuate that people will remain in poverty," Hahn noted. Her research, she added, backed that up.

Work theater is an extension of a popular national attitude about worth. In the fall of 2023, the Republican-led House of Representatives passed a debt ceiling bill to keep the government open that would have reduced spending in part by cutting off healthcare for 1.7 million low-income people and throwing 275,000 people off food stamps. It failed in the Senate, but not before some grandstanding sound bites hit the airwaves. "I don't think hard-working Americans should be paying for all the social services for people who could make a broader contribution and instead are couch potatoes," Florida representative Matt Gaetz argued. (As the journalist David Firestone pointed out, Gaetz's "deep concern about excessive spending didn't stop him from requesting a $141.5 million earmark for a helicopter training hangar . . . in his district.") Gaetz would eventually go on to help lead the ouster of House majority leader Kevin McCarthy for negotiating with President Biden on a markedly less punitive deal to keep the government open. That deal toughened work requirements to qualify for SNAP and TANF and still ended up increasing federal spending, according to the Congressional Budget Office.

Here again, the moth-eaten idea that struggling Americans weren't trying hard enough stood at the heart of the national debate, even if they were unable to work or were battling to find stable, quality jobs where few exist. Hahn, citing an annual survey of Americans experiencing poverty, outlined their torment in more basic terms: One in five respondents had rotating or irregular shifts, where they didn't work the same hours every week. About half of respondents had work schedules that fluctuated by more than ten hours a week. Forty percent of them had less than a week's notice of their upcoming schedule.

For many poorer Americans in this impossible bind, income isn't the only volatile or erratic feature of life; *everything* is volatile or erratic. "You might need multiple jobs because your income is unpredictable, but it's hard to be available for more than one job when you don't know what your schedule is going to be," Hahn explained. "It makes it hard to engage in training if you don't know if you're going to be able to show up for the training." Worse yet, she added, "This makes it really difficult to do other things that are important in your life. It makes it hard to be there for your kids and your family." Finally, in addition to these constraints and uncertainty, there are work requirements, which demand that a person prove that they're working a certain number of hours each week or each month to qualify for help, despite that number often being out of their control.

I suppose this rigmarole could be justified if it yielded positive outcomes. However, most of what it seems to do is reveal how cold and unforgiving a society without built-in support can be, especially when opportunity is unevenly split. "In Europe, there's generally a social contract between the people and the government that involves a much greater role of the government in supporting the people, whereas in the United States, we are so focused on the individual," Hahn said. "Understanding this social ideology is really important for understanding work requirements because we find again and again that work requirements are not helping people get jobs that are going to lift them out of poverty. They don't always even help people get jobs at all."

———————

Waving off collective accountability for individuals is part of what makes America's working way so unique and muscular and zero-sum. Receiving help or being in need is scorn-worthy in a nation built on off-roading Chevys and self-fulfilled destiny. "Our whole system, including our safety net system, is built on this assumption of individual agency and individual responsibility," Hahn said. "This is rooted in the Protestant work ethic; it's the foundation of the American Dream. The American Dream says, 'If you work hard and you're morally upstanding, you will be rewarded.' So in that context, it's really suspicious when people are not financially secure. . . . This shows up very concretely in our policies."

It also shows in our rhetoric. In his notorious "47 percent gaffe," 2012 presidential candidate Mitt Romney was captured on tape during a closed-door fundraiser claiming that his opponent, President Barack Obama, had the support of the 47 percent of Americans who subsist off government programs and contribute little to the country and the economy. "There are 47 percent of the people who will vote for the president no matter what," he began. "There are 47 percent who are with him, who are dependent upon government, who believe that they are victims, who believe the government has a responsibility to care for them, who believe that they are entitled to health care, to food, to housing, to you-name-it. That that's an entitlement. And the government should give it to them. And they will vote for this president no matter what. . . . These are people who pay no income tax."

Romney was actually right about the approximate number of Americans not paying income tax around that time, but not because they were shirkers or malingerers or lollygaggers or freeloaders. Many simply didn't make enough money to have a tax liability. They were too poor. "About half of people who don't owe income tax are off the rolls not because they take advantage of tax breaks but rather because they have low incomes,"

Roberton C. Williams of the nonpartisan Tax Policy Center had explained the year before. As for the other half of the group not paying income tax, he noted that a majority of that half (74 percent) was made up of seniors, the working poor, and low-income families with children, groups whom the tax code is designed to assist by bipartisan acts of Congress.

The reactions to Romney's remarks were overwhelmingly negative, but polling at the time showed that it struck a particularly harsh chord with Americans with family incomes below $30,000, 69 percent of whom disapproved. That probably had to do with the fact that nearly two-thirds of the 47 percent *did* work. And not only did they still pay taxes (including state and local taxes as well as payroll taxes for Social Security and Medicare), but a larger share of their limited earnings ultimately went to flat excise taxes (like on gasoline) that aren't reduced for people with lower incomes.

But most damningly of all, Romney was insinuating that struggling Americans didn't really count. "My job is not to worry about those people," he added. "I'll never convince them they should take personal responsibility and care for their lives." In essence, Romney's determination that any American who relied on government help or didn't pay an income tax would automatically support his opponent served as a means to wash his hands of them. *Abracadabra*. Poof!*

Associations with work, taxpaying, and citizenship (and accompanying veins of anger about work, taxpaying, and citizenship) are embedded in our national identity. In a 1789 letter, Benjamin Franklin cautioned a friend in France that although he felt hopeful about the long-term prospects for the newly ratified U.S. Constitution, "in this world, nothing is certain except death and taxes." (Franklin would die the following year.) Bitter contentions about taxpaying have been formidable if unsexy subplots in fights over British rule (No taxation without representation!), slavery,

---

* Also, not to overdo it on the guy, but that weird assertion was patently untrue. As many pointed out at the time, eight of the top ten states with the highest rates of citizens not paying any income tax in 2012 were deep-red states.

Reconstruction, integration, various U.S. military misadventures abroad, and the space program, which was boycotted by some civil rights activists. The need for the Constitution itself is often attributed by historians in part to fallout from Shays' Rebellion, a deadly farmer uprising in Massachusetts inspired by anger over wage taxes following independence. And though Mitt Romney's father, George, may be best remembered as a governor, presidential candidate, and auto executive, when he was five years old, in 1912, he and his family were part of a Mormon colony fleeing revolution in Mexico. Finding refuge in the United States, they were financially buoyed by the kind of taxpayer-funded federal refugee relief fund that routinely draws derision from deficit hawks.

Through it all, the aggrieved protagonist in the debates about work and spending has been the American taxpayer—overextended, righteous, and angry. "In the United States, we tend to use the word *taxpayer* as a kind of shorthand for an upstanding, contributing citizen," Vanessa S. Williamson, a senior fellow in governance studies at the Brookings Institution, told me, noting the positive connotations with performing one's civic duty and paying a fair share to society. "But," she added, "at the same time we also use the idea of taxpaying as a shorthand for who in the country is seen as contributing and working hard and doing their part. . . . Taxpaying reinforces stereotypes about who deserves and who is shirking. That's the underlying symbolism of taxpaying that undercuts, at least for me, the very positive aspects of this taxpayer culture."

The symbolism around paying taxes, she explained, is complicated by factors that have always fed into American division. Williamson brought up "welfare queen," the infamous slur used by Ronald Reagan during his failed 1976 presidential run to categorize an entire class of welfare recipients as scammers gaming the public. The basis of Reagan's archetype was a Chicago woman named Linda Taylor, thought to be Black, who had brazenly committed welfare fraud but who had also been linked to a grisly assortment of rackets and serious crimes that wouldn't make her representative of much beyond a true-crime podcast episode list.* "A murder in Chicago is mundane," the journalist Josh Levin wrote of the original welfare queen. "A sumptuously attired woman stealing from John Q. Taxpayer is a menace."

Nevertheless, the Gipper's "welfare queen" moniker helped cement a long-standing stereotype that reinforced, as William-son explained, "people's racist ideas about black women not doing their part in terms of working." She added, "Obviously, it's a trope that is utterly violated by the facts of the situation, but that has never stopped a stereotype before." Reagan's public cru-sade against assistance programs would carry into his presidency. As the journalist Bryce Covert noted, not long after his inaugura-tion, "Congress would pass $25 billion in cuts to programs that helped the poor."

Despite its much politicized history, the fact that Americans vastly overestimate the amount of government waste from tax-payer money on social programs for the poor, and the deep internal unpopularity of the U.S. government, the recent rise of antitax political groups like the Tea Party and even the stray political leader who brags about avoiding his tax burden, paying one's taxes remains wildly popular among Americans. "Ninety-plus percent, ninety-five percent sometimes of Americans agree that paying your fair share of taxes is a civic duty," Williamson explained, citing her research. Maybe that's why the taxpayer-citizen trope has been utilized so thoroughly.

Mitt Romney, of course, didn't win the presidency; in a poetic flourish, he got only 47 percent of the popular vote. But the long-held belief that financial success or independence from govern-ment aid is natural proof of character continues to fare well. Its manifestations can be detected in ways as punitive and varied as the cash bail system and debt-related driver's license suspen-sions. "Well into the twentieth century," Nancy Isenberg wrote

---

* Her story brings to mind Al Capone, another Chicago criminal mastermind, who was known for a lot of misdeeds other than the tax evasion charge that ultimately brought him down.

in *White Trash*, "expulsion and even sterilization sounded rational to those who wished to reduce the burden of 'loser' people on the larger economy."

Like income tax and social aid programs, disdain flows from the belief that success is virtue. It shows up in how the challenges facing struggling people are often portrayed as frivolous or self-imposed. In public retellings, an individual drowning in student debt is never someone who took out loans to go to nursing school or dropped out of an engineering program to care for a sick parent; it's always some loafer or wastrel who, in the words of Senator Ted Cruz, "studied queer pet literature" or a "slacker barista who wasted seven years in college" and can't "get off the bong for a minute."

Posturing about the deservingness of the supposedly idle continues to be popular, with or without the discretion usually offered by a closed-door fundraiser. Another eye-opening public debate happened in November 2017, this time out loud on the floor of the Senate. Ohio senator Sherrod Brown was pressing his colleagues over the fact the Senate had designed a trillion-dollar tax cut for the wealthy (financed by taxpayers), but had let the Children's Health Insurance Program (CHIP), the popular social program designed to give healthcare coverage to roughly 10 million low-income uninsured children and pregnant women, go without funding. The late senator Orrin Hatch, at the time the chair of the powerful Senate Finance Committee, took umbrage at that linkage. "The reason CHIP's having trouble is that we don't have any money anymore," he said before fixing his aim on social programs more broadly. "I have a rough time wanting to spend billions and billions and trillions of dollars to help people who won't help themselves, won't lift a finger, and expect the federal government to do everything." He went on to excoriate the liberal agenda for having "created millions of people that way, who believe everything they are or ever hope to be depends on the federal government rather than the opportunities that this great country grants them." In Hatch's argument, like most versions of this ageless sentiment, the fault never lay with policymakers who approved bad trade deals, removed oversight of major financial bodies, failed to protect consumers and workers against monopolies, and allowed the cost of necessities to reach crushing levels; the blame fell on individuals who simply didn't try hard enough.

To be clear, it's not a strictly one-party pastime for leaders to dodge basic accountability for the poor or embattled in America. There are plenty of examples of how high-minded liberal leaders have instituted regressive policies and revealed hypocritical attitudes toward the poor and those cut adrift in communities where Democrats call the shots. "It is in the blue states where affordable housing is often hardest to find, there are some of the most acute disparities in education funding and economic inequality is increasing most quickly," the journalists Johnny Harris and Binyamin Appelbaum outlined in 2021. The mandatory-minimum sentencing recommendations of the 1980s mass incarceration movement that funneled untold poor and mentally ill Americans out of treatment programs, mental health facilities, and the job market and into prisons were, as Ta-Nehisi Coates noted, "backed not just by conservatives such as Strom Thurmond but by liberals such as Ted Kennedy."[*]

Taking a destructively transactional view of American worth remains a bipartisan custom. Describing her unsuccessful presidential run, Hillary Clinton summoned up the image of the electoral map during a 2018 talk. "All that red in the middle, where Trump won," she said, "what the map doesn't show you is that I won the places that represent two-thirds of America's gross domestic product. So I won the places that are optimistic, diverse, dynamic, moving forward." Those remarks weren't far afield from plenty of resistance-themed commentary from the Trump years that painted millions of strangers with the same broad brush.

———

Perhaps the story of how hard people strain to get by is rarely absorbed because it implicates all of us. There's no other way to

———

[*] And as a damning two-year investigation by the Associated Press revealed in 2024, many of these prisoners now work for pennies producing hundreds of millions of dollars' worth of goods for some of the biggest companies in the United States.

explain how the richest country in history has far more poverty (especially among children) than any of its peer nations. For ugly reasons, perceptions of poverty tend to focus only on cities, but it's actually rural areas where enrollment in major federal programs such as Medicare and Social Security (as well as the social aid programs met with the most derision, such as Medicaid and food stamps) is disproportionately higher. That includes places like Ranburne, Alabama.

During my call with Steve Tucker, the town's police chief, I told him that I hoped to come down to visit him after the high heat of the pandemic dissipated. I hoped to meet the person everyone called simply "Chief," who had been handed the impossible challenge of policing—mediating custody battles and domestic disputes, managing mental health crises with limited resources—and who had tried to but couldn't save his good friend John from the crushing sense of incapacity that accompanies struggle in America. Unfortunately, the opportunity to meet in person never came. In April 2021, Tucker fell gravely ill. The town rallied around him, organizing blood drives and directing support toward his family. "Please continue to pray for Ranburne PD Chief, Steve Tucker," a local daycare posted on Facebook. "He is our best grass cutter, the greatest crossing guard & our favorite Dr. Seuss book reader! He's always there any time we need him."

Sadly, Tucker passed away, in his thirtieth year as police chief, and to honor him, the governor of Alabama ordered flags in the county to be lowered to half-mast. Likening Ranburne to Mayberry, the small fictional town of oddballs and busybodies held together by its kindly sheriff, the mayor eulogized Tucker as "our Andy Griffith." Later that year, on the first Friday night of the high school football season, Tucker was posthumously honored at halftime and the Ranburne Bulldogs won a close game against an in-state rival.

———————

The section of Highway 46 that runs through Ranburne is now known as Chief Steve Tucker Memorial Drive. Beyond the honorary road sign, the highway doubles as the town's Main Street, winding through a span of churches and auto body shops. I pull over for coffee at Country Boys, a counter service joint inside a gas station and the town's one full-time restaurant, where chicken livers, country fried steak with brown gravy, and peach cobbler are the specials on offer. I make my way to Freedom Baptist Church, one of the county's thirty-six Southern Baptist churches, where Tucker's memorial service was held. There I find Pastor Jerome Whaley on the rocking chairs outside the church life center. November is mild in eastern Alabama, and he tells me that if I can stand the smell of chicken manure from the pasture nearby, we can sit outside while we talk.

Pastor Whaley, whose assertive kindness would be off-putting were it not so genuine, lets me fumble through a preamble in which I try to explain that I'm thinking a lot about work but also the unseen struggles around work in America and the cumulative cost of them. I tell him I had been drawn to Ranburne by Tucker and the ways his duties had stretched so far beyond the protocols of law enforcement handbooks. That collection of attritions had seemed connected, I thought, and I wanted to know how that manifested in a place where, in Tucker's words, "everybody, some way or another, is kin to one another."

Whaley was fast to praise Tucker as a lost cornerstone of the community and to spell out the special magic of Ranburne—its "laid-back country way of life," the loyalty to the town that runs bone deep, and the absence of what Whaley termed "the hassle" found in nearby cities like Atlanta and Birmingham. "I've heard people say before, 'Man, I can't wait to move out of this town,'" he said with delight. "And then they get married and they have kids, and where do you think they show up?"

At forty-three, Whaley's path to becoming the pastor at Freedom Baptist reinforced both the town's tight-knit ties and its economic dislocation. He had grown up in Ranburne, and his father had been one of the founders of the church. After high school, he had taken a job at a Honda manufacturing plant in Lincoln, Alabama, not far from the famous Talladega Speedway. "My trip to work every day was fifty-six miles one way, and then it was 'turn around and come back,'" he said. "I worked a rotating shift: two weeks of night shift, then two weeks of day shift. Really good money and everything." After the Great Recession hit and Honda downsized, he took a buyout. By then he'd already been working part-time at the church in youth ministry. With the flock growing, the church brought him on full-time.

I asked Whaley how the town had changed over the years, and he told me that the area had seen a lot of growth. He suspected it had come from people retreating from the taxes and higher cost of living across the state line in Georgia and the exurbs of Atlanta. "When I was a kid, we didn't even have a dollar store here," he said. "Now we've got a Dollar General; that's a big deal in our town. We've got two convenience stores, which is a big deal. The school that I went to here has been bulldozed down, and there's a new one that's [been] built."

The growth of the area hadn't necessarily meant prosperity. "It's a fairly poor county. Just within the city limits here . . . I know the average income used to be $20,000 a year not all that long ago," he said. "You know as well as I do, that's nothing. I mean, that's absolutely nothing." Like many small towns, Ranburne is also isolated—nearly twenty miles in any direction from the nearest hospital, hotel, AA meeting group, or major road. There was farmland everywhere you looked, and it hadn't rained in eight weeks.

Initially, Whaley's work as an associate pastor for the church revolved around youth outreach. "I would run the van and pick up kids that were needy," he said. "The best meal they get during the day is at school, and on Wednesday night, we do a home-cooked meal here." An average Wednesday drew anywhere from seventy to ninety teenagers from the area to a town with just over four hundred people. "We picked up kids that were from troubled, broken homes, some a grandparent was raising them, or an aunt or uncle. I picked up kids that, I'll just be honest with you, that typically in a traditional church, they don't pick up. The colored hair, the gauges in the ears, stuff like that. I never did let that faze me. I looked past all of that because that wasn't my motive. My motive was to, of course, to impart something on them as far as their salvation, first and foremost. And then, primarily, my motive was to love them, maybe like they had never been loved before and, and just be like a parent or an example in their life."

In twenty years of ministering, he'd seen a fair share of misery. One summer early on, during the buckling July heat, he'd paid a visit to a home outside town fashioned of two single trailers. A family with several kids, including a newborn, was packed inside. It wasn't just stifling inside but also infested with insects. "As soon as we're delivering the food, you see the bugs just start to swarm. That's a thing that you see all over in this area. And I said to my pastor that mentored me, 'Why aren't these kids in foster care?' He said, 'There's too many . . . there's not enough families.' And so we try to meet as many needs as we possibly can."

For an outsider, at the heart of a story like this lies a divisive question, particularly in a deep-red county in a go-it-alone country. I asked him if he thought the government should play a bigger role in providing more help or infrastructure. Whaley rocked his chair a few times. "I don't think it was ever intended, in my personal opinion, for the government to take total and complete care of those situations. That was supposed to be the church's and the community's responsibility," he said. "I'm grateful for what the government does for people. I think it's a *hand up* and it shouldn't be just a *handout*, if that makes sense. I think, though, that we have the responsibility to fill those gaps."[*]

His philosophy is an ageless one that dates back to the Puritans and the English poor laws that influenced their attitudes toward the social contract. In the face of profound hardship seemingly everywhere, Whaley's lament was that churches on the national level had ceded the role of "providing for widows and orphans and people in need." Still, even in the clergy, there remained questions about deservingness. "Of course, what comes

---

[*] In 2024, Alabama became one of fifteen states to reject federal funds for a new program that would give assistance to food-insecure children during the summer months, when school is out. In rejecting the aid, Nebraska governor Jim Pillen didn't mince words: "I don't believe in welfare."

with the territory is you do have people that take advantage," he said of local efforts. "You learn that, and you sift your way through that, but then there are real, actual needs in this area."

Whaley described Ranburne as a place where interdependence has a fairy-tale quality. Initiatives like school supply and Christmas gift drives are coordinated annually by area churches, civic groups, and the community. During the early days of the pandemic, his father, a manager at a poultry plant across the border in Georgia, secured hundreds of pounds of chicken for the church that would normally have gone to restaurants. "Every week, we would have a drop-off day, and I would hit people with messages," he said. "They would pull up, and no questions asked. I mean, we were just giving away cases of chicken. And then me and my associate pastor, we would ride around in the van to elders that weren't even members of our church that we just knew in our community, and we would knock on the door and say, 'Hey, we got chicken.' When that started happening, we had other people in the community reach out to us and say, 'Hey, I just slaughtered a cow, a steer. I'd like to give away this beef.'" It was workaday holiness mixed with classic American motion— good deeds organically begetting good citizenship in a crisis.

I asked Whaley what would help, what would make his work simpler. "The easy answer is always to say, 'We need more money,'" he explained, "but I can say that our church has done a fairly good job of taking care of those needs." The main challenge, he reckoned, was not always knowing who needed help. "There's the stigma of the beggar, or you don't want to be the needy person, but in some cases, there's people that fall on hard times and hard circumstances, and they can't help that." Those struggling, be it from hunger, a mental health crisis, or addiction have to make themselves and their vulnerabilities known to receive support. Here in the mother country of rugged individualism, though, doing so is neither easily said nor done. Whaley, for his part, understood the obstacles in play. His sermons, he said, increasingly feature calls for congregants to resist demonizing mental health issues and disabilities that are unseen or little understood. He also talked of embracing an ideal of pro-life ideology that extends beyond the unborn. "I told our church, I said, 'The thing about pro-life is if we're going to be pro-life, we have to be pro-life from the cradle to the grave.'"

I'd found my way through another cracked looking glass. We're often socialized to hate asking for help, even when we need it. But in spite of (or maybe because of) our attitudes about work and worthiness, the United States outranks all other countries in charitable giving. By volume and proportion, Americans of all ages, religions, and geographies stand alone in handing over more of their money and more of their time for the benefit of others. In 2020 and 2021, even as the pandemic fueled precarity and discord and social justice protests fueled reevaluation of and collective denial about American prejudices, those seismic crises were accompanied by a surge in individual donations. When asked, we give to and rely on what the writer Alissa Quart described as "the dystopian social safety net"—for example, using crowdfunding sites like GoFundMe to help pay the medical debt or funeral costs of friends and strangers. Around the country, nonprofits and churches run warming stations for the unhoused to stay alive during freezing spells, even as housing costs spiral upward and public services are cut. Various civic organizations have started safe parking initiatives to provide security for the growing number of Americans who live in their cars, while nationally, the number of laws passed against sleeping in vehicles has swelled by over 200 percent since before the Great Recession. And no matter where we rest, we all wake up again in a country whose people are caring and whose chosen policies are not, and we do it all over again.

Driving out of Ranburne on Chief Tucker Highway, I thought again about the collective millstone of the American way and not solely for those in need. As Pastor Whaley had outlined the fraught and highly personal nature of his work, I had caught myself repeating again and again that his community and his congregation were unbelievably lucky to have him. I meant it, of course, but buried within that reaction was an ambivalence— a fear, really—about what we ask people to carry for the American way. My last question for Whaley had been about the pressure of his job, which was obviously nothing like his old work at the Honda plant. In places both like and unlike Ranburne, community fixtures—local clergy, local law enforcement, or simply caring neighbors—have become the last thin line of defense for people in need of help or guidance, people who were slipping through the cracks. Did he feel the weight of that?

"I do," he told me, worrying a thumb across his temple. "There's times that I can't sleep very well; there's some situations that you hold out hope that maybe you can help this person. Then there's situations that are just beyond your control, and you do all that you possibly can. . . . And there's a lot of things that are brought to you, as far as in rural communities, where we take on roles as pastors that maybe we shouldn't have to . . . like getting in the middle of a custody dispute or a marriage dispute, just situations like that or where there's abuse that takes place.

"So you do feel that sense of pressure," he went on. "I'm sure like Steve did at times where he was probably more than a police officer. He was like me, he lived here his whole life. And people were like, 'Well, I can go to that guy, I can trust him.' . . . And then you go home at night and you kind of try to take it off if you can because you got to be husband and dad to your family. But it gets in bed with me. That's the thing about pastoring and ministering. There's not a time clock. You don't clock it out and leave it there. I'm twenty-four/seven. It's like, 'You call me, I'm there.' I keep my phone beside the bed. It's on all night and ready to go."

CHAPTER TEN

SMALL NORMALCIES

A NEW NATIONAL STORY

STUDY FINDS U.S. EMPLOYEES WASTE 2 MILLION HOURS
ANNUALLY SPENDING TIME WITH FRIENDS, FAMILY

—THE ONION

As novelty presidential candidates go, the United States can do (and certainly has done) much worse than Andrew Yang. In a 2020 field overstuffed with some two dozen Democratic hopefuls, Yang stood out by running a campaign filled with data, memes and internet speak, dry self-effacement and dad jokes, funny merch, and an aversion to typical campaign theater. As he eschewed the stiff and hokey symbolism, neatly packaged answers, and Crest Whitestrips optics of the primary trail, small donors poured in pizza money, and a coalition that included disaffected voters, disenchanted Trump supporters, and progressive college kids swooned. Long long long past the normal expiration date of affinity candidates, Yang was still a contender into the second tier of the race, at one point landing fifth in the polling.

Beyond its quirks, the Yang campaign inverted several trusty conventions of American politics. Though he had a biography ready-made for a modern American campaign—he was the son of Taiwanese immigrants; his father, Kei-Hsiung, had grown up in a dirt-floor house on a peanut farm before arriving in the

States, met his wife at UC Berkeley, gotten a PhD, and become a career physicist who secured a nice number of patents (sixty-nine in total)—Yang opted not to relentlessly batter crowds with his story as proof of the country's greatness. Also, though he had managed a successful career as a young entrepreneur, he didn't parlay that into empty assurances about job creation or lecture voters in hushed tones on the rewards of excessive hard work.

Instead, Yang melded a message of economic pessimism with a delivery of easygoing calm. He became best known for unleashing unvarnished doom and gloom about automation and the future of work in the United States ("riots in the street") and proposing a guaranteed basic income (branded a "Freedom Dividend") as his cornerstone solution. "The substance of Yang's campaign is shockingly easy to talk about," the journalist Ben Smith wrote in January 2020, after Yang had already outlasted some credible candidates (two senators, three governors) and some not-so-credible ones (Bill de Blasio). "He wants to give everyone $1,000, and instead of preaching the inherent dignity of work, he looks to an automated future where there's dignity in working less."

Yang's distress about the state of jobs wasn't new; John F. Kennedy had made a fuss about automation during his 1960 campaign, casting it as the "dark menace of industrial dislocation, increasing unemployment, and deepening poverty" (which helped him secure several labor union endorsements). Nor was Yang's solution to the problem novel; Universal Basic Income (UBI) is a centuries-old concept that has been met with favor in one form or another more recently by an unlikely mixture of American leaders (Richard Nixon, Dr. Martin Luther King, Jr.) and assorted tech bros and futurists (Jeff Bezos, Elon Musk, Mark Zuckerberg, Larry Page, Tim Cook) as well as dozens of current mayors, at least three former U.S. Treasury secretaries, the Black Panther Party, and America's most influential conservative economist (Milton Friedman). Residents of the biggest state in the United States have received a small-scale version of a guaranteed income through Alaska's Permanent Fund Dividend since 1982.

I spoke to Yang about his decision to bring UBI to the fore of his campaign, in 2023, long after the chaos and theater of the 2020 election season had subsided. "There was a lot of dubiousness because people are so programmed to think of money as both scarce and also something that only returns to you if you do something—typically work," he told me. But he had driven UBI into mainstream consciousness at just the right time. Prior to the pandemic, a majority of Americans opposed the idea, with the strongest and most predictable opposition among voters over fifty. However, the pandemic, with its direct government assistance through stimulus checks, various recovery funds and debt pauses, and hefty unemployment benefits, shifted some perceptions. "Things have changed pretty dramatically since then because we demonstrated that yeah, actually, it is possible to send everyone money." One Hill-HarrisX poll found a twelve-point jump in approval for UBI (from 43 percent to 55 percent) between February 2019 and August 2020.

It's hard to draw a straight line between the two, but the growing public appetite for UBI was most detectable after the 2021 expansion of the Child Tax Credit (CTC), which, in its generosity and tangibility, became one of the most revolutionary policy achievements in generations. Passed by Congress one year into the pandemic, the enhanced credit sent $250 to $300 per child to most American families each month.* Critically, there were no minimum-income guidelines, which meant that the poorest third of Americans—often excluded from the CTC—automatically received access to the money without conditions. "Let's say you're a kid and you're being cared for by an elderly grandparent who cannot work," the journalist Catherine Rampell explained. "Your household got that funding, too, and was able to use it to pay for those necessities to be lifted out of poverty."

Over six months, the policy led to an unprecedented 46 percent drop in child poverty, as measured by a threshold for basic needs. "There were clear data points that educational resources and results went up," Yang added. "Health improved. Men-

---

* In earlier versions, the Child Tax Credit was a smaller amount that became available to families only when they filed their tax return the following year.

tal health improved. Domestic abuse went down. Nutrition improved." A study of the expanded CTC by Columbia University's Center on Poverty and Social Policy found that most of the funds had been spent by parents and guardians on food, followed by essential bills, clothes, rent or mortgage, paying down debt, and childcare. The pandemic-era CTC momentarily placed the United States close to its peers like Canada, South Korea, France, and Germany, where similar benefits are deployed to minimize child poverty, make parenthood less expensive and difficult to balance, and spur increases in birth rates.

More philosophically, the expanded credit also accomplished something in its brief life that Yang and many others talk about when describing the built-in American association between money and work: it buttressed the idea that care work is labor. "Giving birth to and raising children, tending to the disabled and sick, aiding the elderly, and giving succor to the dying: few things are of more societal importance," the journalist Annie Lowrey wrote in *Give People Money*. "But much of that labor goes unpaid, and when it is paid, it is done with low wages and scant benefits." Citing a study by the research arm of the senior advocacy group AARP, Lowrey estimated that about 40 million family caregivers in the United States—mostly older women—provide a staggering *half-trillion dollars'* worth of unpaid adult care each year.

While thinking about UBI, my focus returned again and again to how it does and doesn't affect employment. After all, beyond the cost, the most common and classically American grumble about a guaranteed income (or any social program, really) is that it devalues work, degrades the supposedly level playing field, and empowers the hypothetical futzers, spongers, and lazybones among us to loaf like never before. But like the expanded CTC, which didn't reduce employment, UBI hasn't seemed to do that so far.

"What people often have forgotten is that we experimented with guaranteed income from the 1960s to the 1980s," Dr. Stacia

West, the founding director of the Center for Guaranteed Income Research at the University of Pennsylvania, told me, referencing four separate experiments that came and went in low-income rural and urban communities across the country. "They provided people with an unconditional cash transfer, which was called a 'negative income tax' at the time, because it brought them up to 150 percent of the federal poverty level." In other words, the cash infusions were designed to give participants space between themselves and the poverty line, all but eradicating poverty. Not surprisingly, the participants enjoyed positive outcomes. There were fewer hospitalizations, more children went on to finish high school, and it didn't seem to reduce the hours worked by primary household earners.

West added that those early trials, which dovetailed with the second wave of the feminist movement, also provided a financial cushion that enabled wives, particularly those in unsafe relationships, to leave their husbands. Now, modern, sane analysis would consider this to be a good thing, but for the liberal sociologist Daniel Patrick Moynihan, who was working on the experiments as President Nixon's assistant for urban affairs, the ensuing rise in divorces posed a threat to the nuclear family and prompted him to withdraw his support for UBI. Following that, West explained, "it goes to shit."

And so UBI went from a viable legislative possibility to an arcane piece of social policy jetsam until it was fished up again by academics and policy wonks in the years after the Great Recession. Those familiar with the current-day debate over guaranteed income probably know about the Stockton Economic Empowerment Demonstration (SEED), the landmark program that gave $500 a month to 125 residents of the poor Central California Valley city for two years, starting in early 2019. In addition to making for a nifty acronym, the "Demonstration" aspect of SEED was deliberately meant to set a model for what UBI could do on a national level. By the end of SEED in 2021, researchers were heartened all over again, as the mental health of participants had improved significantly, with lower levels of stress, anxiety, and depression. After two years, the level of full-time employment also grew, rising from 28 percent to 40 percent, as SEED recipients took on internships, got real estate certifications, and took on training that expanded their reach in the job market. Under the heading of "self-determination," SEED's findings contend that the steady cash payments "generated increased bandwidth for goal-setting and risk-taking, both of which were previously limited by scarcity." Participants' stories spanned a range of small normalcies: one woman exulted in being able to pay both her bills and her church tithes without breaking a sweat, another bought her son shoes and sent him to out-of-town track meets with cash for food. Broadly, there was relief in the testimonies—relief in automating gas and electric bill payments or covering car payments on time, not agonizing over food and medicine, handling car repairs to get back on the road for work, or just being around family more. "What I would really point to is in the negative income tax experiments and the Stockton experiments—and those are really the two that we have concluded at this point—there appears to be no impact on paid work," West explained. "But there may be an impact on women's ability to nurture and stay home with their kids."

In fixating on UBI as an engine for better, steadier work, I'd been limiting my thinking about what else it enabled. And as I peppered West about jobs and employment figures, she kindly steered me back to less obvious perks. "We already work too hard and we already work too much, right?" she eventually said. "The better argument, to me, focuses a lot around caregiving and the benefit that that has to our economy."

Conventional measures of success and attainment in American life tend to take for granted the simple and straightforward—what it means to have the time and energy to plug in to family. "The data clearly shows that sixty-five percent to seventy percent of our students' outcomes are determined outside the school," Yang explained during his presidential run. "We're talking about time spent at home with parents, words read to them when they're young, stress levels in the house, income, type of neighborhood. We're saying, 'You're one hundred percent responsible for educating your kids,' but you can only control thirty percent.

They all know this. The answer is to put money directly into the families and neighborhoods."

About a hundred UBI pilot programs have surfaced in communities around the country since SEED and Stockton, the Yang campaign, the pandemic, and the expanded CTC. "It's like, 'You're not cool if you're not experimenting with guaranteed income as a left-leaning mayor,'" West quipped. More than straight copycats of Stockton or the Freedom Dividend, many of the newer trials have unique missions, the varying characteristics of which give insights into the frontier of hardship out there. Across the map, cash infusions are being sent to young recipients aging out of foster care or formerly incarcerated people trying to get back onto their feet, for whom a reliable source of income could mean the difference between being housed or not, suffering from hunger or not, recidivism or rehabilitation.

After visiting Ranburne, I drove an hour west to Birmingham— a politically mixed city, rather than a progressive font—where a pilot program that sent $375 each month to 110 single mothers had concluded earlier that year. It resembled a pilot in New York State for mothers in poverty. "In New York, when a mom is called in for child neglect, we know about ninety percent of the time, it's poverty related," West explained. In West Hollywood, California, a pilot UBI program was setting its sights on helping low-income, older adults stay in their homes amid an affordable housing crisis. In September 2024, a two-year pilot that sent $50 a week to 470 high school students in Indianapolis and New Orleans wrapped up. "One of the things that stands out most to me is the kids in New Orleans and Indianapolis are spending money in the same way that the adults across the United States are. That is fascinating and very sad to me. That nearly fifty percent is spent on food and household goods, just the very basic expenses," she said before zooming out. "People talk about how folks are going to spend money irresponsibly . . . but we don't ask these same questions of unearned income in the form of dividends for the uber-wealthy that I'm sure have a wine-and-cocaine budget that far exceeds the alcohol or tobacco that some of these lower-income people may need."

I asked West if there was any particular story from the pilots that stood out to her. She had three. One mother regularly took the small gift cards offered for answering UBI pilot surveys and gave them to her daughter so she could buy her favorite brand of deodorant. "It's budgeting down to five or ten dollars and also prioritizing your children," she explained. "That's something that I think that every parent can relate to: just buying the thing that your kid wants." Elsewhere, a grandmother got to hand her grandchildren money in a convenience store to buy a few of whatever snacks they wanted, a generosity that she'd most often experienced vicariously. "She tells the story of how it felt to just be a normal person. She sees these normal people that can make these expenses, and, in that moment, she could do that." Meanwhile, in the New Orleans pilot, there was a teenager who had felt the trivial power and joy of holding total sovereignty over a pizza. "He was like 'An entire pizza just for me. No one else gets this pizza,'" West said. "How can you hear those sorts of stories and think that our system is working?"

Beyond the obvious need, all of these distinct pilot programs are connected by Mayors for a Guaranteed Income, a UBI advocacy group founded by former Stockton mayor Michael Tubbs. "So many of the mayors that are in Mayors for a Guaranteed Income and I have been friends for a long time," Baltimore mayor Brandon Scott told me as we sat down in a conference room in Baltimore City Hall. "And what we all think is important is to showcase how different the groups of folks are who benefit from the program. The data all says the same thing, but as you know, all the pilots are different."

Baltimore Young Families Success Fund, the city's UBI pilot, focused on young parents, guardians, and caretakers (ages eighteen to twenty-four) in households whose incomes are 300 percent below the poverty line. For two years, two hundred participants would receive $1,000 a month, equivalent to a Yang Freedom Dividend and more than most of what the other pilot UBI programs provided.

When Scott and I met, the second year of the pilot had just

gotten under way. I asked him how the city's specific UBI mission had come about, and he put it into simple terms: calling back to his own childhood, he thought about what could make the biggest impact for the people in deepest need. "This comes from my upbringing here and growing up and having friends that were these people," he began. "I lived in a family where I had both parents, gratefully. Now, we were poor. We didn't know it, right? But we also weren't as poor as some of my friends."

Of poverty's several converging stressors, one constant is a lack of time. Or, as West put it, "Income poverty is time poverty." Even at a young age, Scott could feel what it meant to have his parents around when his friends came over and what it meant that he never saw his friends' parents. "Sometimes that was because they were dealing with things like addiction, but most of the time, it was because those parents were working two and three jobs."

Scott stopped for a moment to take in the wood-paneled room, which was lined with portraits of Baltimore's dignitaries, civic celebrities, and other high-office relations in the politics of Maryland. "Imagine living in a family where your mother can't take you to school or pick you up. Or take you to daycare or go to your sports games or even afford for you to play those sports, right? They can't help you with homework. Because they can't afford a car, they have to wake up in the morning, get on the bus at five a.m. to get to work by eight or nine o'clock, and then, by the time they get home from their job, you're asleep," he said. "That's what pushed me to want to focus on those families, because I know when I think about our young people, those who we lose in school, I know not having the complete community and family support plays a significant part in that."

We were back at work and its failure to save us. Like many cities around the United States and on the national level, Baltimore's unemployment rate was at or near record-low numbers. It didn't matter. Not really. During our conversation, the markets had closed for the day; the Dow had jumped 57 points, up for the seventh straight session. That also didn't matter to most residents of Baltimore. I asked him what he thought of the common knock on UBI and on most social programs, namely that they disincentivize work and make people reliant on the government. "That's

just this 1980s, Reagan welfare queen . . . just bullshit. That's
what it is," he said. "People work hard every single day, right?
And I just think it boils down to this mindset that we have to get
out of. Because the truth is that we're talking about guaranteeing income because we, as a country, haven't realized that in the
wealthiest country in the history of the world, one job should be
enough. But it's not for so many people."

In its own specific way, each UBI initiative reflects how people, whether in communities as rural as Ranburne or as bustling as
Baltimore, are impeded by a course of obstacles; some ever changing and unpredictable, others fixed and historic. In providing a
context for Baltimore's UBI pilot, Scott wound the city's story
all the way back to its fixture as the birthplace of redlining, now a
catch-all term for discriminatory real estate practices. Redlining
in Baltimore initially started as a response to the arrival of many
Black Americans, who, spurred to make the Great Migration out
of the Jim Crow South, were seeking economic opportunity farther north. In 1910, the city passed what's thought to have been
the nation's first official residential segregation ordinance after
a Black law school graduate named George W. F. McMechen
and his family moved into a home in an all-white neighborhood
in West Baltimore. Making a proclamation at the time, J. Barry
Mahool (a very *different* mayor of Baltimore) didn't conceal the
animus that inspired the ordinance, the same animus that resulted
in McMechen's home being vandalized, tarred, and pelted with
rocks: "Blacks should be quarantined in isolated slums in order
to reduce the incidence of civil disturbance, to prevent the spread
of communicable disease into the nearby White neighborhoods,
and to protect property values among the White majority." Of
course, Baltimore's ordinance was only one tactic of exclusion and
bias out of many in the playbook. And though the Supreme Court
later struck down a replica of the ordinance in Louisville, redlining
spread both formally and informally in endless ways through the
misdeeds of banks and private lenders, federal agencies and housing commissions, neighborhood associations and individuals.*

---

* The Supreme Court, by the way, didn't rule against the ordinance on the grounds
that it constituted illegal discrimination but rather because it kept white owners from

Within the context of the legacy of U.S. housing inequality, Baltimore's UBI pilot guides us down a long and instructive trail of disparity in America. Homeownership has been a foundational way to build wealth in the United States, but not if you've been denied a conventional home loan or credit, blocked from buying or living in certain areas, or preyed upon by slumlords and contract schemers. Decades after *some* legal protections around housing were enacted, we're still accounting for the consequences of redlining in terms of gaps in generational wealth, property ownership, and levels of financial mobility, as well as health outcomes and mortality rates in areas and communities deprived of investment, opportunities, and resources.

Overtly or not, the concept of guaranteed income has a redemptive bent to it. Advocating for the policy in his final book, Martin Luther King, Jr., imagined it serving a coalition that remains vulnerable nearly sixty years later. "Those at the lowest economic level, the poor white and Negro, the aged and chronically ill, are traditionally unorganized and therefore have little ability to force the necessary growth in their income," he wrote. "They stagnate or become even poorer in relation to the larger society." For King, the answer to this problem was binary: "We must create full employment or we must create incomes."

In the decades since, however, jobs have stopped creating the path toward stability and dignity. According to 2022 research by Brandeis University economists, 35 percent of families in the United States with full-time workers don't earn enough to cover basic needs such as food, housing, and childcare. Even as the country has enjoyed massive economic growth and big jumps in worker productivity, U.S. businesses have concentrated and consolidated—stifling pay, limiting competition through monopoly and monopsony, and passing on higher costs, shoddier goods, and diluted services to patients, passengers, and most other types

---

selling property to whomever they pleased. (The transactional Columbian spirit in America is undefeated.)

of consumers. "AT&T's acquisition of Time Warner netted Time Warner's CEO a $400 million parachute," Sarah Miller of the American Economic Liberties Project wrote in 2021, "while a staggering 45,000 workers were cut from payrolls and consumers saw a steady stream of price hikes on streaming and satellite TV services after the merger cleared."

In 2025, recollections of the days of pensions and union power sound more like urban legends. Around the country, workplaces have become atomized between more secure employees with benefits and their implied lessers—contract workers, permalancers, temps, and third-party staff with little say about their schedules and working conditions. According to the Federal Trade Commission, nearly half of American firms use noncompete agreements, not just to guard proprietary secrets but to keep hourly wage workers from seeking better pay and opportunities down the road. And according to one industry study, roughly half of U.S. employers run credit checks on job applicants when screening potential candidates.

More and more Americans, regardless of their employment status, have been dealt a losing hand. And for the dwindling few with wealth, their winning cards have been filched from the bottom of the deck. Success via sleight of hand, another abracadabra. "There's guaranteed income in other ways by means of tax breaks for billionaires and all these other things," Scott said. "But when you're talking about people, the working class, the people that are working in hospitals, helping to care for everybody, the people that are cleaning facilities? Working people are serving and doing jobs that most people won't do, right? Why should they have to struggle and not be with their families in a country that, quite frankly, can afford to help them?"

I'd been stuck in my thinking about initiatives like the expanded Child Tax Credit, guaranteed income, and universal healthcare strictly as means to spark innovation. Would-be entrepreneurs would have the space to start new businesses, while small businesses could plot expansions. Creative people could take a calculated risk on their artistic pursuits. Workers wouldn't have to move (or commute long distances) to a small handful of cities for the best opportunities and could instead find them or build them in their own backyards and keep those communities vibrant. These all sounded like reasonable fantasies. But what about more basic, worthy aspirations, like freedom from bad jobs? Or more time spent among friends or engaged in the community? Or eliminating the desperate clambering of millions in a country where one of the most shoplifted consumer goods is baby formula and medical debt is the biggest cause of personal bankruptcy? The journalist Annie Lowrey framed the potential of UBI as a de facto "twenty-first-century union," where workers have the power to reject jobs with low pay, lousy benefits, and exploitative conditions and companies have to court workers. As Scott put it, "It allows people to not have to just take the first thing smokin'."

Long before there's the political will for it, passing an initiative like UBI will take public trust. "We're not going to have a blanket situation where we wake up tomorrow and we all receive a UBI of about a thousand dollars a month or a negative income tax," West conceded. But what the flood of direct assistance during the pandemic revealed is that given opportunities, individuals tend not to squander them. During the pandemic years, American workers left crummy jobs for safer, better-paying ones—spurring a slight but overdue reduction in income inequality—and new businesses were launched in the United States at the highest rate in more than a decade.

Moreover, the pandemic assistance that reached American families went to good use. In March 2021, around the time the second set of stimulus checks went out, social media users joked about all the frivolous things they planned to spend their $1,400 on. (Two examples: "Me at Dollar Tree: I'll take 1400 trees" and "Me at Chick-fil-A on Sunday: open it.") In reality, though, the bulk of the three stimulus payments was spent on food, utilities, household products, rent, and later to pay down debt. As for the expanded CTC payments, which lasted for only six months, they mostly went toward paying down debt and for school expenses and childcare.[*] In a similar vein, as of January 2024, about 75 per-

---

[*] Despite the promising results, the expanded CTC never came up for renewal, in part because the deciding voice in the Senate reportedly believed that parents would use the money to buy drugs. The senator in question, Joe Manchin, was also thought to oppose a paid-leave initiative because he worried that parents would use the time off to go on hunting trips during deer season.

cent of spending by participants in UBI pilots around the country had gone toward retail sales and services (everything from Walmart and Target to car repairs), food and groceries, and housing and utilities.

"The data doesn't lie," Scott closed. "As I always say, in the immortal words of one Sean Carter, also known as Jay-Z, 'Women lie, men lie, numbers don't.' And these numbers show that this is working, not just in Baltimore but across the country. But the numbers more importantly show that the recipients are spending this money wisely and on what they need to be successful."

With the exception of a handful of people in a handful of places, the pandemic experiments that almost frictionlessly steadied household incomes and staved off hunger and mass evictions for millions of Americans have all run their course. With poverty and all its secondary symptoms back in force, public officials and advocates are working to claw back any workable piece of the equation. When we spoke, Mayor Scott was gearing up for a tough reelection battle while maintaining hope that the results of Baltimore's pilot UBI program will provide ballast for a different way forward. "We will continue to prove that this works with the hope that our friends, especially in Congress, will wake up to realize this is something that we can do for our country instead of just giving out tax breaks all the time."

Meanwhile, Andrew Yang is currently pursuing a revival of the expanded CTC, which led to a historic drop in U.S. child poverty in 2021, followed by a historic rise in 2022 after it failed to be renewed. "That is the lowest-hanging fruit in this realm," he said. "If you can't do that, it's a very bad sign for humanity because it was an obvious win." For Dr. Stacia West, if handed a magic policy wand, she would bring back the early negative income tax from the 1970s and effectively eliminate poverty among American families. "If they're falling below the poverty level, they would receive a recurring unconditional cash transfer on a monthly basis to bring them to 150 percent of the federal poverty level," she said. Unlike UBI, the price tag would be significantly lower; by one estimate, around $237 billion lower. "We have that sort of money. We just choose to spend it on other shit."

CHAPTER ELEVEN

AUTOMATIC FOR THE PEOPLE

THE POSTWORKER FUTURE

NOT ALL SPEED IS MOVEMENT.

—TONI CADE BAMBARA

No matter how sunny the data or how promising the outcomes, the American immune system has long treated government help as an antigen that must be attacked. "It is common talk that every individual is entitled to economic security," Dr. Ray Lyman Wilbur, the eugenicist and longtime president of Stanford University, once wrote. "The only animals and birds I know that have economic security are those that have been domesticated—and the economic security they have is controlled by the barbed-wire fence, the butcher's knife and the desire of others. They are milked, skinned, egged or eaten up by their protectors." Woof.

Wilbur, who served as Herbert Hoover's secretary of the interior during the onset of the Great Depression, believed that economic distress was character building and had a love of rugged individualism as timeless as child malnutrition. In 2023, not far from the Stanford quad, the Silicon Valley billionaire and influential venture capitalist Marc Andreessen relit Wilbur's torch with a flamethrower. "We believe a Universal Basic Income would turn people into zoo animals to be farmed by the state," he wrote in a widely discussed manifesto on his VC firm's website. "Man was not meant to be farmed; man was meant to be *useful*, to be *productive*, to be *proud*."[*]

The conviction that ensuring a basic level of economic security somehow affronts the natural order is the type of reasoning that flows freely from Silicon Valley to Wall Street. Nevertheless, it'd be easier to buy what some sell about the primal glories of the unregulated jungle if it were actually true. When challenged about the cost of UBI during his presidential run, Andrew Yang liked to point out how predatory banks had been saved during the Great Recession while a mass of Americans had been cleaned out and evicted from their homes. "Even arguing about it in 2019," Yang told me, "I would reference the fact that we printed $4 trillion to bail out the financial system in the first bubble. And I said, 'Does anyone remember being consulted on that? Does anyone remember the government saying, "Oh, we don't have enough money"?'" Similar charges could be leveled at Silicon Valley Bank, the extremely risk-tolerant bank in which Marc Andreessen and other moneyed tech luminaries steered their start-ups to park their money. The reckless bank's collapse in 2023—the second largest bank failure in U.S. history—was kept from blowing into a global catastrophe only because the FDIC took the extraordinary step of guaranteeing that the bank's depositors wouldn't lose their money. One Silicon Valley observer lamented, "These guys didn't fulfill their fiduciary responsibility to anybody, they almost took the whole system down."

Silicon Valley's "Move fast and break things" ethos, its kettle-black anti-elitist posturing, and its words-and-deeds hostility toward *social responsibility*—a concept referred to in Andreessen's manifesto as "the enemy"—all resonate here for a particular reason. In charting the ways a measure like UBI might fix our crooked world of work, at least one more noteworthy point has emerged in the postpandemic years. Outside the potential ben-

---

[*] A few months before publishing his manifesto, when Mark Zuckerberg and Elon Musk were publicly discussing settling their differences via cage fight, Andreessen signaled his earnest approval: "I consider Mark and Elon to be role models to children in their embrace of fighting."

efits of direct government assistance—the promotion of entrepreneurship, the creation of stronger ties among families and
communities, freedom for workers to leave bad jobs and dangerous personal situations, fewer work hours and a healthier work
culture, a better-trained workforce, and maybe even a simplifica-
tion of America's sprawling welfare apparatus—a tech-dominated
future is looming.

Though plenty of pundits and economists scoffed at the
apocalyptic scenarios suggested by Andrew Yang during the 2020
campaign, recent fretting over jobs being automated has become
compounded by fretting over jobs being lost to artificial intelligence (AI), especially as sophisticated new tools have entered
the market. "AI has become real, and so now people think, 'Wow,
this actually might be important sooner rather than later,'" Yang
said. Indeed, on my way to meet Mayor Scott in Baltimore to
talk UBI, I'd seen a different sort of pilot program in action that
struck at the heart of that worry.

———————

Maybe the only prospect more terrifying than a fleet of self-
driving trucks putting a million American truck drivers out of
work is imagining a fleet of self-driving trucks crossing the Chesapeake Bay Bridge in Maryland. Over four miles long and nearly
two hundred feet above the water with narrow lanes, no shoulders, and low railings for a dramatic view, travelers understandably hate this bridge with a nervous passion. The bridge unites
two sections of Maryland, yes, but as you reach an ascending turn
that makes it look like the road runs out, the bridge unites the
darkest horrors of gephyrophobia (fear of bridges) and acropho-
bia (fear of heights) and, if you *really* dwell on plunging into the
frigid bay below, aquaphobia (fear of water) and kabourophobia
(fear of crabs). In naming the Chesapeake Bay Bridge one of
the scariest bridges in the world, *Travel + Leisure* noted that the
seventy-year-old structure is "subjected to frequent—and often
violent—storms" that can obscure all land from view. For years
now, a popular local business has ferried panicky travelers across
the bridge in their own cars for the going rate of $40 each way.

"We've taken airline pilots, raceboat drivers, policemen, fire-fighters," one operator claimed. "We took a couple who were both in the Navy—neither could drive over the bridge." When I posted video taken from my ride over the Chesapeake Bay Bridge on social media,* a few Mid-Atlantic faithful responded to curse me for triggering their past travel traumas. What I didn't have the heart to tell them was that I'd gambled my life (and their psychological well-being) just to visit an outpost of America's seventh largest burger chain.

The Hardee's in Stevensville on Maryland's Eastern Shore is, for now at least, one of just a few hundred restaurants in the United States where an AI chatbot takes the orders at the drive-thru. It's a technology that seems both futuristic (I'm talking to a machine!) and unexceptional (I'm ordering a $6 hamburger from a machine?). Unlike its Silicon Valley peers, Presto Automation, the company that created the AI chatbot for Hardee's as well as Carl's Jr., Del Taco, and Checkers, doesn't hype it as something revolutionary or messianic so much as utilitarian—a tool that "improves order accuracy" and "increases revenue for superior drive-thru and dine-in experiences."

In addition to grabbing lunch and taking in a bite of the future, my biggest goal was to see if I could stump the chatbot. As I inched up to the speaker, a sign before the menu boards introduced my nemesis. "Hello! I'm your automated drive-thru ordering assistant," it read. According to the sign, if I began to freak out about a robot takeover, all I needed to say was "Team member, please," a person would step in, and the nightmare would end. After I reached the speaker and an unmistakably nonhuman voice welcomed me to Hardee's, I ordered the Frisco Burger, Hardee's very sturdy 830-calorie, quarter-pound power-house burger on toasted, buttered sourdough bread. Since the Frisco Burger already came with two slices of Swiss cheese, two strips of bacon, mayonnaise, and over 70 percent of my recommended daily allowance of sodium, I asked the chatbot to add lettuce because that would immediately make it healthy. "Sure," it responded confidently. Though I didn't try ordering in Spanish,

---

* (From the passenger seat, Mom.)

which Presto claims a diner can do, when my friend and intrepid driver, Dan, ordered a honey mustard chicken tender wrap in his Canadian brogue, the chatbot didn't stumble over it. So far, so good.

In addition to allowing restaurant workers to focus on other tasks, the fast-food AI chatbot is said to earn its keep through its mechanical dedication to upselling customers. Both times we ordered, the bot asked if we wanted to add two apple pies to our orders for $1.59. (Yes, we did.) But when Dan was urged to turn his chicken wrap into a combo, the bot fritzed out when—as any Canadian would—he politely said "No, thank you" to the upsell. At that point, Kristi, a kind but no-nonsense employee listening in on us, stepped in. All told, the hiccup added maybe five seconds to the transaction, but we made it through.

As we downed our food in the parking lot, we fought through a sodium-induced haze to ponder the future that had arrived. During a few years of reporting on the fast-food industry, I'd always been somewhat surprised to hear that handling the drive-thru is considered by many to be one of the worst assignments, even compared to emptying the grease traps or handling the bathrooms. But then again, we were talking about fast-food work, which appears relentlessly in American pop culture as a punishment for what happens if you don't buckle down in school and have enough ambition. The term "McJob" appears in several dictionaries as a pejorative for work with few prospects. With this level of scornful prompting, drive-thru diners are often abrasive, abusive, rude, or violent toward the people serving them. If AI could cure the toughest part of an already brutal job, that seemed worthwhile enough.

Still, on the second go-around at the drive-thru, I decided to go straight for the chatbot's jugular (or mainframe or whatever). First, I asked if it was still breakfast time even though it was over an hour into lunchtime and the breakfast menu boards had disappeared from the drive-thru. When the bot said yes, I ordered one of Hardee's unacknowledged early-hour gems, the potato Hash Rounds. Here, Kristi stepped in again and apologized. "Okay, honey, I don't know why the AI told you that we're still serving breakfast, but we're not," she said. In addition to calling me "honey," which unfortunately a bot would never do, Kristi also generously flexed against the script by offering to throw some Hash Rounds into the fryer for me if I didn't mind waiting a few minutes for them. Feeling like a colossal dickhead, I said, "No, thank you," and just got a Coke for the road. As we pulled up to the window, I asked Kristi how she liked the chatbot. "I actually like it," she said in a way that didn't sound programmed. "It's very helpful when we're shorthanded."

The first arrival of fast-food AI chatbots followed a significant moment of upheaval in the American workplace. Dubbed "the Great Resignation," the pandemic-era trend of people walking away from their jobs actually turned out to be a much less snappy Great Reshuffling. Those quitting tended to be workers in low-wage sectors, parents and guardians (mostly women) forced to drop out of the workforce to pick up slack as schools and childcare options remained closed, and career longtimers who saw the pandemic as a good enough reason to retire. In the case of low-wage workers, they were working people who, given a little leverage, were leaving lackluster jobs to seek out better pay and protections like sick leave during a deadly public health crisis. With the labor market still tight, open positions in the service industry remained unfilled around the country for months as stores, restaurants, and hotels struggled to find workers willing to take middling work for the same old pay and conditions.

To be extremely sure, not everyone saw the worker shortage this way. In April 2021, a video circulated on TikTok featuring a nurse at a McDonald's in Texas who encountered a sign taped to a drive-thru speaker. It read, "We are short-staffed. Please be patient with the staff that did show up. No one wants to work anymore." She approvingly captioned the sign "Savage." Later appearing on *Fox & Friends Weekend*, she blamed generous government pandemic benefits for the lack of staffing and her wait at the drive-thru. A few weeks later, a bigger uproar ensued when Congressman David Rouzer posted a photo of a similar note from a Hardee's in North Carolina. "Due to NO STAFF," read the sign, "WE ARE CLOSED." The notice also mentioned that the store was hiring and included a phone number for interested applicants. "This is what happens when you extend unemployment benefits for too long and add a $1400 stimulus payment to it," Rouzer posted on Twitter/X. "Right when employers need workers to fully open back up, few can be found." On social media, Rouzer was skewered for blaming workers and pandemic protections for the shortage instead of the employers who were offering too little. "The free-market solution is to pay people more to work for you," went one critique.

These weren't isolated events; public-facing notes like these were documented at businesses around the country, with some employers offering surreal incentives such as signing bonuses for minimum-wage jobs and others implying that lazy, entitled workers were worsening a labor shortage and destroying the economy with government complicity. The data supporting the theory was hard to come by. Hoping to force workers back into the trenches, half of the states opted out of the federal pandemic emergency benefits in June and July 2021. Labor Department data showed that by the end of August, the highest job growth appeared to have happened in states that had kept some form of the benefits alive.

Though the circumstances of the pandemic labor shortage may have been unique, the messaging wasn't. Paul Fairie, a Canadian researcher, made that point by unearthing the complaint that Americans simply didn't want to work anymore from old newspaper clips. Starting in the 2020s, he posted one example from every decade, going all the way back to the coal miner strikes of 1894. And the grievance predated even that. Speaking with Bloomberg, the labor historian Joseph McCartin referenced the "vagabond scare" in the shakeout from the 1873 recession, when people were thought to be roaming blithely from place to place instead of working for a living. "Really what was happening is often these are migrant workers looking for work elsewhere," he explained. "But in the public imagination at the time, there was this idea that there are people that just don't want to work."

———

Squint at this drama just a little, and you may be reminded again of the early Puritans, who saw work as the chief way to win divine favor and also saw poverty as a moral failing. "Lazy hands make a man poor, but diligent hands bring wealth," goes a popular verse from Proverbs, a Puritan favorite among the books of the Bible. As we already know, they weren't alone in the belief that the grind always yields its reward. Writing on the "management of the poor" in 1766, Benjamin Franklin, our knight-errant of the American way, described traveling abroad and being troubled by how in other countries, "the more public provisions were made for the poor, the less they provided for themselves, and of course became poorer." He added, "on the contrary, the less was done for them, the more they did for themselves, and became richer." And finally, sensing complacency among women in business in 2022, the celebrity socialite and entrepreneur Kim Kardashian dished some straightforward advice: "Get your fucking ass up and work. It seems like nobody wants to work these days."

These splinters help form the plank of a faith—an idea that only some combination of work and tough love and individual grit can deliver us to some promised land of dignity and prosperity. What it also implies is that any other approach to creating prosperity is naive, the indulgent fantasy of someone a Yiddish bubbe would call a *freier*, a sucker, a mug.

If we were to anoint a modern priest of the pure and inflexible American faith in work, Andy Puzder would make a terrific nominee. The son of a working-class midwest family, he cleared the 1960s counterculture bingo card with gusto: long hair, guitar, Woodstock, a march on Washington to protest the Vietnam War. He was even enrolled at Kent State when the Ohio National Guard infamously opened fire on a crowd of antiwar protesters, killing four students and bringing about the symbolic end of the 1960s. But whatever antiestablishment notions he'd collected, Puzder packed them away in his moon bag. He became the first in his family to graduate from college; he married and had kids, went on to law school, flourished as a commercial trial lawyer, and then ascended in the world of corporate fast food.

During his sixteen-year run as the chief executive of CKE Restaurants, which owns Hardee's and Carl's Jr., Puzder was a loud critic of the Affordable Care Act and unions and liked to air an unabashed contempt for labor laws, workplace regulations, overtime pay, and paid sick leave, much of which he saw as business-crushing overreach by the government. As the national movement for a $15 minimum wage coalesced around fast-food work in the mid-2010s, Puzder argued that the federal minimum wage—still stuck at $7.25 since 2009—shouldn't be increased because, well, many workers just weren't worth the money. "The point is simple: The feds can mandate a higher wage, but some jobs don't produce enough economic value to bear the increase," he wrote in *The Wall Street Journal*. "If government could transform unskilled entry-level positions into middle-income jobs, the Soviet Union would be today's dominant world economy. Spain and Greece would be thriving."[*]

Now, one *might* argue that there aren't enough Frisco Burgers in Maryland to match the empty calories baked into this popular line of thinking. We've already dug into how investments in worker-friendly policies and benefits would save companies billions of dollars each year in employee turnover, wasted training, and lost morale and productivity, but these points hit even harder when it comes to punishing low-wage service work, like fast food, which has the highest worker turnover of all U.S. industries. And for all their small-government bravado and deep-pocketed lobbying, several of America's biggest employers have supercharged their profits for decades by passing on labor costs to taxpayers. More than half of fast-food workers—overwhelmingly women—rely on public assistance, and according to the latest data, low-earning employees of highly profitable behemoths like Walmart, McDonald's, Dollar Tree, and Dollar General are the biggest recipients of programs like SNAP and Medicaid. Yet instead of praising these programs, it's become corporate ceremony to campaign to weaken or destroy them and shame the recipients. Like many others, Puzder has condemned public assistance for

---

[*] Perfect to theme, during Puzder's tenure at the helm of CKE, the company was acquired by Roark Capital, the sprawling private equity firm named for the protagonist in *The Fountainhead*, Ayn Rand's literary accolade to the religion of individualism and free markets. (Roark's company, by the way, also owns Arby's, Baskin-Robbins, Dunkin', Subway, Sonic, Jimmy John's, Jamba Juice, the Cheesecake Factory, Cinnabon, and Buffalo Wild Wings, along with a handful of fitness and beauty chains.)

"discouraging work rather than encouraging independence, self-reliance and pride."

In degrading the worth of low-paid labor, opponents of a living wage also inadvertently make a startling point about the state of American work. Just ahead of the pandemic, researchers from the Brookings Institution estimated that a mind-blowing 44 percent of Americans work jobs that qualify as low wage. These aren't just teens working for walk-around money but adults, often with dependents, making a median income of $18,000 a year. And in several regions, low-wage workers make up the majority of the workforce.

The cheapening of worker value was one big reason I'd ended up talking to an AI chatbot at a Hardee's on the Eastern Shore of Maryland. Automation is about many things: efficiency and technology, cost reduction and profit, investor hype and stock value. But it's also a statement about employers' perception of workers. In 2025, the jobs being automated or replaced by machines aren't limited to beleaguered washerwomen doing laundry over boiling cauldrons. And in a *freier*'s world, the untold riches being sunk into deploying virtual assistants, medical diagnostic bots, and self-driving rideshares are treasure that could be devoted instead to cultivating talent, shoring up a loyal workforce with solid pay, and providing better service. Among many things, these investments would keep interactions human and better guarantee that there will be enough consumers who can participate in the economy in the future. Illustrating at least a few of these sentiments, in late 2023, there was a brief boomlet of stories about major grocers and retailers either ditching or reducing their self-checkout stations because consumers missed interacting with cashiers, found the machines clumsy to use, or were shoplifting goods at a higher frequency.

A renewed investment in workers would require a certain level of belief in people, an ideal that's been supplanted by contempt in many boardrooms. Describing the hiring process in his chosen industry, Puzder once explained, "In fast food, you sort of compete for the best of the worst. In other words, you're not getting the Microsoft guys. At Hardee's, we were getting the worst of the worst." (This address, by the way, was delivered not to a shad-

owy conference of fast-food execs but to young college students.)
During the pandemic, when a chorus of pundits, employers, and
free-market absolutists was disparaging workers as entitled and
lazy for wanting better pay, it was another way of saying that their
labor and potential weren't worth enough.

Though his press team didn't respond to an interview
request, what makes an industry figure like Puzder stand out is
that he is unbowed by and unambiguous about his beliefs. He
doesn't hedge or mince words. Questioned about a controversial
TV ad for "The Most American Thickburger," which featured
a swimsuit model in a stars-and-stripes bikini eating a massive
cheeseburger topped with a hot dog in a hot tub in the flatbed of
a pickup truck on an aircraft carrier beneath the Statue of Liberty, he responded, "I like beautiful women eating burgers in
bikinis. I think it's very American."[*] And as automation became
an emerging topic of speculation in the service industry, he didn't
conceal how and why it would be utilized. "You're going to see
automation not just in airports and grocery stores, but in restaurants," he warned the journalist Kate Taylor. "If you're making
labor more expensive, and automation less expensive—this is not
rocket science." In making the case for substituting machines for
people, he explained, "They're always polite, they always upsell,
they never take a vacation, they never show up late, there's never
a slip-and-fall, or an age, sex, or race discrimination case."

In isolation, the cranky misanthropy of a stray corporate
executive or a few Silicon Valley billionaire blowhards wouldn't
matter much in the scheme of the universe. But as pieces of a
popular political philosophy—in which most basic regulations or
social safeguards aren't just bad but evil—it's a problem. It's a
problem in a country where the alternative to any credible form
of governance is concentrated wealth and oligarchy and where
private interests surmount public ones, and it's also a problem in
a society where the struggles of hard-bitten people are demeaned
and diminished as self-inflicted.

---

[*] A company press release defending the strategy of airing ads with erotic themes
likewise asserted, "We believe in putting hot models in our commercials, because ugly
ones don't sell burgers."

The grim arc of work in the United States has had its share of record-scratch moments, but early 2017 delivered a recent standout when Andy Puzder was nominated to serve as U.S. secretary of labor. Though the Department of Labor's founding purpose may have been "to foster, promote and develop the welfare of working people, to improve their working conditions, and to enhance their opportunities for profitable employment," it hadn't mattered that under Puzder, CKE Restaurants had outsourced its help desk workers to the Philippines, its two burger chains (Carl's Jr. and Hardee's) had been hit with more race discrimination and sexual harassment lawsuits than any other burger chains relative to their sales, and the company had settled class action lawsuits over accusations of not paying its workers. Puzder's nomination was partially framed in terms of how he might protect businesses from "the crushing burdens of unnecessary regulations." (True to form, Puzder gushed about the prospect of serving in President Donald J. Trump's cabinet by calling it "the most fun you could have with your clothes on.")

Puzder withdrew his nomination, not because his love of automation, his record, or his hostile outlook toward workers made him unconfirmable in the U.S. Senate. What ultimately torpedoed his support was a series of accusations—among them that he'd hired an undocumented immigrant and never paid employment taxes on their salary. The following month, Puzder resigned as the CEO of CKE Restaurants; years later, he remains active as a public figure on the pundit and think tank circuit. In lieu of Puzder, the attorney Alexander Acosta would be confirmed and would serve as labor secretary for more than two years until renewed outrage about his role in facilitating a secret plea deal for the accused sex trafficker Jeffrey Epstein forced him to resign.

———————

After another bracing journey over the Chesapeake Bay Bridge, I thought about the Hardee's chatbot and the enduring appeal of stories about the technology that will save us from overwork and hunger and inefficiency. Steam power and internal combustion engines made us mobile; household appliances cut the burden of domestic labor. Throughout history, the futurists who have envisioned a tech-propelled utopia have come from all ideological corners; they've been prominent economists and theorists, scientists, radical socialists, and unrepentant capitalists. In 1911, *Cosmopolitan* asked Thomas Edison to envision what the world would be like one hundred years into the future. Though he accurately forecast a world in which farming would be mechanized, phones would be smart enough to "whisper the quotations from the drug markets," and "colossal machines" would enable easy air travel across great distances, what Edison couldn't fathom was poverty in the technologically advanced universe of 2011. "Poverty was for a world that used only its hands," he wrote, predicting that "there will be no poverty in the world a hundred years from now." More recently, the headline of a white paper by economists at Goldman Sachs claimed that generative AI, the same technology that powered the Hardee's chatbot, could deliver $7 trillion in global GDP growth over the next decade. Only a bit further down did the economists break the bad news that the technology might also make 300 million full-time jobs—almost one out of every ten jobs on planet Earth—susceptible to automation.

Edison's optimism about the future strikes me as particularly American. The received wisdom about technology as an inevitable, equalizing force sounds a lot like the national attitude about hard work. And in both cases, this optimism comes at a cost.

In a fascinating study, the economists Alberto Alesina, Stefanie Stantcheva, and Edoardo Teso charted how the belief in social mobility in the United States compares with that in four European countries. Their paper begins with a classic truism, attributed to John Steinbeck, about how the working poor in America never see themselves as a static, entrenched class so much as "temporarily embarrassed millionaires," one game plan away from the American Dream. The heart of the paper gets at how, despite the fact that the odds of moving up the economic ladder in Europe are roughly the same as (or even better than) in the United States these days, optimism about social mobility is much stronger among Americans (stronger than the actual rate of mobility, in fact). Interestingly, this rock-steady American confidence in freedom of opportunity is even more robust in the states "where actual mobility is particularly low."

What Steinbeck really wrote was "Everyone was a temporarily embarrassed capitalist," but by now, none of this should surprise us. As the authors noted, much of Europe has the shared legacy of feudalism, where status was widely determined by birth for centuries, while the United States has the epic myth of arrival, triumph, and riches.

One tangible expression of Americans' irrepressible cheer and Europeans' gloom can be seen in the ways that countries organize their social safety nets. In the United States, the people who believe most in social mobility also tend to reject policies that would level the playing field. On the other hand, the study also shows how those who see the path of opportunity as fundamentally crooked or largely determined by arbitrary luck— a more common outlook in Europe—"tend to favor more generous redistributive policies and higher levels of government involvement."

What stuck out to me most about the study's data was that everyone was a little bit off; Europeans tended to be too pessimistic about social mobility and the freedom to advance, while Americans were not pessimistic enough. Put another way, the ceiling of American life is often higher, but the basement is also usually lower. It's possible to be rich or poor in the United States in ways that don't translate to other advanced nations. In extreme ways, life here fledges and falters in the margin between ambition and reality.

Traveling the country in the late-pandemic fog—a time in which optimism about the future had hit both generational highs and generational lows—I found that the conventional indicators of national health felt beside the point. Wages had jumped, only to be undone by inflation and basic costs like housing. Unemployment hovered at historic, rock-bottom levels even as clashes over new workplace standards had created new tensions. American-led science had mostly stopped a virus, but only after an excruciating rending of the country's social fabric and a million agonizing deaths. Support for unions had reached its highest point in six decades, even as membership in private-sector unions was at a hundred-year low. Talk of worker power and work-life balance was ascendant, but only if the recession on everyone's lips didn't wreck the momentum. The government had given citizens an unprecedented taste of support and security, only for it to disappear and for the old precarity to return. And for all that new technological advances had done to ease the way we work, spend our time and money, and interact with one another, it had become undeniable that technology had degraded all these facets of life, reshaping norms for the worse and elevating tech oligarchs to incalculable levels of wealth and influence.

If there is a cure, a better version of American optimism, it's one where instead of nurturing fantasies about technology or unchecked markets or ambition as the synchronizing forces in life, we'd invest in people. And we'd do so explicitly and without conditions. That starts with a trust borne out by the evidence that, given a reasonable chance, people will do their best. This reordering won't be accomplished strictly through direct assistance or government outlays; it can't be. What's required is a split from what work and the American ethic have robbed us of: time and rest, community and public collaboration, and a faith in the secular calling of good citizenship. To be clear, these fixes make for a tall task. But as more and more of us are finding out each day, the alternative is worse.

CHAPTER TWELVE

BLINDNESS

THE CRISIS OF AMERICAN SELF-ESTRANGEMENT

**THE GROWING GOOD OF THE WORLD IS PARTLY
DEPENDENT ON UNHISTORIC ACTS.**

—GEORGE ELIOT

Back in Paris, I'd more or less nailed the tourist checklist. I'd selfied on several bridges over the Seine, scoffed at the winding line for the Louvre before spending thirty-five minutes in line for Instagram-famous falafel, gotten scolded for wearing headphones in the Musée d'Orsay, crushed a croque madame at an outdoor café in a miasma of Gauloises smoke, and strolled the Tuileries with a sappy grin on my dumb American face.

For extra credit, I'd also stumbled across one of the several protests over national pension reform in France. To keep the country's pension system solvent even with an aging population, longer life expectancies, and a declining birth rate, the French government had recently proposed an unpopular measure that would slowly raise the retirement age from sixty-two to sixty-four. For months running, a million or so French protesters had blocked roads, stopped river traffic, scuffled with police, and fired flares inside the headquarters of Louis Vuitton, all in a quest to not work more than previously agreed. Striking energy sector workers, inspired by Robin Hood, diverted free gas and electricity to hospitals, daycares, libraries, and low-income households. At another point, sanitation workers, whose retirement ages would be boosted from fifty-seven to fifty-nine, let ten thousand tons of garbage pile up in the streets. I was on my way out of Paris when a demonstration led by one of France's major trade unions suddenly materialized in Gare du Nord, one of the world's biggest train stations. My Duolingo-level French had only prepared me to order a croissant from a cat, so I couldn't exactly make out the chants of the crowd. When I asked Léa, a young protester in a red vest, what they were basically saying, she told me that instead of forcing people to work later in life, French president "Macron's friends, the rich, should pay more taxes." Léa then returned to blowing a whistle with earsplitting vigor. Chaos aside, it was affecting to see an intergenerational body of workers come together in solidarity for a common cause—in this case, to advocate working less in life.

This send-off from Paris stayed with me as my train pulled into Bayeux on the northwestern coast of France. To knit a cosmic balance with the *Emily in Paris* tour, I had signed up for an intensive outing in Normandy. I would be spending ten hours in a dude-heavy Sprinter van of American retirees and amateur World War II buffs, who'd come to France to make a patriotic pilgrimage to the D-Day landing sites. We looked out at the English Channel from inside the still-intact German batteries at Longues-sur-Mer, which had (and had not) enjoyed a catbird view of the largest amphibious assault in history on June 6, 1944. We were ferried among the beaches, the memorials, and the battle sites, where the guys on the tour quizzed one another about artillery and took pictures with the jack-shaped metal hedgehogs that had blocked American landing craft from getting ashore. When we arrived at Sainte-Mère-Église, the first town in France liberated on D-Day, there was a brief competition over who could pronounce it the most like John Wayne in the popular war flick *The Longest Day*.

Laying eyes on Normandy's military sanctums had a humbling resonance. One set of my grandparents had managed to escape Berlin just as the horrors there had begun to unfold—stopping in France and then carrying on to Brooklyn—and so, for me at least, the heroic sweep of the Allied advance into Europe had a righteous quality to it, something more biblical than national. But among my fellow history nerds, their fascination had a different character, a sort of dutiful longing.

Taking in the scene at Omaha Beach, the grisly carnage of which was memorialized in the opening moments of *Saving Private Ryan*, one fellow tourgoer walked out to the surf to pick up a handful of sand and drop it into a Ziploc as a keepsake. Later, standing among the bloodstained pews inside a small rural twelfth-century church, our guide explained how two medics from the 101st Airborne had holed up there and, despite the mortal danger, managed to save dozens of injured U.S. and German troops as the ground around them kept exchanging hands. They'd been sent into battle with only two weeks of training. At that point, another pilgrim from our pack interrupted the story to demand collective reverence. "Two weeks of training?" he said in awe and disbelief. This was Ron, our unelected Additional Comments Guy. He wore a baseball cap with a picture of a Douglas C-47 warbird on it, and, back on Long Island, he'd once gotten to ride around in a Sherman tank. "No suspension at all. I don't know how they did it! I was aching from those vibrations." Next year, he was going to island-hop the Pacific theater with his son. "Ten thousand bucks!" he said.

Ron had brought along small American flags he had bought from his local Home Depot so he could plant them at each spot we visited. And resentfully photographing Ron at each stop was Allie, his twentysomething daughter, who seemed less than thrilled to be spending a day in France hearing how American paratroopers had missed their drop zones in excruciating detail.

Coming to France, Ron told me, had actually been Allie's idea. When she and her boyfriend had broken up on Christmas Eve, she'd been left with a nonrefundable ticket to Paris. "She said, 'Dad, you want to go to France?' I said, 'Yeah, with stipulations.'" Poor Allie was now living out those stipulations. In addition to spending ten hours in a Sprinter van with people naming their favorite scenes from *Band of Brothers*, she had to absorb her father's mild disappointment when she failed to muster up adequate excitement about Operation Overlord's more trivial subplots. "What are they teaching her in school?" Ron asked with slightly jokey exasperation. "I know! Teaching her to freaking hate America."

––––––––––

Speaking about the differences between generations, the writer and American sage Kurt Vonnegut once theorized that what older generations want is "credit for having survived so long, and often imaginatively, under difficult conditions." At the same time, what younger generations want is "acknowledgement, and without further ado, that they are without question women and men now." Complicating everything, Vonnegut added, is the fact that both groups are "stingy" about giving what the other one wants.

Among the many silly fault lines of American life, generational combat is one of the most irritating and artificially imposed of all. And surprise, surprise, the modern origins of this battle emerged in big part from the realm of work.

Back in 1900, less than 15 percent of Americans between the ages of fourteen and seventeen went to school. The rest mostly worked and, by doing so, garnered ammunition to browbeat future generations with tales of their youthful hardships. But by 1940, just before the United States began sending its troops to Europe again, 73 percent of that same cohort were going to school. The mass enrollment of teens initiated a huge collective shift in the American life cycle. As the critic and essayist Louis Menand explained, "A social space had opened up between dependency and adulthood, and a new demographic was born: 'youth.'"* In the decades that followed the war, an upsurge in both college attendance (thanks to the GI Bill) and a young population (thanks to the baby boom) expanded the ambit of youth and its grip on Americans' cultural consciousness.

Now, even outside those specific social conditions, young people have never exactly been popular. Going back at least as far as the ancient Greeks, the alleged softness, self-absorption,

––––––––––

* Menand added that the 1940s also saw the convenient arrival of the term "youth culture," which became a way to market to and profit from that new cohort.

arrogance, and foolish idealism of the young have been fixations of the older set. As an elder millennial, I saw the best minds of my generation denigrated for their shoddy work ethic, avocado toast–fueled spendthriftery, and apparent hatred of home buying, dating, marriage, office dress codes, and handshakes. Like the savages we are, we replaced hotel stays with home shares and fabric softener with ignorance. Eventually, with enough time, our crimes were attributed to Gen Z, the cohort now charged with the murders of paper cash, beer drinking, phone calls, and face-to-face conversations, the American worth ethic (once again!), and Madison Avenue's purchase funnel.

As work in America has grown to both occupy more of life and fulfill fewer of its basic needs, it's only natural that workplaces have become bigger conflict zones between our generations. In recent years, popular verdicts about young American adults have gone from dismissive to outright hostile. One 2023 survey found that 74 percent of managers and business leaders said their Gen Z employees were difficult to work with, compared to workers from other generations. What's more, an astonishing 12 percent of those bosses claimed to have fired a Gen Z employee less than one week after their start date. (More generally, a leading reason for Gen Z dismissals was their tendency to be "too easily offended.")

For their part, Gen Z and younger millennials have started giving as good as they've gotten. Across social platforms, cold-blooded takedowns of older coworkers proliferate about their supposed love of pointless meetings, their animosity toward taking personal time off, and their possible exposure to lead paint in childhood, as well as their unwillingness to adopt technology to communicate, handle tasks, answer basic questions, and so on. A few short years ago, "OK, boomer" became the rallying cry of enraged youths returning fire at baby boomers, the longtime stand-ins for an American establishment rightly considered to be too critical of young adults, too obsessed with work, too reluctant to share control, and, at best, indifferent to the unsustainable cost of living, the changing climate, and the country's entrenched social ills. Considering the ease with which young adults could be labeled "snowflakes" for apparently being too sensitive and outspoken, the fuming public response to the brief "OK, boomer" fever offered a nice reset of perspective.

To say the very least, it's a supreme bummer that generational warfare fails to serve up little beyond popcorn, fireworks, and flame wars. In spite of our eternal national preoccupation with individualism, we've somehow settled for these divisive and sweepingly cockeyed generational stereotypes to guide our understanding of one another, even as we know, for example, that not every young person was smoking pot and protesting the Vietnam War on college campuses in the 1960s and 1970s. (Plenty of them were binge drinking and founding local chapters of the John Birch Society!) As Pew Research Center president Michael Dimock pointed out, "many high-quality surveys at the time showed that younger Americans—most of whom were not attending college—were *more* supportive of the war than older generations who had lived through previous conflicts."* Lamenting the way that generational perceptions have been hijacked to focus on the negatives and divisions, Kim Parker added, "The field has been flooded with content that's often sold as research but is more like clickbait or marketing mythology." Making matters worse, there are no universal experiences in a country as large and variegated as ours.

If there's good news here, it's that our attraction to deciphering generational differences in America speaks to a curiosity we have about one another. "When you're clicking on an article about generation concepts, it may be because you're irritated or cackling at the stereotype that's being portrayed in the headline, but it's also because you're trying to understand how the culture is changing," the sociologist Philip N. Cohen told the journalist Kelli María Korducki when asked about generational animosity. "And I think there's a great impulse there."

This is perhaps another way of saying that our curiosities could be satisfied in more productive ways, like finding real-life

---

* Traces of this disconnect are evident in the lopsided attention given to what goes on at Ivy League colleges, despite the fact that the entire population of the Ivies could be held within the combined enrollment at Texas A&M and the University of Central Florida.

ways to interact with each other. As our tour of Normandy began to wrap up, I checked in on Ron and found that he'd changed his tune a bit about his day with Allie. "I was proud of her!" he said. "She was asking questions by the end." I asked him what was next, and he told me that they were heading back to Paris the following day to see the *Mona Lisa* at the Louvre, which had been on her wish list. "I'll probably stay outside and smoke cigarettes," he said in a tone that suggested that maybe he'd go along after all.

What our antagonistic framing of generations obscures is that most everyone is struggling to flourish in a country with a go-it-alone ethos, where we're defined by our productivity. It gnaws at each American cohort in a very specific way. Gen Z, for example, is coming of age having never experienced the country even feign political unity; polls show that beneath their general optimism about the future lies a deep pessimism about the American system. Likewise, being online from a young age has meant cultivating a real-world identity and a digital persona on extractive and unforgiving platforms with little oversight. In 2023, Surgeon General Vivek Murthy went as far as to issue a lengthy advisory on the effects of digital stress on younger Americans, citing extensive research that connects social media use by kids and teens with depression, anxiety, disordered eating, self-harm, and suicide.

Graduating into adulthood with its various debts and financial sleeper holds hasn't seemed to offer much reprieve. As recently as July 2022, half of U.S. adults between the ages of eighteen and twenty-nine were living with their parents. Meanwhile, for Americans in their prime years, the devolution of salaried, middle-income jobs into low-wage service work doesn't just betoken future instability without pensions or savings but also limits and colors the interactions among people from different economic backgrounds.

Then, of course, for older Americans, the national obsession with utility means that they often face scorn and social isolation upon (voluntarily or involuntarily) exiting the workforce. Owing in part to our unrelenting focus on self-reliance and independence, the proportion of older Americans living alone is higher than ever before, with poorer health outcomes and shorter life spans to show for it.* In declaring a national and all-encompassing "epidemic of loneliness and isolation" in 2023, the surgeon general estimated that in addition to the painful and unseen costs, "social isolation among older adults alone accounts for an estimated $6.7 billion in excess Medicare spending annually, largely due to increased hospital and nursing facility spending." They weren't alone in being alone; the number of Americans who report having no close friends has quadrupled since 1990, and by one account, Americans actually spent less time with friends between 2014 and 2019 than during the pandemic.

In order to solve for what keeps us at each other's throats, we first have to chart the deep depths to which we've sunk. Misapprehensions about America's generations are plenty of trouble on their own, but unfortunately, they're not the only gophers pocking up the social landscape. We are physically divided as well, the handiwork of income inequality, gerrymandering, bad policies, bad leadership, racism, and partisan mistrust.

Even as U.S. society has grown much more diverse, Americans now overwhelmingly live in communities that are segregated by income, race, and political affiliation. Between 1970 and 2009, as wealth concentrated and the middle class hollowed out, Stanford researchers estimated that "the share of families living in middle-income neighborhoods dropped from 65 percent to 44 percent." In those years, higher-income households wended their way to wealthier neighborhoods while low-income households went to poorer ones. Back in 1980, you could live in a city with a high level of income inequality and it didn't necessarily map geographically. The kid of a doctor and the kid of a dockworker were more likely to play ball in the same street and go to the same school. But by 2015, that, too, had changed. "Cities with higher levels of income inequality now also have higher levels of income segregation," the economists Hannah Rubinton and Maggie Isaacson wrote in a 2023 report for the Federal Reserve

---

* According to a 2020 study, 27 percent of U.S. adults ages sixty and older live alone, compared with an average of 16 percent of adults in 130 countries.

Bank of St. Louis. These divergences influence everything in a neighborhood from its crime rate, the quality of its schools, its degree of social mobility, and its stock of good-paying jobs to the presence of environmental hazards, the likelihood of developing chronic health conditions, and the life expectancies of both old and young.

Simply put, these changes are bad news for democracy and, in addition to their big-scheme implications, freight everyday experiences with undisguised indignities. We are increasingly split by the growing number of separate entrances, cut-throughs, velvet ropes, and separate seating built into theme parks and sports stadiums for VIPs and the sad service and long waits for everyone else, and not just to board a plane but to get medical care.

Worse yet, these divisions are growing deeper and more entrenched. What makes American life feel most like it's happy hour on the *Titanic* is our intensifying retreat into partisan echo chambers; we're going blind on terms that are social and fundamental and increasingly unbridgeable.

Using the voter registration data of 180 million U.S. voters, Harvard researchers Jacob R. Brown and Ryan D. Enos analyzed how geographic polarization—the growth of physical partisan clusters—has evolved from perceptible regional phenomena (red counties, blue metro areas, for example) down into individual neighborhoods and blocks. "A large proportion of voters live with virtually no exposure to voters from the other party in their residential environment," they wrote in 2021. "Such high levels of partisan isolation can be found across a range of places and densities and are distinct from racial and ethnic segregation." According to their estimate, somewhere between 98 and 99 percent of Americans live in areas that are politically segregated—in other words, basically everyone everywhere, from the densest block of the Big Apple to the most desolate tract of West Texas.

Geographic polarization is a complicated trend to unpack, and not everyone agrees on its causes. In some cases, it's obvious: people move to places where the prevailing policies and culture feel safe and welcoming. But other observers attribute geographic polarization in the United States to a natural drift in the major political parties; Democratic strongholds centering more on cities and Republicans taking control of less densely popular areas in recent decades. "The realignment has increased geographic polarization without anyone having to physically move," Professors Greg Martin and Steven Webster argued in 2018.* As a result, voting districts have become less politically diverse, making them more extreme and their elected representatives exponentially more annoying.

Arriving at a consensus about what causes this isolation and sorting may be elusive, but what everyone seems to agree on is that geographic polarization is broadly Not Good. Bad things happen in theory when people are shielded from an understanding of one another, and bad things are happening in practice as a result of our ideological self-quarantines. The pandemic provided proof of how social cooperation breaks down when simple strangers become abstractions and collective trust erodes. Working for months as a census enumerator during the 2020 count, I knocked on thousands of doors between the urban warrens north of New York City and the ploughlands and exurbs of Georgia and found out just how little a mask, a government badge, or the promise of a greater share of federal money for roads and schools endears you to folks.

Our atomized ways tell us a lot. Why some lawmakers feel no pressure to seek common ground or compromise, why conspiracy theories flourish, why cynical media types relish in calling cities full of working people "lawless hellholes," why a phrase like "flyover country" exists, and why the same people who post "Refugees welcome" signs in their windows go on to oppose affordable housing initiatives in their neighborhoods. "You have this increasingly incoherent tribalized political narrative where our quality of life becomes less and less relevant," Andrew Yang told me. "And you can see that from the fact that American life expectancy has been declining over the last number of years in a way that's unique to industrialized countries. So you think to yourself, *Okay, like what's the feedback mechanism?* And the feedback mechanism doesn't really exist anymore."

---

* They also noted that the United States is more geographically polarized now than it has been at any point going back to 1860, which was not a banner year for social unity.

Our reigning tribal estrangement is part of why we fail to see how others are struggling; it's what keeps the American abracadabra from seeming bogus. To be isolated from each other and our communities by work, financial status, and political affiliation in a time when technology alienates us and the algorithmic incentives of social media inflame us points the dim way toward an irreparably broken society. These separations have collectively robbed us of a basic responsiveness to one another and to a collective good; moreover, we're in danger of losing the perspective and empathy needed to understand our problems and fix what's broken. The sums of our division have created a domestic foreignness that's both dispiriting and dangerous. We need a unifying experience that hammers at the barriers that seem to be everywhere. And it's why we need national service—a mechanism of renewal to pull all the disparate threads of American life together through a variety of meaningful work across the country.

A few weeks before I left for France, I met Robert Gibson. A World War II veteran, Gibby had been eighteen when he was part of the second wave to hit Utah Beach at two in the afternoon on D-Day. "I was in the 116th AAA Gun Battalion," he told me. "We had a four-man crew, thirty-six rounds of ammunition, and a hundred gallons of gas." Six months later, when he got to the Battle of the Bulge, there was no fuel left. "We used to run the equipment to keep warm, but we couldn't even do that."

Gibby came to mind during the free hour I'd been given to wander the sprawling grounds of the Normandy American Cemetery by myself. Set upon a bluff overlooking the Atlantic and Omaha Beach, it's almost certainly visible in your mind if you've spent any Saturday afternoon watching TBS. The iconic weave of nine thousand bone-white headstones of crosses and Stars of David, including forty-five sets of brothers. Among the known, unknown, and unidentified is the grave of Theodore Roosevelt, Jr., who died a few weeks after leading troops onto the beach; his kid brother Quentin, who had died in World War I, had been reburied next to him. On my way around, I passed a tour of professional gardeners who were visiting on behalf of memorials across Europe. The expert maintenance of the Normandy cemetery grounds—the green standard, if you will—has been led by the same gardener for nearly forty years now, and they had come to study his work. Near a reflecting pool, I found a group from the U.S. Army Corps of Engineers assembled in their yellow vests. They were already penciling out the festivities for the eightieth anniversary of D-Day, even though it was still fifteen months away. Later, when a chime played "The Star-Spangled Banner," everyone stopped in place and stood still as the flag ruffled somberly in the ocean breeze.

There seemed to be an immense sense of purpose to everything and everyone there. Having already spent hours with a group of Americans in the thrall of the heroic deeds and battle valor of Normandy, I'd felt a dull ache accompanying our bystanding and nostalgia and vicarious patriotism. What had stayed with me about Gibby was how he had cut the noble snare drum out of his war story and let it play as a sad adagio instead. "I hate to say this, but when we landed on the beach, we came in on what they call a rhino ferry and I was driving a full track with a ninety-millimeter gun on it," he told me. "And there wasn't a one of us—in that tractor or on that barge coming in—that wasn't crying. Believe me. That's about all I have to say. We had to do it."

Gibby wore this purpose home with him like a uniform. After the war, he went back to Hampton, his small New Jersey town fifteen miles east of Allentown, and has lived the rest of his life there, serving as a Presbyterian church elder, a town council member, the town mayor for eight years, and a member of the fire department for seventy-four. When he was ninety-eight, he needed a member of Congress to help him get a passport so he could travel back to Normandy for a D-Day commemoration; born at home in 1923, he'd never been issued a birth certificate, and he hadn't left the United States since coming back from Europe after the war. A few months after we talked, the town threw him a parade on Labor Day for his hundredth birthday, complete with fire trucks and a flyover by a World War II–era plane.

It's easy to be romantic about the beaches and to forget that the war was also won on the home front, which relied on the largest surge in internal migration in American history to take on vital production jobs. It was won through victory gardens and war bonds and in the factories and shipyards, where women and people of color stepped into work previously limited to white men, even as they were often underpaid for the same efforts. Its heroes were not only the ordinary people who fought but also the ordinary people who got married in their living rooms and car-pooled on their honeymoons to save gas and preserve tires, which had been rationed, and led scrap metal drives. Of the 160,000 D-Day troops, slightly more than half were from other Allied nations including Canada and Great Britain, who brought their own resources and values to the fight.

"Nothing can get done alone," General Stanley McChrystal, the former head of Joint Special Operations Command, told me a few months later. "You see movies about soldier-heroes, *Sergeant York* or whatever, but the reality is nothing in the military gets done without a combination of capabilities and people that are brought together to solve a problem. The logisticians, the signal people. Everybody's just as important as everybody else. And that becomes, through experience, evidence of people. And so what that does is it widens your peripheral vision of views a bit."

McChrystal was talking about the benefits of military service as a cohering social force, but he was also talking about the collective good. In the years since he left active duty, he has taken up the mantle of advocating for national service—not as a mandatory feature of American life and certainly not limited to the military but as a part of a cultural shift with the means to restore what's been lost to the vast sorting and ongoing fragmentation. "We tend not to travel outside of our economic group. We tend to go places with people of our race or background or our tribe. And maybe that's just cultural habit. But now we tend to communicate that way as well," he said, referring to the vitriol and chaos that govern online life. The expansion of this void, he explained, has created a way for misinformation to thrive and for bad actors and opportunists to exploit new technology for selfish, extreme aims. All the while the rest of us have been becoming outsiders to each other.

The growing domestic estrangement among Americans has another casualty, a crucial interdependence that can't be fulfilled by work or solved by government. "The idea of community as being this knitted-together entity to which we all have responsibility and from which we all derive benefit has been weakened," McChrystal said. Outside rigid self-reliance and careerism lay the makings of a corrective, what he called a "practical experience" that civics books alone can't quite capture. "When you have the opportunity to do service or receive service, in fact, you start to have this sense that *Wow, the volunteer fire department came and they saved my house. How about that?*"

One model that McChrystal and others have endorsed is service that focuses on younger Americans: opportunities for paid work in the real world that directly benefits communities and imparts useful skills and experience. Picture a country in which every year, millions of recent high school graduates commit to specialized projects—teaching seniors to use new technology, working on community climate change projects or public health initiatives, helping rural areas come online, partnering with army veterans returning to civilian life, or mentoring younger underserved students—before heading to college or vocational school or into the workforce.*

Several of these programs already exist, but oftentimes they attract only applicants who can afford to pay high out-of-pocket costs or live on a small stipend, theoretically cutting against the inequities these programs are meant to address. Others have been criticized for sending young people into high-need environments without adequate training or support. Ultimately, what McChrystal argues is that they don't match the demands of our dysfunctional moment. "I've gotten to the point where I think that the only way national service is going to be substantively effective in the U.S. is going to be for the president, whoever it is, to get up

---

* I would never hold my experience up for emulation because I was a bit insufferable about it, but after high school and before college, I participated in a gap-year program abroad, where I volunteered, interned at a newspaper, and almost learned a language. At minimum, I did my own laundry and was thoroughly humbled by having left a comfort zone where everything seemed to make sense to me.

in front of the nation and make the case that this is important."
He suggests that the mass adoption of post–high school service—
with incentives such as student debt relief, health insurance, college or trade school credit, and paid work experience—would
improve the American life cycle and forge a more focused and
durable workforce, much as the mass adoption of high school
did last century. Service would not only help level the unwieldy
weight of higher education in America and create an inclusive
national experience where there hasn't been one before; it would
also have the power to efface the long-standing social insulation
in American life, reset our transactional relationship with ambition, and redefine what work is and what it could be.

"Most of us go off to either our job or our college—if we go
to college—and we don't know what we want to do," McChrystal said. "If we do go off to college, for example, we go off and
we study finance, and then we become finance people for the
rest of our lives. But if we spend a year or maybe two, and you
do something like Teach for America or you do some equivalent
hard work—maybe you're doing conservation, maybe you're out
cutting trails, maybe you're helping build a home—you get an
appreciation for what that is. You get an appreciation for what
other people in society are going to do for their whole lives.
It gives you a grounding that is remarkably humbling in many
ways."

At least some of these aims can be met by taking on work
experiences that don't fit neatly or strategically on a résumé.
McChrystal's call for humility brought to mind the Osage educator Patrick Martin, whom I had met back in Oklahoma. After
our trip around Pawhuska, the conversation had drifted toward
our early work lives. My first job after college had been as a bartender, covering three twelve-hour shifts a week at a smoky and
extremely corny cigar and whiskey bar on New York's Upper East
Side.* I told him that I'd grown up around people who had been
set up for success, worked hard, and done well. But I also hadn't

---

* The bar played early James Bond movies on a loop on mute, and I had to wear a
double-breasted blue captain's blazer with a Windsor-knotted tie.

understood what work really was in America until I'd seen the porters and barbacks at the bar, who knew its operations better than everyone else, who were paid too little money under the table, and who worked six days a week, took long subway rides home to their families after we closed at 4 a.m., and came back by noon to do it all over again. Before teaching, Martin had taken a few years to do something else and reform his outlook. "I worked on a farm in Kansas after I graduated college," he told me. "I knew I was gonna go into education, but I just wanted to do some hard work to learn what it was like. And so I worked for this farmer who had this market, and he grew fruit and vegetables. . . . I really learned to work, I worked my butt off for several years . . . and it changed my life." His own daughters had now logged time working at a coffee shop and an Olive Garden and had often arrived home reeking of espresso and endless breadsticks.

The same hard-work culture that has always chastised American kids for being too self-involved or slothful has increasingly robbed them of a youth of exploration, a time in which work can actually be good and formative and expansive. Since the 1990s, the number of sixteen- to nineteen-year-olds taking up summer gigs and after-school jobs has plummeted. Many of the reasons are complex and depressing, whether because teenagers are now competing with adults for entry-level work, or more teens are needed to take up caretaking roles in their households, or they've been steered by consultants toward unpaid internships so they can stand out on college applications. As an outcome, a familiar wisdom has been washed out. McChrystal relayed a story about his son, who delivered pizzas for years and took away a deep appreciation of how hard a job can be. "It creates respect and linkages for people with different backgrounds . . . and a grudging acceptance of the fact that their perspective may be just as right as mine," he added. "They've had a different life journey. I tell people, 'If you've ever had to pick up trash, you tend not to litter as much as you did before.' You learn that somebody's picking it up."

It doesn't take the battle-won wisdom of a four-star general to grasp that our preternatural focus on the individual, with its at-all-costs devotion to work and self-driven destiny and its thumb-in-the-eye economic absurdities, is keeping us from fully being what George Washington called "citizens of a common country" in his farewell address. Our moment demands a new patriotism; an ideal strong enough to hold the truth that no singular American success has happened without help and sweat from the greater whole; and that for each high-water triumph of collective sacrifice like June 6, there has also been a rock-bottom calamity of collective dysfunction like January 6.

Finally, we have to invert the civic disparity that pushes us to ask too much of each other as individuals and too little of each other as citizens. "People think that if they vote, they pay their taxes, they've checked the box as citizens," McChrystal told me. "But in reality, most of us got citizenship by accident at our birth. We didn't do anything to earn it."

For all the hoary sermonizing about independence, communities would actually be more self-reliant if there weren't a sense of shame about needing help. We'd be better if we didn't demand the sacrifice of Yea Ji Sea, who looks out for the veterans no one else will, or Pastor Jerome Whaley, who sleeps with his phone by his bed with the ringer on. We could solve deeper problems if people didn't have to choose among eating, getting medical care, and staying in their homes.

It's incredibly easy to tune out in the despair of this ugly, crisis-laden moment. But, bleakness aside, we've been here before and found ways out by admitting our position and deploying the best of our national principles. The context delivered in the opening line of the Declaration of Independence—"When in the Course of human events"—acknowledges the exhaustion of options and begins the admission of a breaking point. The end of the Civil War enabled us to create massive infrastructure, build a national network of public universities, and set a course (however tragically brief) toward addressing our historic inequities. The Great Depression led to a raft of federal laws that reduced inequality, protected workers, and set the stage for unprecedented human progress. The social and political upheaval of the pandemic years has to be our twenty-first-century breaking point, an opportunity to construct a viable American Dream, one that's actually attainable and less ethically confused.

It begins with the understanding that we haven't lived up to our democratic, equalizing values, not yet at least—and that the answer isn't to give up on these values; it is to finally make them true. It's the kind of hard work that's worth it.

ACKNOWLEDGMENTS

Like all work, this book would have been impossible to make happen without the help of many hands. First, I'm grateful to everyone who shared their stories, time, and expertise with me.

Writing a book with Pantheon has been an honor. I'm indebted to my editors, Concepción de Leon and Amara Balan, who understood this idea immediately and pushed me to think more expansively about it . . . and everything really. This project was aided immensely by the efforts of the wonderful Pantheon team, who did a million things seen and unseen alike. A special thanks to Lisa Lucas, Beatrice Chaudoin, Julianne Clancy, Rose Cronin-Jackman, Kathleen Cook, Karen Dziekonski, Victoria Hernandez, Kate Keating, Juliane Pautrot, and Matt Chase, who designed the rad cover. An additional million thanks to Amelia Possanza.

To Sarah Levitt, my eternal gratitude for being the best agent, editorial copilot, and psychoanalyst that a neurotic like me could have ever hoped for. I also would have been lost in the wilderness without the bighearted guidance of my unofficial rebbe Michael Maze and the good-natured annoyance of my unofficial priest Kathy Gilsinan. I'm also thankful for Apoorva Tadepalli, who brought deep research and sharp insights, as well as Amy Berman, Sara Mirsky, AZA's Dan Sacks, and Benjamin Ariel Smith, who read some chaotic early drafts of this thing.

When the writing was slow, which was often, I texted and meme-bombed Jason Methner, Albert Rubinsky, Jacob Silverman, and Andy Weil, who were especially forgiving victims and are better friends than I deserve. Grudging thanks to Jose Altuve, Yordan Alvarez, Dusty Baker, Alex Bregman, Christian Javier, Jeremy Peña, Ryan Pressly, Kyle Tucker, Framber Valdez, and Justin Verlander for two deep October runs that turned my deadlines into adventures.

For their friendship, support, hospitality, and willingness to indulge in tiresome conversations, I owe a debt to an impossibly long list of people: Alex Aciman, Aaron Aft, Ben Apatoff, Yoni Appelbaum, Jo Ann Beard, Russell Berman, Lisa Bonos, Taffy Brodesser-Akner, Jacob Brogan, Jimmy Capo and Travis Rush, Marcia Chatelain, Bryn Clark, Hassan Damluji, Nicky Dawidoff, Jason Diamond, Eva Dickerman, Damien Dupont, Jeremy Elias, Kimberly Escobar, Stephen Fidgeon, Mike Fisherman, the Frames of Tulsa, the Friedmans of Philly, Michael Furman, Hadass Gerson, Brad Girson, Adam Goldberg, Jeffrey Goldberg, Rebecca Goldfarb, Gabe Goodwin, Barrie Gordon, David A. Graham, Emma Green and Michael Schulson, Barrie and Jared Gruner, Jim Hamblin and Sarah Yager, Ben Hart and Mallory Kass, the Hernandi, Marisa Kabas, Kelly and Paul Kennedy, Nicole Loving, Paul Lucas, Stephen Marche, Alicia Miller, Gaby Moss and Jesse Rifkin, Robert S. Nooromid, Bill Oakley, Lizzie O'Leary, Spencer Peeples and Rebecca Ramsey, Brooks Rich, the Rinskys, Daniel Robbins, Morty Rosenbaum and Jonathan Vatner, Jennie Rothenberg, Joe Saka, Felix Salmon, Ben Schwade Schmidt, Matt Shaer, Maya Sigel, Charlie Smith and Meghan Steinbrecher, the Sobels, Liz Stevenson, Simo Stolzoff, Jake Weixler, and Jeffrey Yoskowitz. Stephen Silverman, may the drinks be stiff wherever you are; I will miss talking craft with you.

Thank you to my family, Mom, Amelia, Ziva, Bo, and Noma, along with the Fischers, Hoffmans, Mazzurcos, Orsecks, Saladinos, and the Crestwood crew, who fed me hamburgers and support along the way. Lastly, thank you to Emily, whose love, patience, intelligence, empathy, and sugar cookies make everything better.

NOTES

INTRODUCTION THE AMERICAN ABRACADABRA

3 twice the state's minimum wage: "Minimum Wage in N.C.," N.C. Department of Labor.

3 "Wages never match": Author interview with Nakitta Long, August 2, 2022. Unless otherwise noted, all quotes and data about Long come from this August 2 interview.

3 tens of millions of other American workers: Lauren Hall and Catlin Nchako, "A Closer Look at Who Benefits from SNAP," Center on Budget and Policy Priorities, April 25, 2022.

3 tens of millions of American jobs: "American Opportunity Study," McKinsey & Company, August 23, 2022.

4 disproportionately affecting hourly workers: Nicole Bateman and Martha Ross, "Why Has COVID-19 Been Especially Harmful for Working Women?," Brookings Institution, October 2020.

4 only 14 percent: Jonnelle Marte, "As U.S. Jobless Claims Surged in March, Some States Lagged with Payments," Reuters, May 1, 2020.

6 "Genius is another name": "Doing One's Best," *Idaho Daily Statesman*, May 6, 1901, 4.

7 "Stuff!": Frank Lewis Dyer and Thomas Commerford Martin, *Edison: His Life and Inventions* (New York: Harper & Brothers, 1910), vol. 2, 607.

7 he arranged to have: "Test Tube, 'Edison's Last Breath,' 1931," Henry Ford Museum; Atlas Obscura, "Edison's Last Breath."

7 "There are way easier places": Elon Musk (@ElonMusk), Twitter/X, November 26, 2018, https://twitter.com/elonmusk/status/1067173497909141504.

7 "varies per person": Elon Musk (@ElonMusk), Twitter/X, November 26, 2018, https://twitter.com/elonmusk/status/1067175527180513280.

7 more than six hundred: Marisa Taylor, "At SpaceX, Worker Injuries Soar in Elon Musk's Rush to Mars," Reuters, November 10, 2023.

7 Despite naming his most celebrated: "Importance of Thomas Edison's

Quotes," Thomas Alva Edison Foundations; Joe Berkowitz, "Who Said It? Ethan Hawke's 'Tesla' or Tesla-Worshipping Elon Musk?," Fast Company, August 21, 2020.

8 "Those of us": Abby Livingston, "Texas Lt. Gov. Dan Patrick Says a Failing Economy Is Worse than Coronavirus," *Texas Tribune*, March 23, 2020.

8 "The message is": Caroline Kelly, "Chris Christie Says the Country Will Just Have to Accept More Deaths," *Mercury News*, May 4, 2020.

9 more than 10 percent: Jennifer Tolbert and Kendal Orgera, "What Does the CPS Tell Us About Health Insurance Coverage in 2020?," Kaiser Family Foundation, September 23, 2021.

9 That figure in all other industrialized countries: "America Is a Health-Care Outlier in the Developed World," *The Economist*, April 26, 2018.

9 Americans working from home: Jo Craven McGinty, "With No Commute, Americans Simply Worked More During Coronavirus," *Wall Street Journal*, October 30, 2020; Joan C. Williams, "The Pandemic Has Exposed the Fallacy of the 'Ideal Worker,'" *Harvard Business Review*, May 11, 2020.

9 became the highest percentage: Yea-Hung Chen et al., "Excess Mortality Associated with the COVID-19 Pandemic Among Californians 18–65 Years of Age, by Occupational Sector and Occupation," PLOS One, June 4, 2021.

9 3 million U.S. women: Tyler Boesch et al., "Pandemic Pushes Mothers of Young Children Out of the Labor Force," Federal Reserve Bank of Minneapolis, February 2, 2021.

10 The rate of child poverty: Jeff Stein, "Child Poverty Spiked 41 Percent in January After Biden Benefit Program Expired, Study Finds," *Washington Post*, February 17, 2022.

10 "I promise you": Seanna Adcox, "'Over Our Dead Bodies': Graham Promises Congress Won't Extend $600 Weekly Extra for Jobless," *Post & Courier*, April 29, 2020.

10 By the end of 2020: Megan Cerullo, "U.S. Poverty Jumps the Most in 60 Years," CBS News, December 17, 2020.

10 "If a person is making $23": Adcox, "'Over Our Dead Bodies.'"

11 In an earlier variation: Personal Responsibility and Work Opportunity Reconciliation Act of 1996—Conference Report, *Congressional Record* 142, no. 116 (August 1, 1996): S9387–415.

13 A 2023 economic opportunity poll: Lydia Saad, "Americans Still Glum About State of the Union in Most Areas," Gallup, February 2, 2023.

14 In 2023, an astounding: Kim Parker and Rachel Minkin, "What Makes for a Fulfilling Life?," Pew Research Center, September 14, 2023.

15 "He reached up": Ian Frazier, *Travels in Siberia* (New York: Farrar, Straus and Giroux, 2010), 4.

CHAPTER ONE COLUMBIA

19 "Go there!": Lewis Black, "The End of the Universe," *The CBC Show*, 2001. This section's rendering also contains language from Black's other performances of the bit in 2001.

20 "culture and way of life": "American Values Survey," Public Religion Research Institute, November 1, 2021.

20 almost a third: Jamie Ballard, "How Americans Believe the World Will End," YouGovAmerica, March 18, 2020.

20 St. Croix holds: Valerie Strauss, "Christopher Columbus: 3 Things You Think He Did That He Didn't," *Washington Post*, October 14, 2013.

20 "He stopped in search": "Columbus Cove Marina—Salt River, St. Croix," StCroixTourism.com.

20 the Columbus landing spot: "America's 11 Most Endangered Historic Places," National Trust for Historic Preservation.

21 he went to his grave: Carrie Gibson, *Empire's Crossroads: A History of the Caribbean from Columbus to the Present Day* (New York: Grove Atlantic, 2014), 23.

21 The reason the United States: Erin Allen, "How Did America Get Its Name?," Library of Congress, July 4, 2016.

21 the name *America* is a historical fluke: "Creating the Declaration: A Timeline," National Archives, https://www.archives.gov/.

21 "His voyages were significant": Russell Freedman, *Who Was First? Discovering the Americas* (New York: Clarion, 2007), 19.

21 Columbus' inaugural journey west: Freedman, *Who Was First?*, 8.

22 he scored seventeen ships: Christopher Minster, "The Second Voyage of Christopher Columbus," ThoughtCo., September 28, 2020.

22 "reknit the torn seams": Harrison Smith, "Alfred Crosby, Environmental Historian of 'Columbian Exchange,' Dies at 87," *Washington Post*, April 5, 2018.

22 "With the Columbian Exchange": Charles C. Mann, *1493: Uncovering the New World Columbus Created* (New York: Knopf, 2012), 23.

22 were all grown exclusively: Alfred W. Crosby, Jr., *The Columbian Exchange: Biological and Cultural Consequences of 1492* (Westport, CT: Greenwood Press, 1972), 211.

23 One long-standing estimate: Charles C. Mann, *1491: New Revelations of the Americas Before Columbus* (New York: Knopf, 2005), 92–96, 132–33.

23 which got its name: "St. Croix, V.I.: Salt River Bay National Historical Park and Ecological Preserve," National Park Service.

23 It was the first documented: "St. Croix, V.I.," National Park Service.

24 "A startlingly large proportion": Mann, *1491*, 78.

24 Between 1600 and 1800: Jill Lepore, *These Truths: A History of the United States* (New York: W. W. Norton, 2023), 101.

24   that first figure comprises: Steven Mintz, "Historical Context: Facts About the Slave Trade and Slavery," Gilder Lehrman Institute of American History.

24   In 1860, the enslaved: "1825 to 1860: Slavery," Virginia Museum of History & Culture.

24   In Mississippi and South Carolina: "Chart: Slave Population in 1860," Bill of Rights Institute.

25   many across the North: Julie Zauzmer Weil, Adrian Blanco, and Leo Dominguez, "More than 1,800 Congressmen Once Enslaved Black People. This Is Who They Were, and How They Shaped the Nation," *Washington Post*, January 10, 2022.

25   Nearly half of the wealth: Lepore, *These Truths*, 100.

25   enslaved workers were calculated: Matthew Desmond, "In Order to Understand the Brutality of American Capitalism, You Have to Start on the Plantation," *New York Times Magazine*, August 14, 2019.

25   Thomas Jefferson financed: Desmond, "In Order to Understand."

25   there were more millionaires: Desmond, "In Order to Understand."

25   "the unchristian prejudice": Harriet Beecher Stowe, *Uncle Tom's Cabin: A Tale of Slave Life in the United States of America* (London: Ingram, Cooke, and Company, 1853), 351.

25   "It is uncanny": Tiya Miles, "How Slavery Made Wall Street," *New York Times Magazine*, August 14, 2019.

25   second only to Charleston: Sylviane A. Diouf, "New York City's Slave Market," New York Public Library, June 29, 2015.

26   As recently as 2019: Juliana Menache Horowitz, "Most Americans Say the Legacy of Slavery Still Affects Black People in the U.S. Today," Pew Research Center, July 17, 2019.

26   median wealth of white households: Aditya Aladangady, Andrew C. Chang, and Jacob Krimmel, "Greater Wealth, Greater Uncertainty: Changes in Racial Inequality in the Survey of Consumer Finances," Board of Governors of the Federal Reserve System, October 18, 2023.

26   "So you have an institution": Clint Smith, "'Monuments to the Unthinkable' Explores How Nations Can Memorialize Their Atrocities," *Fresh Air*, December 1, 2022.

26   But he was also the first: "Slavery in the President's Neighborhood," The White House Historical Association.

27   "Our journey has never": Barack Obama, "President Barack Obama's Inaugural Address," The White House, January 20, 2009.

27   constructed in part: "Slavery and the White House," White House Historical Association.

27   Columbus came up in Genoa: Carrie Gibson, *Empire's Crossroads: A History of the Caribbean from Columbus to the Present Day* (New York: Grove Press, 2015).

27 "He was also a weaver's son": Gibson, *Empire's Crossroads*, 20.

28 various royal establishments: Gibson, *Empire's Crossroads*, 20.

28 The deal would double: "Louisiana Purchase Treaty (1803)," National Archives, https://www.archives.gov/.

28 the biggest literary sensation: Robert McCrum, "The 100 Best Novels: No 35—*The Call of the Wild* by Jack London (1903)," *The Guardian*, May 19, 2014.

28 And a century after that: Andrew Dansby, "50 Cent Tops 2003," *Rolling Stone*.

29 "Americans were actively looking": Michael D. Hattem, "Columbus Never Set Foot Here. Why Do We Remember Him?," *Washington Post*, June 15, 2020.

29 public campaigns in the young country: Timothy Winkle, "The Monument That Created Columbus," National Museum of American History.

29 "The strength of the Columbus symbol": Timothy Kubal, *Cultural Movements and Collective Memory: Christopher Columbus and the Rewriting of the National Origin Myth* (New York: Palgrave Macmillan, 2008), 2.

29 A few of the many other: Yoni Appelbaum, "How Columbus Day Fell Victim to Its Own Success," *The Atlantic*, October 8, 2012.

29 "Fix'd are the eyes": Phillis Wheatley, "Enclosure: Poem by Phillis Wheatley, 26 October 1775," National Archives.

29 In 1899, for example: Alessandra Bocchi, "Columbus Day Stands for Diversity," *Wall Street Journal*, October 11, 2020.

29 On New Year's Day 1892: "Ellis Island," Statue of Liberty–Ellis Island Foundation.

30 President Benjamin Harrison created: Benjamin Harrison, "Proclamation 335—400th Anniversary of the Discovery of America by Columbus," American Presidency Project, July 21, 1892.

30 Schools began to install: Appelbaum, "How Columbus Day Fell Victim."

30 the newly founded Daughters: "A Colonial Ball," *New York Times*, October 12, 1892, 11.

30 Harrison's motives for boosting: Associated Press, "New Orleans to Apologise for Worst Mass Lynching in America's History," *The Guardian*, March 31, 2019.

31 "300 marching Indian boys": William J. Connell, "What Columbus Day Really Means," *American Scholar*, October 4, 2012.

31 A flotilla of warships: "The Triumph of America," *New York Times*, October 13, 1892, 1–2.

31 "the regulation, every-day": "The Triumph of America."

31 "The celebration of Erikson": Appelbaum, "How Columbus Day Fell Victim."

31 One conspicuous absence: Ronald G. Shafer, "The First Columbus Day

Was Born of Violence—and Political Calculation," *Washington Post*, October 10, 2021.

31 In the mid-1930s: Dan Fletcher, "A Brief History of Columbus Day," *Time*, October 12, 2009.

32 Roosevelt would designate: David A. Taylor, "During World War II, the U.S. Saw Italian-Americans as a Threat to Homeland Security," *Smithsonian Magazine*, February 2, 2017.

32 "don't have their heads": Michael Tomasky, "Nixon: Irish Were Bad Drinkers," *The Guardian*, December 13, 2010.

32 "expressions of man's": Richard Nixon, "Proclamation 3929—Columbus Day, 1969," American Presidency Project.

32 Columbus Day had been replaced: Scott Gleeson, "What Is Indigenous Peoples Day? Is It Offensive to Celebrate Columbus Day? Everything to Know," *USA Today*, October 10, 2022.

32 the U.S. Mint: "Christopher Columbus Quincentenary Dollar," United States Mint.

32 "If some of these folks": "Obama: GOP Candidates 'Would Have Been Members of the Flat Earth Society,'" March 5, 2012, https://www.youtube.com/watch?v=Rsz3uLxTwQs; Byron Tau, "Newt vs. Obama on Gas Prices, Round 3," Politico, March 15, 2012.

33 "Powerful interests": Christina M. Desai, "The Columbus Myth: Power and Ideology in Picturebooks About Christopher Columbus," *Children's Literature in Education* 45, no. 3 (2014): 183.

33 "It is difficult to grapple": Emma Bowman, "Goodbye, Columbus? Here's What Indigenous Peoples' Day Means to Native Americans," NPR, October 10, 2022.

33 "For generations, Federal policies": Joseph R. Biden, "A Proclamation on Indigenous Peoples' Day, 2021," White House, October 8, 2021.

33 "It is a measure of our greatness": Joseph R. Biden, "A Proclamation on Columbus Day, 2021," White House, October 8, 2021.

33 "to root out the teaching": Donald J. Trump, "Proclamation on Columbus Day, 2020," White House, October 9, 2020.

34 in at least two states: Meena Venkataramanan, "Two States Still Observe King-Lee Day, Honoring Robert E. Lee with MLK," *Washington Post*, January 16, 2023.

34 "It sometimes gets overlooked": William J. Connell, "What Columbus Day Really Means," *American Scholar*, October 4, 2012.

CHAPTER TWO EXCEPTIONAL AND EXCEPTIONALLY VAGUE

35 "I never knew": Christopher Hitchens, "Charles Dickens's Inner Child," *Vanity Fair*, January 5, 2012.

35 "No other nation": Margaret Thatcher, "Speech at Hoover Institution Lunch," Margaret Thatcher Foundation, March 8, 1991.

35   Even when it came: Jill Lepore, *These Truths: A History of the United States* (New York: Norton, 2023).

36   only about one-third: Maya Jasanoff, *Liberty's Exiles: American Loyalists in the Revolutionary World* (New York: Knopf, 2011), 8.

36   So deep was their rift: Paul A. Stellhorn and Michael J. Birkner, eds., *The Governors of New Jersey, 1664–1974: Biographical Essays* (Trenton: New Jersey Historical Commission, 1982), 72–76.

38   "We had in Camp": James E. Seelye, Jr., and Shawn Shelby, eds., *Shaping North America: From Exploration to the American Revolution* (Santa Barbara, CA: ABC-CLIO, 2018), 970–71.

38   "Most were working-class": Joseph J. Ellis, *The Cause: The American Revolution and Its Discontents, 1773–1783* (New York: Liveright, 2021), 240.

39   "The road to glory": George Washington, "7 August 1782, General Orders," in *The Writings of George Washington*, ed. John C. Fitzpatrick (Washington, DC: Government Printing Office), 329.

39   Harry Washington: Francine Uenuma, "Enslaved by George Washington, This Man Escaped to Freedom—and Joined the British Army," *Smithsonian Magazine*, June 14, 2023.

40   "Every other aspect": Paul H. Smith, ed., *Letters of Delegates to Congress, 1774–1789: August 1774–August 1775* (Washington, DC: Library of Congress, 1976), 378.

41   "in his first message": James M. McPherson, "Out of War, a New Nation," *Prologue Magazine* 42, no. 1 (Spring 2010).

42   "King George": Ellis, *The Cause*, 14.

42   "the final Articles of Confederation": Lepore, *These Truths*, 183.

42   Its most recent amendments: "The 26th Amendment," Richard Nixon Presidential Library and Museum, June 17, 2021; "The Twenty-seventh Amendment," United States House of Representatives.

43   "It has exacted": Ryan D. Doerfler and Samuel Moyn, "The Constitution Is Broken and Should Not Be Reclaimed," *New York Times*, August 19, 2022.

43   "Our myths have not": Nikole Hannah-Jones, *The 1619 Project: A New Origin Story* (New York: Random House, 2021), xxxii.

43   In 2023, the United States: "Global Gender Gap Report 2023," World Economic Forum, June 2023, 11, https://www3.weforum.org/docs/WEF _GGGR_2023.pdf.

43   The word *meritocracy* was born: "The History and Future of Meritocracy," *The Economist*, June 3, 2021.

43   The phrase *American exceptionalism*: Donald E. Pease, "American Studies After American Exceptionalism? Toward a Comparative Analysis of Imperial State Exceptionalism," in *Globalizing American Studies*, ed. Brian T. Edwards and Dilip Parameshwar Gaonkar (Chicago: University of Chicago Press, 2010), 58–59.

43   The term *bootstrapping*: Melissa Mohr, "How the 'Bootstrap' Idiom
     Became a Cultural Ideal," *Christian Science Monitor,* October 4, 2021.

44   The embiggening concept: Herbert Hoover, "Principles and Ideals of the
     United States Government," October 22, 1928, UVA Miller Center.

44   Then there's the *American Dream*: James Truslow Adams, *The Epic of
     America* (New York: Little, Brown, 1931), 214–15.

44   *the pursuit of property*: Arthur M. Schlesinger, "The Lost Meaning of the
     'Pursuit of Happiness,'" *William and Mary Quarterly* 21, no. 3 (1964):
     326–27.

44   the state's lawmakers: Arika Herron, "'Divisive Concepts' in Indiana Anti–
     Critical Race Theory Bill Found in 26 States," *Indianapolis Star,* Janu-
     ary 14, 2022.

44   More than a few: Sarah Schwartz, "Where Critical Race Theory Is Under
     Attack," *Education Week*, February 16, 2023.

45   "One line of questioning": Aleksandra Appleton and Stephanie Wang,
     "How Indiana's Anti-CRT Bill Failed Even with a GOP Supermajority,"
     Chalkbeat, March 10, 2022.

45   "In practice, it is unclear": Ana Ceballos, "What's Ahead for Florida Stu-
     dents, Parents After Passage of 'Don't Say Gay' Bill?," *Tampa Bay Times*,
     March 8, 2022.

46   The town: "Our History," Frankton, Indiana, https://www.townoffrankton
     .com.

46   "Frankton is a community": "Our History," Frankton, Indiana.

50   "Our histories tend": W. E. B. Du Bois, *Black Reconstruction in America: An
     Essay Toward a History of the Part Which Black Folk Played in the Attempt to
     Reconstruct Democracy in America, 1860–1880* (London: Oxford University
     Press, 2014), xx.

50   the Green Feather Movement: "The Green Feather Movement," Indiana
     University, August 1, 2019.

50   slavery had provided: Kevin Sullivan and Lori Rozsa, "DeSantis Doubles
     Down on Claim That Some Blacks Benefited from Slavery," *Washington
     Post*, July 22, 2023.

50   the American Library Association reported: "Top 10 Most Challenged
     Books List," American Library Association.

51   "Social studies": "Education Code," Texas State Legislature, May 30,
     1995, https://statutes.capitol.texas.gov/Docs/ED/htm/ED.28.htm.

51   "The yawning gap": Dana Goldstein, "Two States. Eight Textbooks. Two
     American Stories," *New York Times*, January 12, 2020.

52   overwhelming majority of Americans: "Census Bureau Releases New
     Educational Attainment Data," United States Census Bureau, Febru-
     ary 24, 2022.

52   the gap in adult life expectancy: Anne Case and Angus Deaton, "Without a
     College Degree, Life in America Is Staggeringly Shorter," *New York Times*,
     October 3, 2023.

53 "Doll cannot stand alone": "Madam C. J. Walker Barbie Inspiring Women Doll, Collectible Gift for 6 Years & Older," Mattel.

CHAPTER THREE LANDFALL

54 "For my own part": Benjamin Franklin, "From Benjamin Franklin to Sarah Bache, 26 January 1784," National Archives, https://founders.archives .gov/.

55 "often very lousy": Franklin, "From Benjamin Franklin to Sarah Bache, 26 January 1784."

55 his whispered battles: *The Colbert Report*, March 1, 2006; *The Office*, February 1, 2007; Allen B. Schwartz, "Medical Mystery: A Founding Father's Foot Infirmity," *Philadelphia Inquirer*, October 6, 2017.

55 an inventor: "Benjamin Franklin's Inventions," Franklin Institute.

55 "Dost thou love life?": "Benjamin Franklin's Famous Quotes," Franklin Institute.

55 "There are no gains": Julia Hanna, "Ben Franklin's 'Way to Wealth' Was a Worldwide Introduction to American Capitalism," *Forbes*, August 31, 2015.

55 "the first great American": Walter A. McDougall, "William Penn, Benjamin Franklin, and the American Founding: The Philadelphia Factor," Foreign Policy Research Institute, July 16, 2020.

55 possibly fathering: Thomas A. Foster, "Ben Franklin: Ahead of His Time?," Huffington Post, July 2, 2014.

55 "I followed Ben Franklin's schedule": Stephanie Vozza, "What Happened When I Followed Ben Franklin's Schedule for a Month," Fast Company, January 15, 2019.

56 "The Way to Wealth": "The Way to Wealth," Baker Library Bloomberg Center, Harvard Business School.

56 Franklin's general approach: "Financial Independence Lessons from Ben Franklin," Wealthy Doc.

56 "was published in expensive folios": Hanna, "Ben Franklin's 'Way to Wealth.'"

56 of which he claimed to sell: "Poor Richard, 1733," National Archives, https://founders.archives.gov/.

56 "a proper vehicle": Benjamin Franklin, *The Autobiography of Benjamin Franklin*, ed. Leonard W. Labaree et al. (New Haven, CT: Yale University Press, 1964), 146.

56 "inculcated industry and frugality": Franklin, *The Autobiography of Benjamin Franklin*.

56 "written in part": Steven Forde, "Benjamin Franklin's *Autobiography* and the Education of America," *American Political Science Review* 86, no. 2 (1992): 357.

56 The private letters: William B. Evans, "John Adams' Opinion of Benja-

min Franklin," *Pennsylvania Magazine of History and Biography* 92, no. 2 (1968): 220–38.

57 "Why then did": D. H. Lawrence, *Studies in Classic American Literature*, eds. Ezra Greenspan, Lindeth Vasey, and John Worthen (Cambridge, UK: Cambridge University Press, 2003), 30.

57 "He was always proud": Mark Twain, "The Late Benjamin Franklin," *The Galaxy*, July 1870, 138–40.

58 "A few poor souls": Joshua Mitchell, *The Fragility of Freedom: Tocqueville on Religion, Democracy, and the American Future* (Chicago: University of Chicago Press, 1999), 38.

59 "The latter narrative": Annette Gordon-Reed, "Estebanico's America," *The Atlantic*, July 2021, 64.

59 "Some preferred and chose": Alden Vaughn, *The Puritan Tradition in America, 1620–1730* (Lebanon, NH: University of New England Press, 1972), 42.

59 "Her new assignment": John McPhee, "Travels of the Rock," *New Yorker*, February 26, 1990, 108.

60 the workers each received: "The English Establish a Foothold at Jamestown, 1606–1610," Library of Congress.

60 "just and equal Laws": "The Mayflower Compact," Mayflower Society, https://themayflowersociety.org/.

60 Governance over Jamestown: John Smith, *The Generall Historie of Virginia, New-England, and the Summer Isles* (London: Printed by I. D. and I. H. for Michael Sparkes, 1631), 83.

61 "perhaps, the only instance": John Quincy Adams, "Oration at Plymouth, Delivered at Plymouth Mass. December 22, 1802 in Commemoration of the Landing of the Pilgrims," *Daily Republican*, December 22, 2002.

61 "They were among": James T. Kloppenberg, *Toward Democracy: The Struggle for Self-Rule in European and American Thought* (New York: Oxford University Press, 2016), 80.

62 "Religion and profit jump together": Kloppenberg, *Toward Democracy*, 81.

62 One of the many *Mayflower* passengers: This section is drawn from various parts of Nathaniel Philbrick's terrific *Mayflower: A Story of Courage, Community, War* (New York: Penguin, 2006). Four stars, great holiday fun.

62 For example, one 2017 study: Kira Schabram and Sally Maitlis, "Negotiating the Challenges of a Calling: Emotion and Enacted Sensemaking in Animal Shelter Work," *Academy of Management Journal* 60, no. 2 (2017), 584–609.

63 he would show the Pilgrims: Much of this section on Tisquantum comes from these sources: Charles C. Mann, *1491: New Revelations of the Americas Before Columbus* (New York: Knopf Doubleday, 2006), 36–39; Eric Jay Dolin, *Fur, Fortune, and Empire: The Epic History of the Fur Trade in America* (New York: Norton, 2011), 41.

63 "their pilot to bring": William Bradford, *Of Plymouth Plantation, 1620–1647* (New York: Knopf, 1952), 81.

64 the original Thanksgiving: Alice Hutton, " 'The Gooey Overlay of Sweetness over Genocide': The Myth of the 'First Thanksgiving,' " *The Guardian*, November 25, 2021.

65 "For peace and for survival": Philbrick, *Mayflower*, 348.

65 "Thus the true sinners": Robert S. Michaelsen, "Changes in the Puritan Concept of Calling or Vocation," *New England Quarterly* 26, no. 3 (1953), 329.

65 the Englishman Thomas Morton: Sue Scheible, "Remembering Some Great May Day Celebrations in Quincy," *Patriot Ledger*, May 2, 2020.

66 "most full of humanity": John Adams, "John Adams to Thomas Jefferson, 12 October 1812," National Archives, https://founders.archives.gov/.

66 "observing any such day": Stephen Nissenbaum, *The Battle for Christmas: A Cultural History of America's Most Cherished Holiday* (New York: Knopf, 1996), 14.

66 "They for whom": "When Americans Banned Christmas," *The Week*, January 8, 2015.

66 "there was no": Ellis, *The Cause*, 22.

66 Horatio Alger: Timothy Noah, "The Mobility Myth," *New Republic*, February 7, 2012.

66 As noted before: Wendy Warren, *New England Bound: Slavery and Colonization in Early America* (New York: Liveright, 2017).

66 Copying the design and cynicism: John E. Hansan "Poor Relief in Early America," VCU Libraries Social Welfare History Project, 2011.

67 "Some colonies required": Randy Albelda and Chris Tilly, *Glass Ceilings and Bottomless Pits: Women's Work, Women's Poverty* (Boston: South End Press, 1997), 89.

67 "the separation": Michaelsen, "Changes in the Puritan Concept."

68 "where the Streets are said": Benjamin Franklin, "Information to Those Who Would Remove to America [before March 1784]," *The Papers of Benjamin Franklin*, vol. 41, *September 16, 1783, through February 29, 1784*, ed. Ellen R. Cohn (New Haven: Yale University Press, 2014), 597–608.

CHAPTER FOUR EARN THIS

70 a solid majority of Americans: Jens Manuel Krogstad, Mark Hugo Lopez, and Jeffery S. Passel, "A Majority of Americans Say Immigrants Mostly Fill Jobs U.S. Citizens Do Not Want," Pew Research Center, June 10, 2020; Ana Gonzalez-Barrera and Phillip Connor, "Around the World, More Say Immigrants Are a Strength Than a Burden," March 14, 2019; "Immigration," Gallup.

70 Immigrants are 80 percent: Pierre Azoulay et al., "Immigration and Entre-

preneurship in the United States," *American Economic Review: Insights* 4, no. 1 (2022): 71–88.

70 immigrant-founded businesses: Azoulay et al., "Immigration and Entrepreneurship in the United States."

70 are far less likely: Michael T. Light, Jingying He, and Jason P. Robey, "Comparing Crime Rates Between Undocumented Immigrants, Legal Immigrants, and Native-Born US Citizens in Texas," *Proceedings of the National Academy of Sciences of the United States of America*, December 7, 2020.

70 pay $1.38 in taxes: Elizabeth Trovall, "Immigrants' Taxes Play an Outsized Role in the U.S. Government's Fiscal Health," Marketplace, April 11, 2023.

70 each year, undocumented Americans: "Undocumented Immigrants' State & Local Tax Contributions," Institute on Taxation and Economic Policy, March 1, 2017.

71 "I came to America": Jill Young Miller, "Immigration Jewels," *South Florida Sun Sentinel*, December 26, 1996.

71 There are roughly 11 million people: A. K. Sandoval-Strausz, "A Path to Citizenship for 11 Million Immigrants Is a No-Brainer," *Washington Post*, February 24, 2021.

72 "helping people is on": Ronny Chieng, *Asian Comedian Destroys America!*, Netflix, December 5, 2019.

74 The harshest action: Alisa Reznick, "'Show Me Your Papers': A Decade After SB 1070," Arizona Public Media, July 30, 2020.

75 By 2018, the army: Martha Mendoza and Garance Burke, "US Army Quietly Discharging Immigrant Recruits," Associated Press, July 5, 2018.

76 It's there that his host: Nick Bilton and Evelyn M. Rusli, "For Founders to Decorators, Facebook Riches," *New York Times*, February 1, 2012.

76 "There's nowhere else": *Anthony Bourdain: Parts Unknown*, CNN, season 1, episode 2, April 21, 2013.

77 Even before roughly two dozen: Kat Stafford et al., "Deep-Rooted Racism, Discrimination Permeate US Military," Associated Press, May 27, 2021.

77 In 2018, a *Military Times* poll: Leo Shane III, "White Nationalism Remains a Problem for the Military, Poll Suggests," *Military Times*, February 28, 2019.

CHAPTER FIVE FORDING THE RIVER

80 "We have made": Grover Cleveland, "President Cleveland's Address," *Chicago Daily Tribune*, May 2, 1893, 12.

80 Next came cannon fire: *Dedicatory and Opening Ceremonies of the World's Columbian Exposition* (Chicago: Stone, Kastler & Painter, 1893).

81 many reportedly wept: Robert Muccigrosso, *Celebrating the New World:*

Chicago's Columbian Exposition of 1893 (Chicago: Ivan R. Dee, 1993), 176–78.

81 a showcase of the Gilded Age zeitgeist: Erik Larsen, *The Devil in the White City: Murder, Magic and Madness at the Fair That Changed America* (New York: Crown, 2003).

81 Paris' new marvel: Kristi Finefield, "The Washington Monument: A Long Journey to the Top," Library of Congress, September 19, 2019.

81 a six-month run: Neil Steinberg, "Aunt Jemima Welcomes Us into an 1893 World's Fair That's Not So Fun to Recall," *Chicago Sun-Times*, May 1, 2018.

82 Attractions like the World's Congress of Beauty: Stephen M. Silverman, *The Amusement Park: 900 Years of Thrills and Spills, and the Dreamers and Schemers Who Built Them* (New York: Black Dog & Leventhal, 2019), 121.

82 three thousand lights: "George Ferris: The Ferris Wheel," Massachusetts Institute of Technology.

82 The Columbian Exposition: Chella Vaidyanathan, "Columbian Exposition of 1893," Johns Hopkins Sheridan Libraries, March 12, 2012.

82 Despite its success: "Ashes of George W. G. Ferris," *New York Times*, March 8, 1898, 5.

83 legends persist about hard-hit citizens: "World Exhibitions First Flower'd Magically in London in Queen Victoria's Time," *New York Times*, August 22, 1964, 5; Phil Patton, "'Sell the Cookstove if Necessary, but Come to the Fair,'" *Smithsonian Magazine* 24, no. 3 (1993): 38–51.

83 "Its exhibits displayed": Silverman, *The Amusement Park*, 111.

83 iconic American brands: Maggie Borden, "Food History: The 1893 Columbian Exposition in Chicago," James Beard Foundation, September 15, 2014.

83 The familiar blue ribbon: Katherine Nagasawa, "From Vienna Beef to PBR: Five Food and Drink Legacies of the 1893 World's Fair," WBEZ Chicago, May 18, 2019.

83 The company Vienna Beef: Nagasawa, "From Vienna Beef to PBR."

83 the vast array of goods: Thorstein Veblen, *The Theory of the Leisure Class* (London: Macmillan, 1912), 91.

84 After seeing a demonstration: Borden, "Food History."

84 in a poem that became: Elizabeth Dunlop Richter, "'America the Beautiful': The Chicago Connection," *Classic Chicago Magazine*, November 7, 2018, https://classicchicagomagazine.com/america-the-beautiful-the-chicago -connection/.

84 Helen Keller: Larson, *The Devil in the White City*, 291.

84 Henry Ford also passed: "Brochure and Map of Ford Exhibition Building and 'The World of Tomorrow,' New York World's Fair, 1939–1940," The Henry Ford Museum.

84 L. Frank Baum modeled: Silverman, *The Amusement Park*, 111.

84 "a dry run": Patton, "'Sell the Cookstove if Necessary.'"

84 Nancy Green: Nagasawa, "From Vienna Beef to PBR."

84 "He evidently feels": 1893 advertisement for Aunt Jemima's pancake flour, Chicago *Inter Ocean*, January 2, 1893, at Scott, "Remembering Nancy Green, Aunt Jemima, and the 1893 World's Fair," World's Fair: Chicago, 1893, September 9, 2020.

85 In the summer of 2020: Alexandra Olson and Matt Ott, "Aunt Jemima Brand Retired by Quaker Due to Racial Stereotype," Associated Press, June 17, 2020.

85 Buffalo Bill Cody: Silverman, *The Amusement Park*, 118–20.

85 Similarly impressive: "Bertha Honoré Palmer," Britannica Money, May 15, 2024; Terri Colby, "Taste the Palmer House Brownies for a Bit of Chicago History," *Forbes*, August 31, 2018.

85 Sophia Hayden: Larson, *The Devil in the White City*, 84.

85 the vast efforts made: Don Behm, "Waukesha, Once Swimming in Water Resources, Now Struggles," *Milwaukee Journal Sentinel*, April 19, 2010.

85 Carter Harrison III: Alison Martin, "This Week in History: Mayor Carter Harrison Shot in Mansion," *Chicago Sun-Times*, October 29, 2020.

86 In a standout moment: Elliott M. Rudwick and August Meier, "Black Man in the 'White City': Negroes and the Columbian Exposition, 1893," *Phylon* 26, no. 4 (1965): 355.

86 "Theoretically open to all Americans": Ida B. Wells, *The Reason Why the Colored American Is Not in the World's Columbian Exposition*, 1893, https://digital.library.upenn.edu/women/wells/exposition/exposition.html.

86 the fair's planners added: Rudwick and Meier, "Black Man in the 'White City,'" 359–60.

86 "The real problem has been": Christopher Robert Reed, *"All the World Is Here!": The Black Presence at White City* (Bloomington: Indiana University Press, 2002), 135.

86 Douglass implored the group: Reed, *"All the World Is Here!,"* 135.

87 in 1896, the U.S. Supreme Court: *"Plessy v. Ferguson* (1896)," National Archives, https://www.archives.gov/.

87 The next World's Fair: Nneka Okona, "These World's Fair Sites Reveal a History of Segregation," *National Geographic*, February 8, 2021.

87 its 1898 counterpart: David J. Peavler, "African Americans in Omaha and the 1898 Trans-Mississippi and International Exposition." *Journal of African American History* 93, no. 3 (2008): 337.

88 "Since the days": Frederick J. Turner, "The Significance of the Frontier in American History (1893)," Annual Report of the American Historical Association, 1893, 197–227.

89 "prevalent in political speech": Colin Woodard, "How the Myth of the American Frontier Got Its Start," *Smithsonian Magazine*, January–February 2023.

90 "The American cowboy is often": "When Chicago and the West Were One," *Chicago Tribune*, September 14, 1999.

90 "They put little": Patrick J. Kiger, "10 Ways the Transcontinental Railroad Changed America," History, September 4, 2019.

90 railroad companies had created: John Steele Gordon, "Standard Time: We All Live By What Happened on November 18, 1883," *American Heritage* (July/August 2001): 22–23.

91 presidents Dwight D. Eisenhower, Ronald Reagan, and Bill Clinton: Meryl Gottlieb, "Here Are 13 American Presidents' Favorite Movies of All Time," Business Insider, September 10, 2016.

91 "Movement has been": Turner, "The Significance of the Frontier in American History (1893)."

92 "No one assimilates": Gilbert Seldes, *The Stammering Century* (New York: New York Review Books, 2012), 39.

92 By one account: Alexandre Tanzi, "Americans Have Never Been So Unwilling to Relocate for a New Job," Bloomberg, May 16, 2023.

94 Route 66 has: Patton, "'Sell the Cookstove if Necessary,'" 230.

95 "I challenge anyone": Robert Antonson, *Route 66 Still Kicks: Driving America's Main Street* (Toronto: Dundurn, 2012), 80; "Route 66: Radiance, Rust, and Revival on the Mother Road," online history exhibition, Albuquerque Museum, https://www.cabq.gov/.

95 "a thoroughfare for freedom": Patton, "'Sell the Cookstove if Necessary,'" 243.

98 "The only essential thing": Paul Graham, "Startup = Growth," September 2012.

99 over half of Fortune 500 companies: "Insight Report Finds 52% of Companies in the Fortune 500 List Have Disappeared over the Last 20 Years," Yahoo! Finance, November 15, 2023.

99 "The evidence of": Ryan Beck and Amit Seru, "Short-Term Thinking Is Poisoning American Business," *New York Times*, December 21, 2019.

99 one bellwether survey: John R. Graham, Campbell R. Harvey, and Shiva Rajgopal, "The Economic Implications of Corporate Financial Reporting," *Journal of Accounting and Economics* 40, nos. 1–3 (2005): 3–73.

101 "The 1920 census": Chris M. Messer, Thomas E. Shriver, and Alison E. Adams, "The Destruction of Black Wall Street: Tulsa's 1921 Riot and the Eradication of Accumulated Wealth," *American Journal of Economics and Sociology* 77, nos. 3–4 (2018): 792.

101 every dollar that entered: Shomari Wills, *Black Fortunes: The Story of the First Six African Americans Who Escaped Slavery and Became Millionaires* (New York: Amistad, 2019).

CHAPTER SIX RIGHT OF WAY

103 the song had been: "Billboard Hot 100," Week of April 13, 1974, *Billboard*.

105 Later, the buzz: Nuria Martinez-Keel, "Can 'Killers of the Flower Moon' Be Taught in Oklahoma Classrooms? Teachers Not Sure Under Law," *The Oklahoman*, October 16, 2023.

107   "The boarding schools": "History and Culture: Boarding Schools," Part-
        nership with Native Americans, https://nativepartnership.org/.

107   the students were taught: David R. M. Beck, *Unfair Labor?: American
        Indians and the 1893 World's Columbian Exposition in Chicago* (Lincoln: Uni-
        versity of Nebraska Press, 2019), 40.

107   "It shows concretely": Daniel M. Browning, "Annual Report of the
        Commissioner of Indian Affairs, for the Year 1893," in *The Abridgment:
        Containing Messages of the President of the United States to the Two Houses of
        Congress with Reports of Departments and Selections from Accompanying Papers*
        (Washington, DC: Government Printing Office, 1894), 698.

108   "Almost immediately our names": James E. Seelye, Jr., and Steven A. Lit-
        tleton, *Voices of the American Indian Experience*, vol. 2: 1877–present (Lon-
        don: Bloomsbury, 2013), 517.

108   In the classroom: "Boarding Schools," Partnership with Native Americans.

108   One chilling quote: Richard Henry Pratt, *Battlefield and Classroom: Four
        Decades with the American Indian, 1867–1904* (New Haven, CT: Yale Uni-
        versity Press, 1964), 335.

109   nearly went bankrupt: Victoria A. Baena, "The Harvard Indian College,"
        The Harvard Crimson, March 24, 2011.

111   "The Pioneer Woman": Amanda Fortini, "O Pioneer Woman!," *New
        Yorker*, May 2, 2011.

112   the Drummonds rank: Christabel Duah, "Government pays 'The Pioneer
        Woman' $2 Million a Year to Use Her Massive Estate," *Atlanta Journal-
        Constitution*, November 15, 2017.

112   "They were put in charge": Rachel Adams-Heard, "Land Is Power,
        and the Osage Nation Is Buying Theirs Back," Bloomberg, October 12,
        2022.

112   In a 2023 statement: "Osage Nation on 'Killers of the Flower Moon,'"
        the Osage Nation, accessed July 22, 2024, https://www.osagenation-nsn
        .gov/news-events/news/osage-nation-killers-flower-moon.

114   "Whole continents of contemporary worry": Fortini, "O Pioneer
        Woman!"

115   "replicated in the Philippines": Maggie Blackhawk, "How 'Killers of the
        Flower Moon' Presses Up Against the Limits of Empathy," *New York
        Times*, January 25, 2024.

115   Though descended from ancestors: "Life of Thomas Alva Edison,"
        Library of Congress.

116   he was a bad student: Casey Cep, "The Real Nature of Thomas Edison's
        Genius," *New Yorker*, October 21, 2019.

116   He hustled newspapers: Cep, "The Real Nature of Thomas Edison's
        Genius."

116   regarding sleep as a "criminal": James B. Maas, *Power Sleep: The Revolu-
        tionary Program That Prepares Your Mind for Peak Performance* (New York:
        William Morrow, 1998), 1.

116 "The Edison symbol": Wyn Wachhorst, *Thomas Alva Edison, an American Myth* (Cambridge, MA: MIT Press, 1981), 328.

117 One analysis of early-twenty-first-century start-ups: Haje Jan Kamps, "Breaking a Myth: Data Shows You Don't Actually Need a Co-founder," TechCrunch, August 26, 2016.

117 Similar research also found: Kamps, "Breaking a Myth."

117 "were more likely": Sheena Iyengar, *The Art of Choosing* (New York: Grand Central Publishing, 2010), 47.

117 "referred more to institutional factors": Iyengar, *The Art of Choosing*, 48.

118 Disney's amusement parks: Christopher Palmieri, "Disney's Black Princess Replaces 'Song of the South' in Ride," Bloomberg, June 25, 2020.

118 Cream of Wheat: Marie Fazio, "Cream of Wheat to Drop Black Chef from Packaging, Company Says," *New York Times*, September 27, 2020.

119 a chain reaction: Allegra Frank, "What's in a Name? For Some Brands, a Racist History Primed to Be Toppled," Vox, December 14, 2020.

119 "Taking the stereotypical image": Fazio, "Cream of Wheat to Drop Black Chef."

119 Jamie Dimon: Thorton McEnery, "Jamie Dimon Drops into Mt. Kisco Chase Branch, Takes a Knee with Staff," *New York Post*, June 5, 2020.

119 the bank giant urged: Levi Sumagaysay, "Hours After CEO Decried Inequality, JPMorgan Seeks to Quash Call for Racial-Equity Audit," MarketWatch, April 7, 2021.

119 "it saddens me": Prem Thakker, "Republican Lawmaker Says Abortion Makes Us Lose Potential Laborers," *New Republic*, June 15, 2023.

119 over a million dollars: Clare O'Connor, "Report: Walmart Workers Cost Taxpayers $6.2 Billion in Public Assistance," *Forbes*, April 15, 2014.

120 over 25 percent: Peyton Bigora, "Walmart Captures Nearly 26% of SNAP Grocery Dollars," Grocery Dive, May 19, 2023.

CHAPTER SEVEN BUSTLE

123 physically resistant to the barricades: Jess McHugh, "Old Paris Is No More," *Lapham's Quarterly*, July 29, 2019.

125 "*Emily in Paris* Is like": Sangeeta Singh-Kurtz, "*Emily in Paris* Is like Happy Hour for the Brain," The Cut, October 2, 2020.

125 "Emily's story": Alex Abed-Santos, "The Seductive Absurdity of Netflix's *Emily in Paris*," Vox, October 7, 2020.

125 "At times, I wondered": Rebecca Nicholson, "*Emily in Paris* Review—an Excruciating Exorcism of French Cliches," *The Guardian*, October 2, 2020.

125 "Beneath the Bambi-like visage": Iva Dixit, "Emily Is Still in Paris. Why Are We Still Watching?," *New York Times Magazine*, December 23, 2022.

126 "Maybe the creators": Elaine Sciolino, "'Ridicule': The French Reaction to 'Emily in Paris,'" *New York Times*, October 2, 2020.

127 "the right to disconnect": Hugh Schofield, "The Plan to Ban Work Emails Out of Hours," BBC, May 11, 2016.

127 "Employees physically leave": Schofield, "The Plan to Ban Work Emails Out of Hours."

128 a number of countries: Megan Cerullo, "After-Hours Work Emails and Calls Are Facing More Legal Restrictions," CBS News, February 3, 2023.

128 a version of the law: Alec Regimbal, "Calif. Bill That Would Punish Bosses for Texting Workers After Hours Shelved," SFGATE, April 2, 2024.

128 created a cherished standard: Peter Weber, "France Aspires to Work by Working Less. Is It Working?," *The Week*, March 29, 2023.

128 "I mean . . . the Senate": Michael Barbaro, "The Disciple Strikes Back: Rubio Bests Bush in a Key Moment," *New York Times*, October 28, 2015.

128 "Article 8 said": Gregory Warner and Katz Laszlo, "Lunching@Work: When Eating at Your Desk Is Forbidden," *Rough Translation*, season 7, episode 2, June 8, 2022.

128 As presidential politics go: Paul Harris, "Newt Gingrich's Attack Ad Gives Mitt Romney a French Dressing-Down," *The Guardian*, January 13, 2012; Roger Cohen, "The Republicans' Barb: John Kerry 'Looks French,'" *International Herald Tribune*, April 3, 2004.

129 Companies are obliged by law: "Titres-restaurant: les 5 informations à connaître" [Meal vouchers: the 5 things you need to know], Ministère de l'Économie des Finances et de la Souveraineté Industrielle et Numérique, March 13, 2023, https://www.economie.gouv.fr/entreprises/titres-restaurant.

129 Employers are required: "Titres-restaurant [Meal vouchers]."

129 "less like a place to eat": Jia Tolentino, *Trick Mirror: Reflections on Self-Delusion* (New York: Random House, 2019), 66.

129 "The lunch and dinner rush": Claire Suddath, "How Chipotle's DJ, Chris Golub, Creates His Playlists," Bloomberg, October 17, 2013.

129 62 percent of Americans: Malia Wollan, "Failure to Lunch," *New York Times Magazine*, February 25, 2016.

129 Food52 launched a column: "Not Sad Desk Lunch," Food52.

130 "We believe desk lunches": Food52, *The Not Sad Desk Revolution*, YouTube, October 14, 2015, https://www.youtube.com/watch?v=xikXIbPLY40.

130 One of the earliest uses: "Lunch al Desko," *Bon Appétit*.

130 "Meal periods": "Breaks and Meal Periods," U.S. Department of Labor.

131 The growing inaccessibility: Norimitsu Onishi, "Holidays Are a Way of Life in France in August. Yellow Vests Can't Afford Them," *New York Times*, August 29, 2019.

131 "Of course your boss": Eleanor Beardsley, "For French Law on Right to 'Disconnect,' Much Support—and a Few Doubts," NPR, January 3, 2017.

132 enjoys levels of productivity: "Productivity Insights," Organisation for Economic Co-operation and Development, February 2019, https://www.oecd.org/france/oecd-productivity-insights-france.pdf.

132 almost on par: "GDP per Hour Worked," Organisation for Economic Co-operation and Development.

132 "The French chose time": Eduardo Porter, *The Price of Everything: Finding Method in the Madness of What Things Cost* (New York: Penguin, 2011), 64.

132 roughly a third of whom: Jagdish Khubchandani and James H. Price, "Short Sleep Duration in Working American Adults, 2010–2018," *Journal of Community Health* 45 (2020): 219–27.

132 France's longer life expectancy: Munira Z. Gunja, Evan D. Gumas, and Reginald D. Williams II, "U.S. Health Care from a Global Perspective, 2022: Accelerating Spending, Worsening Outcomes," Commonwealth Fund, January 31, 2023.

133 only about 25 percent: "Employee Benefits in the United States, March 2023," U.S. Bureau of Labor Statistics, September 2023.

133 "No one should be": David Burkus, "The Real Reason Google Serves All That Free Food," *Forbes*, July 2, 2015.

133 "Maybe they'll hit": Burkus, "The Real Reason Google Serves All That Free Food."

134 it turned the problem: "The Google Diet: Search Giant Overhauled Its Eating Options to 'Nudge' Healthy Choices," ABC News, January 17, 2013.

134 "In seven weeks": "The Google Diet," ABC News.

134 "It is used to attract": Alix Martichoux, "Is Unlimited Vacation Time Really Unlimited?," The Hill, June 25, 2023.

135 American workers take: Bryan Lufkin, "The Smoke and Mirrors of Unlimited Paid Time Off," BBC, May 23, 2022.

136 John Maynard Keynes predicted: Derek Thompson, "Workism Is Making Americans Miserable," *The Atlantic*, February 24, 2019.

136 "How to use his freedom": Derek Thompson, "The Free-Time Paradox in America," *The Atlantic*, September 13, 2016.

136 "The economists of the early": Thompson, "Workism Is Making Americans Miserable."

136 "Conspicuous abstention from labor": Steven G. Medema and Warren J. Samuels, *The History of Economic Thought: A Reader*, 2nd edition (London: Routledge, 2013), 651.

137 In a 2023 survey: "The Wealth Report: Closing the Protection Gap in a Time of Increasing Risk," Chubb, 2023, 4–6.

137 "They valued self-sufficiency": Rachel Sherman, *Uneasy Street: The Anxieties of Affluence* (Princeton, NJ: Princeton University Press, 2019), 22.

138 "knowledge-intensive" economy: Silvia Bellezza, Neeru Paharia, and Anat Keinan, "Research: Why Americans Are So Impressed by Busyness," *Harvard Business Review*, December 15, 2016.

138 "By telling others": Bellezza, Paharia, and Keinan, "Research."

138 the top 10 percent: Carmen Ang, "Do Top Earners Work More Hours? It

Depends Which Country They Live In," World Economic Forum, September 27, 2022.

140 "Industry experts predicted": "Taylor Swift Reacts to Selling Nearly 1.3 Million Album Copies by Lip-Syncing a Kendrick Lamar Rap," ABC News, November 5, 2014.

141 owe Apple a "creator fee": Paul Kunert, "Apple Owes Brit iOS App Devs Millions from Excessively High Commission, Lawsuit Claims," The Register, July 25, 2023.

141 approved by Barbie's parent company: Eliana Dockterman, "How Barbie Came to Life," *Time*, June 27, 2023.

141 a list of more than forty: Bella Arnold, "What Else Is in Mattel's Toy Box?," Vulture, July 27, 2023.

142 "Stop by a Danish office": "Work-Life Balance," Ministry of Foreign Affairs of Denmark, https://denmark.dk/society-and-business/work-life-balance.

142 "the need to demonstrate": "Work-Life Balance," Ministry of Foreign Affairs of Denmark.

142 try ordering their groceries: "Work-Life Balance," U.S. Department of State; Jen Uscher, "5 Tips for Better Work/Life Balance," WebMD, March 28, 2013.

143 "Our very idea": Jenny Odell, *How to Do Nothing: Resisting the Attention Economy* (London: Melville House, 2020), 25.

143 "saying no to something at work": Rainesford Stauffer, *All the Gold Stars: Reimagining Ambition and the Ways We Strive* (New York: Hachette Books, 2023), 167.

144 neither measure affects a firm's profitability: Morten Bennedsen, Elena Simintzi, Margarita Tsoutsoura, and Daniel Wolfenzon, "Research: Gender Pay Gaps Shrink When Companies Are Required to Disclose Them," *Harvard Business Review*, January 23, 2019; Conny Overland and Samani Niuosha, "The Sheep Watching the Shepherd: Employee Representation on the Board and Earnings Quality," *European Accounting Review* 31, no. 5 (May 28, 2021).

144 "Shift as much as possible": Jena McGregor, "How 'Busyness' Became a Bona Fide Status Symbol," *Washington Post*, December 20, 2016.

144 In 2018, Senator Elizabeth Warren: Senator Elizabeth Warren, "Companies Shouldn't Be Accountable Only to Shareholders," *Wall Street Journal*, August 14, 2018.

145 "Only 41 percent": "Vacation Time Recharges US Workers, but Positive Effects Vanish Within Days, New Survey Finds," American Psychological Association, June 27, 2018.

145 take at least fifteen days off: Sarah Green Carmichael, "Goldman Sachs Now Has Wall Street's Best Vacation Policy," Bloomberg, May 19, 2022.

145 which once doled out bonuses: Stephen Grocer, "Wall Street Compensation—'No Clear Rhyme or Reason,'" *Wall Street Journal*, July 30, 2009.

146 Gallup put a *conservative* price tag: Shane McFeely and Ben Wigert, "This Fixable Problem Costs U.S. Businesses $1 Trillion," Gallup, March 13, 2019.

146 "The cost of replacing": McFeely and Wigert, "This Fixable Problem."

CHAPTER EIGHT   HUSTLE

149 36 percent of American workers: "Freelance, Side Hustles, and Gigs: Many More Americans Have Become Independent Workers," McKinsey & Company, August 23, 2022.

149 levels of income inequality: Chad Stone, Danilo Trisi, Arloc Sherman, and Jennifer Beltrán, "A Guide to Statistics on Historical Trends in Income Inequality," Center on Budget and Policy Priorities, January 13, 2020.

149 "You work three jobs?": George W. Bush, "President Discusses Strengthening Social Security in Nebraska," George W. Bush White House Archives, February 4, 2005.

149 The word *hustle*: Isabella Rosario, "When the 'Hustle' Isn't Enough," NPR, April 3, 2020.

149 "By the late 19th": Rosario, "When the 'Hustle' Isn't Enough."

150 Initially narrowed to Black vernacular: Rosario, "When The 'Hustle' Isn't Enough."

150 "forever frustrated, restless, and anxious": Malcolm X, *The Autobiography of Malcolm X* (New York: Random House, 2015), 359.

150 a fashion brand: Marisa Meltzer, "The Ladies Who Launch," The Cut, January 7, 2020.

150 "It doesn't work": Elizabeth Dilts Marshall, "Working from Home 'Doesn't Work for Those Who Want to Hustle': JPMorgan CEO," Reuters, May 4, 2021.

151 "On the one hand": Reeves Wiedeman, "The I in We," *New York*, June 10, 2019.

151 The Red Hot Chili Peppers and Deepak Chopra: Lizzie Widdicombe, "The Rise and Fall of WeWork," *New Yorker*, November 6, 2019.

151 tequila shots were dispensed: Wiedeman, "The I in We."

151 janitor strikes were crushed: David Gelles, "WeWork Ends Combative Dispute with Former Janitorial Workers," *New York Times*, October 13, 2015.

151 a private jet was purchased: Sarah Jackson, "WeWork Founder Adam Neumann Once Threw a Celebratory Bottle of Tequila Through a Glass Panel in His Office, Which Had a Kickboxing Bag and Smoke Eater to Erase Marijuana Fumes, New Book Says," Business Insider, July 19, 2021.

151 collapsed from its dizzying: Stephen Moore, "WeBroke," Medium, June 21, 2023.

151 parachuted out of the mess: Taylor Telford, "Adam Neumann to Exit

WeWork with $1.7 Billion as SoftBank Takes Over," *Washington Post*, October 22, 2019.

152 the writer Jean-Luc Bouchard: Jean-Luc Bouchard, "I Paid $47 an Hour for Someone to Be My Friend," Vox, July 1, 2019.

153 "Workin' five to nine": Dave Paulson, "Dolly Parton changes '9 to 5' song for Super Bowl ad," *The Tennessean*, February 2, 2021.

153 16 percent of Americans: Monica Anderson et al., "The State of Gig Work in 2021," Pew Research Center, December 8, 2021.

153 That growth was led: Andrew Garin et al., *The Evolution of Platform Gig Work, 2012–2021*, Becker Friedman Institute, University of Chicago, May 2023, https://bfi.uchicago.edu/wp-content/uploads/2023/05/BFI _WP_2023-69.pdf.

153 nearly a third: Anderson et al., "The State of Gig Work in 2021."

153 an astonishing 29 percent: Ben Zipperer et al., "National Survey of Gig Workers Paints a Picture of Poor Working Conditions, Low Pay," Economic Policy Institute, June 1, 2022, https://files.epi.org/uploads/250647 .pdf.

153 "Always be hustlin'": Oliver Staley, "Uber Has Replaced Travis Kalanick's Values with Eight New 'Cultural Norms,'" QZ, November 7, 2017.

154 "Some people don't like": Eric Newcomer, "In Video, Uber CEO Argues with Driver over Falling Fares," Bloomberg, February 28, 2017.

154 57 percent of Americans: Britney Nguyen, "Over Half of US Workers Surveyed Want to Work Overtime or Get Extra Shifts to Make More Money as Cost-of-Living Expenses Continue to Rise," Business Insider, October 23, 2022.

154 44 percent of employed Americans: Carmen Reinicke, "44% of Americans Work a Side Hustle to Make Ends Meet—but It May Not Be an Efficient Way to Earn More, Says Expert," CNBC, July 27, 2022.

154 to keep hourly, low-wage workers: Te-Ping Chen, "A Little-Noticed Reason Workers Quit: Too Little Work," *Wall Street Journal*, February 28, 2022.

154 the bottom 20 percent of earners: Ethan Dodd, "Why So Many Americans Hate Their Work Hours," Business Insider, April 5, 2023.

155 Between 1979 and 2021: "The Productivity–Pay Gap," Economic Policy Institute, October 2022.

155 the hourly pay: "The Productivity–Pay Gap," Economic Policy Institute.

155 "Compared with the economy": Jim Tankersley, *The Riches of This Land: The Untold, True Story of America's Middle Class* (New York: PublicAffairs, 2020), 65.

155 the average U.S. household: "Consumer Expenditure Survey, April, 2019," U.S. Bureau of Labor Statistics.

156 credit card debt: Alicia Wallace, "Americans' Credit Card Debt Hits a Record $1 Trillion," CNN, August 8, 2023.

156 a record share of 401(k) participants: Aimee Picchi, "Record Share of

Americans Are Raiding Their 401(k) Plans Due to Hardship," CBS, February 6, 2023.

156 "They are jammed up": Picchi, "Record Share of Americans Are Raiding Their 401(k) Plans Due to Hardship."

156 President Biden had appeared there: Evan Casey, "President Joe Biden Visits Milwaukee Ahead of Inflation Reduction Act Anniversary," Wisconsin Public Radio, August 15, 2023.

157 "Some call it the heartland": CQ Staff, "Transcript: GOP Presidential Hopefuls Debate in Milwaukee," Roll Call, August 24, 2023.

157 The origin of the term: Anne Trubek, "Our Collective Ignorance About the Rust Belt Is Getting Dangerous," *Time*, April 3, 2018.

161 a full two-thirds of U.S. adults: Alec Tyson, Cary Funk, and Brian Kennedy, "What the Data Says about Americans' Views of Climate Change," Pew Research Center, August 9, 2023.

161 70 percent of Americans: Dante Chinni, "Most Americans Want Societal Change but Are Divided over Specifics, Poll Finds," NBC, April 30, 2023.

162 not a single candidate: Rebecca Leber, "The First GOP Debate Reveals a Disturbing Level of Climate Change Denial," Vox, August 24, 2023.

163 Data and modeling: Chang-Tai Hsieh et al., "The Allocation of Talent and U.S. Economic Growth," *Econometrica* 87, no. 5 (2019): 1439–74.

163 "What this paper did": Tankersley, *The Riches of This Land*, 93.

CHAPTER NINE WORTH

167 For most of his career: Katherine Webb-Hehn, "Rural Residents Who Struggle with Mental Illness Are Isolated, Stigmatized, Not Near Help," Youth Today, April 12, 2020.

168 "I always could talk": Webb-Hehn, "Rural Residents Who Struggle with Mental Illness."

169 "Man is dominated": Max Weber, *The Protestant Ethic and the Spirit of Capitalism* (New York: Dover Publications, 2012), 43.

169 6 percent of American workers: Simone Stolzoff, *The Good Enough Job: Reclaiming Life from Work* (New York: Penguin, 2023), 50.

169 "Twenty years later": Stolzoff, *The Good Enough Job*, 50.

169 "do not imagine a career": Charles A. Reich, *The Greening of America* (London: Random House, 1970), 240.

170 "If we recalled": Sarah Jaffe, *Work Won't Love You Back: How Devotion to Our Jobs Keeps Us Exploited, Exhausted, and Alone* (New York: PublicAffairs, 2021), 16.

171 "deflects attention away": Stephen Fineman, "On Being Positive: Concerns and Counterpoints," *Academy of Management Review* 31, no. 2 (2006): 277.

171 "Most Incompetent Coworker": "Most Incompetent Coworker Once Again Shines at Office Halloween Party," The Onion, October 27, 2017.

172 "These hip, shiny workspaces": Apoorva Tadepalli, "Smells like Work," *Los Angeles Review of Books*, April 11, 2018.

172 "When I hear something": Joe Pinsker, "The Dark Side of Saying Work Is 'like a Family,'" *The Atlantic*, February 16, 2022.

172 "In the late '90s": Jody Kohner, "The Real Meaning Behind 'Salesforce Community,'" Salesforce, February 6, 2017.

173 "We Are Ohana": Salesforce, *We Are Ohana*, YouTube, February 10, 2017, https://www.youtube.com/watch?v=g80dO8nfCMQ.

173 "This reminds me": Salesforce, *We Are Ohana*.

173 referencing company layoffs in 2023: Isabella Simonetti and Kalley Huang, "Salesforce to Lay Off 10% of Staff and Cut Office Space," *New York Times*, January 4, 2023.

173 "It's nice to be thought of": Michelle Nugent, "Stop Calling Essential Workers Heroes and Start Actually Helping Us," Broad Street Review, February 1, 2021.

174 "When I work": Nugent, "Stop Calling Essential Workers Heroes."

174 In 2021, four researchers: Zhenyu Yuan et al., "Sacrificing Heroes or Suffering Victims? Investigating Third Parties' Reactions to Divergent Social Accounts of Essential Employees in the COVID-19 Pandemic," *Journal of Applied Psychology* 106, no.10 (2021): 1435–47.

174 "At a broader level": Yuan et al., "Sacrificing Heroes or Suffering Victims?," 1442.

175 47 percent of upper-income workers say: Juliana Menasce Horowitz and Kim Parker, "How Americans View Their Jobs," Pew Research Center, March 30, 2023.

175 that figure drops: Horowitz and Parker, "How Americans View Their Jobs."

176 likening the cognitive effects: Scott Sleek, "How Poverty Affects the Brain and Behavior," Association for Psychological Science, August 31, 2015.

176 "honorable, decent man": "Transcript: Joe Biden's DNC Speech," CNN, August 21, 2020.

176 "Joey, a job": "Transcript: Joe Biden's DNC Speech," CNN.

176 the rise of insecure scheduling: Daniel Schneider and Kristen Harknett, "Consequences of Routine Work-Schedule Instability for Worker Health and Well-Being," *American Sociological Review* 84, no. 1 (2019): 82–114.

176 Income volatility has at least doubled: Matthew Desmond, *Poverty, by America* (New York: Crown, 2023), 16.

176 affects roughly a third: Judith Siers-Poisson, "The Connection Between Unpredictable Work Schedules and Meeting Basic Household Needs," Institute for Research on Poverty, November 29, 2021.

177 "Families close to": Hannah Rubinton and Maggie Isaacson, "Income Volatility as a Barrier to Food Stamp Takeup," Federal Reserve Bank of St. Louis, October 27, 2022.

177 "levy of paperwork": Annie Lowrey, "The Time Tax," *The Atlantic*, July 27, 2021.

177 "Historically, with welfare programs": Grace Segers, "A Nationwide Fight over Food Insecurity Is Just Beginning," *New Republic*, January 27, 2023.

177 "I think the goal was": Laurel Wamsley, "Gov. Says Florida's Unemployment System Was Designed to Create 'Pointless Roadblocks,'" NPR, August 6, 2020.

178 "food stamps ($13.4 billion)": Desmond, *Poverty*, 89–90.

178 "I really think": Sarah Kliff, "Why Obamacare Enrollees Voted for Trump," Vox, December 13, 2016.

178 "In 2020 the federal government": Desmond, *Poverty*, 91.

179 roughly eight thousand Americans: "Social Security Disability: Information on Wait Times, Bankruptcies, and Deaths Among Applicants Who Appealed Benefit Denials," U.S. Government Accountability Office, August 13, 2020, https://www.gao.gov/assets/710/708835.pdf.

179 less than 40 percent: "What Is the Approval Rate for Social Security Disability Benefits?" USAFacts, March 3, 2023.

179 That audit, by the way: "Wait Times to Receive Social Security Disability Benefit Decisions Reach New High," USAFacts, May 8, 2023.

180 "I personally broke": Gwyneth Paltrow, "My $29 Food Stamp Challenge—and the Recipes (& Brouhaha) That Ensued," Goop, April 9, 2015.

181 "I don't think": David Firestone, "How to Use the Debt Ceiling to Inflict Cruelty on the Poor," *New York Times*, May 17, 2023.

182 increasing federal spending: Mary Clare Jalonick, "Changes to Food Aid in Debt Bill Would Cost Money, Far from Savings GOP Envisioned," Associated Press, May 31, 2023.

183 Mitt Romney was captured: Steve Mullis, "Leaked Video Shows Romney Discussing 'Dependent' Voters," NPR, September 17, 2012.

183 "There are 47 percent": Mullis, "Leaked Video Shows Romney Discussing 'Dependent' Voters."

183 "About half of people": Roberton C. Williams, "Why Do People Pay No Federal Income Tax?," Tax Policy Center, July 27, 2011.

184 69 percent of whom disapproved: "Romney's '47%' Comments Criticized, but Many Also Say Overcovered," Pew Research Center, October 1, 2012.

184 nearly two-thirds: William G. Gale and Donald B. Marron, "5 Myths About the 47 Percent," *Washington Post*, September 21, 2012.

184 not only did they still pay: Williams, "Why Do People Pay No Federal Income Tax?"

184 "My job is not": Mullis, "Leaked Video Shows Romney Discussing 'Dependent' Voters."

184 "in this world": "Benjamin Franklin's Last Great Quote and the Constitution," National Constitution Center, November 13, 2022.

184 Also, not to overdo: Glenn Kessler, "Mitt Romney, Caught on Video Tape," *Washington Post*, September 17, 2012.

185 they were financially buoyed: Michael Kranish, "Much Unsaid as Mitt Romney Cites His Tie to Mexico," *Boston Globe*, January 31, 2012.

186 "A murder in Chicago": Josh Levin, "The Welfare Queen," Slate, December 19, 2013.

186 "Congress would pass": Bryce Covert, "The Myth of the Welfare Queen," *The New Republic*, July 2, 2019.

186 he got only 47 percent: "2012," American Presidency Project.

186 "Well into the twentieth century": Nancy Isenberg, *White Trash: The 400-Year Untold History of Class in America* (New York: Penguin, 2017), xxvii.

187 "studied queer pet literature": Gino Spocchia, "Ted Cruz Mocked for Strange Rant About 'Queer Pet Literature,'" *The Independent*, September 7, 2022.

187 "get off the bong": Aila Slisco, "Ted Cruz Slams 'Slacker Baristas' in Rant Against Student Loan Forgiveness," *Newsweek*, August 26, 2022.

187 Ohio senator Sherrod Brown: Daily Kos, *Hatch, Author of $1.5 Trillion Tax Cut, Hasn't Found Money for Social Programs*, YouTube, November 30, 2017, https://www.youtube.com/watch?v=M_GoY7liUf8.

187 give healthcare coverage: Martin Pengelly: "Orrin Hatch Comments on Chip Health Program at Heart of Social Media Storm," *The Guardian*, December 3, 2017.

187 "The reason CHIP's": Daily Kos, *Hatch, Author of $1.5 Trillion Tax Cut.*

188 "It is in the blue states": Johnny Harris and Binyamin Appelbaum, "Blue States, You're the Problem," *New York Times*, November 9, 2021.

188 "backed not just by conservatives": Ta-Nehisi Coates, "The Black Family in the Age of Mass Incarceration," *The Atlantic*, October 2015.

188 "All that red": "Clinton Says Trump Won on Vows to Take Country 'Backwards,'" CBS News, March 13, 2018.

188 And as a damning: Robin McDowell and Margie Mason, "Prisoners in the US Are Part of a Hidden Workforce Linked to Hundreds of Popular Food Brands," Associated Press, January 29, 2024.

189 far more poverty: OECD, "Government at a Glance 2021, United States," 2021.

189 it's actually rural areas: Paul Krugman, "Can Anything Be Done to Assuage Rural Rage?," *New York Times*, January 26, 2023.

189 "Please continue to pray": Pride & Joy Preschool and Child Care Center, Facebook, April 9, 2021.

189 "our Andy Griffith": Town of Ranburne, "Note from the Mayor," April 19, 2021.

190 "everybody, some way or another": Webb-Hahn, "Rural Residents."

192 In 2024, Alabama became: Annie Gowen, "Republican Governors in 15 States Reject Summer Food Money for Kids," *Washington Post*, January 10, 2024.

194 the United States outranks: Erica Pandey, "America the Generous: U.S. Leads Globe in Giving," Axios, March 12, 2022.

194 "the dystopian social safety net": Alissa Quart, *Bootstrapped: Liberating Ourselves from the American Dream* (New York: CCC, 2023), 105.

194 laws passed against sleeping: "Housing, Not Handcuffs," National Law Center on Homelessness & Poverty, December 2019, https://homesslaw .org/wp-content/uploads/2019/12/HOUSING-NOT-HANDCUFFS -2019-FINAL.pdf.

CHAPTER TEN SMALL NORMALCIES

196 landing fifth in the polling: Kristen Sze, "Andrew Yang's 'Yang Gang' Drives His Unconventional Campaign," ABC News, February 11, 2020.

196 a dirt-floor house: Andrew Yang (@AndrewYang), "'My father grew up on a peanut farm in Asia with no floor and now his son is running for president.' #DemDebate," Twitter/X, September 12, 2019, https://twitter .com/AndrewYang/status/1172318741566115844.

197 a career physicist: Daniel Johnson, "Former US Presidential Candidate Andrew Yang to Speak at Sonoma Event," *Sonoma Index-Tribune*, May 13, 2024.

197 "riots in the street": Kevin Roose, "His 2020 Campaign Message: The Robots Are Coming," *New York Times*, February 10, 2018.

197 "The substance of Yang's campaign": Ben Smith, "Andrew Yang Could Win This Thing," BuzzFeed News, January 2, 2020.

197 "dark menace of industrial dislocation": John F. Kennedy, "Remarks of Senator John F. Kennedy at the AFL-CIO Convention, Grand Rapids, Michigan, June 7, 1960," John F. Kennedy Presidential Library and Museum.

198 with the strongest: Matthew Sheffield, "Poll: Younger Voters Want Universal Basic Income While Older Ones Reject It Overwhelmingly," The Hill, March 22, 2019.

198 One Hill-HarrisX poll: Gabriela Schulte, "Poll: Majority of Voters Now Say the Government Should Have a Universal Basic Income Program," The Hill, August 14, 2020.

198 sent $250 to $300 per child: Janet Nguyen, "Here's What's in the New Bill to Expand the Child Tax Credit," Marketplace, January 17, 2024.

198 "Let's say you're a kid": Stephanie Sy, "Child Poverty Increases Sharply Following Expiration of Expanded Tax Credit," *PBS NewsHour*, September 12, 2023.

198 an unprecedented 46 percent drop: Sy, "Child Poverty Increases Sharply."

199 most of the funds: "Research Roundup of the Expanded Child Tax Credit: The First 6 Months," Center on Poverty & Social Policy at Columbia University, December 23, 2021.

199 "Giving birth to": Annie Lowrey, *Give People Money: How a Universal Basic Income Would End Poverty, Revolutionize Work, and Remake the World* (New York: Crown, 2018), 151.

199   *half-trillion dollars'* worth: Lowrey, *Give People Money*, 151.

199   But like the expanded CTC: "Research Roundup of the Expanded Child Tax Credit," Center on Poverty & Social Policy at Columbia University.

200   landmark program that gave $500: Rachel Treisman, "California Program Giving $500 No-Strings-Attached Stipends Pays Off, Study Finds," NPR, March 4, 2021.

201   rising from 28 percent: Treisman, "California Program Giving $500 No-Strings-Attached Stipends Pays Off, Study Finds."

201   Under the heading of "self-determination": SEED, "Self-Determination," https://www.stocktondemonstration.org/self-determination.

201   "sixty-five percent to seventy percent": Ryan Brooks, "Andrew Yang Keeps Winning the Internet Primary," BuzzFeed News, September 19, 2019.

202   a pilot program that sent $375: All forthcoming data about UBI experiments in this section comes from the Mayors for a Guaranteed Income portal, which is an invaluable resource (https://www.mayorsforagi.org/), or from my interview with Dr. Stacia West.

204   the Dow had jumped 57 points: "How Major US Stock Indexes Fared Tuesday, 11/7/2023," Associated Press, November 7, 2023.

205   "Blacks should be quarantined": Paige Glotzer, *How the Suburbs Were Segregated: Developers and the Business of Exclusionary Housing, 1890–1960* (New York: Columbia University Press, 2020), 58.

205   the Supreme Court later struck down: Glotzer, *How the Suburbs Were Segregated*, 60.

206   "Those at the lowest economic level": Martin Luther King, Jr., *Where Do We Go from Here: Chaos or Community?* (1967; Boston: Beacon Press, 2010), 162.

206   35 percent of families: Pamela Joshi et al., "Families' Job Characteristics and Economic Self-Sufficiency: Differences by Income, Race-Ethnicity, and Nativity," *RSF: The Russell Sage Foundation Journal of the Social Sciences* 8 no. 5 (2022): 67–95.

207   "AT&T's acquisition": Sarah Miller, "Corporate Mergers Hurt Workers—and Drag Down the Job Market," *Washington Post*, October 21, 2021.

207   nearly half of American firms: Samuel Estreicher and Alexander Gelfond, "The FTC's Initial Policy Case for Banning All Non-Compete Clauses in Employment Agreements," Justia's Verdict, October 24, 2023.

207   roughly half of U.S. employers: "SHRM Survey Findings: Background Checking—The Use of Credit Background Checks in Hiring Decisions," Society of Human Resources Management, July 19, 2012.

208   one of the most shoplifted consumer goods: Peter C. Earle, "Why Is Baby Formula Kept Under Lock and Key?," American Institute for Economic Research, September 30, 2023.

208   medical debt is the biggest cause: Jesse Bedayn, "States Confront Medical Debt That's Bankrupting Millions," Associated Press, April 12, 2023.

208   "twenty-first-century union": Lowrey, *Give People Money*, 53.

208 new businesses were launched: Abha Bhattarai, "American Entrepreneurship Is on the Rise," *Washington Post*, September 14, 2023.

208 "Me at Dollar Tree": Allie Hayes, "23 Tweets About the Next Round of Stimulus Checks That Are Equal Parts Funny and Ridiculous," BuzzFeed, March 14, 2021.

208 the bulk of the three stimulus payments: Lorie Konish, "How Effective Were Those Stimulus Checks? Some Argue the Money May Have Fueled Inflation," CNBC, June 11, 2022.

208 about 75 percent of spending: "The Guaranteed Income Pilots Dashboard," Stanford Basic Income Lab and Center for Guaranteed Income Research.

208 Despite the promising results: Rachel Scott and Benjamin Siegel, "Sen. Joe Manchin Suggests Child Tax Credit Payments Would Be Used to Buy Drugs," ABC News, December 20, 2021.

CHAPTER ELEVEN   AUTOMATIC FOR THE PEOPLE

210 "It is common talk": "Dr. Wilbur Was Famous for Clear and Pithy Phrases," *Peninsula Times Tribune*, June 29, 1949, 12.

210 "We believe a Universal Basic Income": Marc Andreessen, "The Techno-Optimist Manifesto," Andreessen Horowitz, October 16, 2023.

211 the second largest bank failure: Max Reyes, "First Republic Becomes Second-Largest Ever US Bank Failure," Bloomberg, May 1, 2023.

211 "These guys didn't": Sindhu Sundar, "Venture Capitalists 'Almost Took the Whole System Down' by Having Startups Stow All Their Cash at Silicon Valley Bank, Says One Tech Billionaire CEO," Business Insider, March 13, 2023.

212 "subjected to frequent": Lyndsey Matthews, "World's Scariest Bridges," *Travel + Leisure*, September 18, 2022.

213 "We've taken airline pilots": Mary Clare Glover, "Bay Bridge: One of America's Ten Scariest," *Washingtonian*, August 5, 2011.

213 "improves order accuracy": Presto Automation Inc., "Presto Moves Fiscal Third Quarter 2023 Earnings Call to May 18," news release, May 15, 2023, https://investor.presto.com/news-releases/news-release-details/presto -moves-fiscal-third-quarter-2023-earnings-call-may-18.

215 they were working people: Robert O'Neill, "For Young Service Sector Workers the 'Great Resignation' Often Led to an Upgrade," Harvard Kennedy School, March 29, 2023.

215 "We are short-staffed": Michael Hollan, "McDonald's Drive-Thru Customer Spots 'Savage' Sign Telling People to Be Patient: 'No One Wants to Work,'" Fox News, April 12, 2021.

215 "This is what happens": David Rouzer (@RepDavidRouzer), Twitter/X, April 30, 2021, https://twitter.com/RepDavidRouzer/status/13881387665 99086080.

216   "The free-market solution": Mikael Thalen, "'This Is What Happens When Y'all Work TF Outta People for Only $7.25': Viral Fast-Food Sign Sparks Debate on Minimum Wage, Working Conditions," Daily Dot, May 2, 2021.

216   half of the states opted out: Trevor Hunnicut and Howard Schneider, "Half of U.S. States to End Biden-Backed Pandemic Unemployment Early," Reuters, June 2, 2021.

216   the highest job growth: Ben Casselman, "Cutoff of Jobless Benefits Is Found to Get Few Back to Work," *New York Times*, September 6, 2021.

216   he posted one example: Paul Fairie (@paulisci), "A Brief History of Nobody Wants to Work Anymore," Twitter/X, July 19, 2022, https://twitter.com/paulisci/status/1549527748950892544.

216   "Really what was happening": Jo Constantz, "'No One Wants to Work Anymore' Is a Complaint as Old as Work Itself," Bloomberg, August 10, 2022.

217   "the more public provisions": Howell V. Williams, "Benjamin Franklin and the Poor Laws," *Social Service Review* 18, no. 1 (1944): 78.

217   "Get your fucking ass up": Elizabeth Wagmeister, "'Money Always Matters': The Kardashians Tell All About Their New Reality TV Reign," *Variety*, March 9, 2022.

217   If we were to anoint a modern priest: This paragraph's background on Andrew Puzder comes from this excellent profile: Susan Berfield and Craig Giammona, "Trump's Labor Pick Loves Burgers, Bikinis, and Free Markets," Bloomberg, February 9, 2017.

218   "The point is simple": Andy Puzder, "Minimum Wage, Maximum Politics," *Wall Street Journal*, October 4, 2015.

218   More than half of fast-food workers: Ken Jacobs, Ian Perry, and Jenifer MacGillvary, "The High Public Cost of Low Wages," UC Berkeley Center for Labor Research and Wages, April 2015, https://laborcenter.berkeley.edu/pdf/2015/the-high-public-cost-of-low-wages.pdf.

218   highly profitable behemoths: Eli Rosenberg, "Walmart and McDonald's Have the Most Workers on Food Stamps and Medicaid, New Study Shows," *Washington Post*, November 18, 2020.

218   Perfect to theme: Roark Capital, "Roark Capital Group Closes Acquisition of CKE Restaurants, Marks 17th Restaurant Investment," December 26, 2013, https://www.roarkcapital.com/files/CKE%20Release%20FINAL.pdf.

219   "discouraging work": Andy Puzder, "More Work, Less Welfare," The Hill, June 22, 2015.

219   44 percent of Americans: Martha Ross and Nicole Bateman, "Low-Wage Work Is More Pervasive Than You Think, and There Aren't Enough 'Good Jobs' to Go Around," Brookings Institution, November 21, 2019.

219   a median income of $18,000 a year: Ross and Bateman, "Low-Wage Work

Is More Pervasive Than You Think, and There Aren't Enough 'Good Jobs' to Go Around."

219 ditching or reducing: See, e.g., Nathaniel Meyersohn, "Walmart, Costco and Other Companies Rethink Self-Checkout," CNN, November 13, 2023.

219 "you sort of compete": Andrew Kaczynski, "Trump Labor Pick in 2011 on His Fast-Food Workers: We Hire 'The Best of the Worst,'" CNN, January 23, 2017.

220 "I like beautiful women": Berfield and Giammona, "Trump's Labor Pick Loves Burgers, Bikinis, and Free Markets."

220 "You're going to see automation": Kate Taylor, "Fast-Food CEO Says He's Investing in Machines Because the Government Is Making It Difficult to Afford Employees," Business Insider, March 16, 2016.

220 A company press release: Tiffany Hsu, "Carl's Jr.'s Marketing Plan: Pitch Burgers, Not Sex," New York Times, November 13, 2019.

221 Andy Puzder was nominated: Berfield and Giammona, "Trump's Labor Pick Loves Burgers, Bikinis, and Free Markets."

221 "to foster, promote and develop": Judson MacLaury, "A Brief History: The U.S. Department of Labor," U.S. Department of Labor.

221 CKE Restaurants had outsourced: William Finnegan, "The Rejection of Andy Puzder," The New Yorker, February 15, 2017.

221 more race discrimination and sexual harassment lawsuits: Robin Urevich, "Civil Rights Suits Plague Corporation Run by Labor Pick Andrew Puzder," Newsweek, January 23, 2017.

221 "the crushing burdens of unnecessary regulations": Marianne Levine and Cogan Schneier, "Trump Chooses Puzder as Labor Secretary," Politico, December 12, 2016.

221 "the most fun you could": Levine and Schneier, "Trump Chooses Puzder as Labor Secretary."

221 Puzder resigned: Ezequiel Minaya, "Andy Puzder, Former Labor Secretary Pick, to Step Down as CEO of CKE Restaurants," Wall Street Journal, March 21, 2017.

221 Acosta would be confirmed: Nandita Bose, "Trump's Labor Secretary Acosta Resigns Amid Epstein Case," Reuters, July 12, 2019.

222 "whisper the quotations from the drug markets": Josh Jones, "In 1911, Thomas Edison Predicts What the World Will Look Like in 2011: Smart Phones, No Poverty, Libraries That Fit in One Book," Open Culture, December 21, 2015.

222 could deliver $7 trillion: Goldman Sachs, "Generative AI Could Raise Global GDP by 7%," April 5, 2023.

222 In a fascinating study: Alberto Alesina, Stefanie Stantcheva, and Edoardo Teso, "Intergenerational Mobility and Preferences for Redistribution," American Economic Review 108, no. 2 (2018): 521–54.

223 "where actual mobility is particularly low": Alesina, Stantcheva, and Teso, "Intergenerational Mobility and Preferences for Redistribution," 522.

223 "Everyone was a temporarily embarrassed capitalist": John Steinbeck, *America and Americans and Selected Nonfiction* (New York: Penguin Publishing Group, 2003), 35.

223 "tend to favor more generous redistributive policies": Alesina, Stantcheva, and Teso, "Intergenerational Mobility and Preferences for Redistribution," 523.

CHAPTER TWELVE BLINDNESS

225 the French government had recently: Kathryn Armstrong, "France Pension Reforms: Macron Signs Pension Age Rise to 64 into Law," BBC, April 14, 2023.

225 a million or so French protesters: Thomas Adamson and Jade le Deley, "Nearly 1 Million French March in 4th Day of National Protests Against Pension Changes," Associated Press, February 11, 2023; Nick Kostov and Stacy Meichtry, "LVMH's Paris Headquarters Stormed by Protesters," *Wall Street Journal*, April 13, 2023.

226 ten thousand tons of garbage: Thomas Adamson, "Long Paris Trash Strike Ends, Workers Face Daunting Cleanup," Associated Press, March 29, 2023.

228 "credit for having survived so long": Susan Farrell, "Kurt Vonnegut's Advice to College Graduates Is Still Relevant," *Smithsonian Magazine*, May 8, 2023.

228 less than 15 percent of Americans: "On the Fringe of a Golden Era," *Time*, January 29, 1965.

228 73 percent of that same cohort: "On the Fringe of a Golden Era," *Time*.

228 "A social space had opened": Louis Menand, "It's Time to Stop Talking About 'Generations,'" *New Yorker*, October 11, 2021.

229 74 percent of managers: Daniel De Visé, "Gen Zers Make 'Difficult' Employees, Managers Say," The Hill, June 30, 2023.

229 12 percent of those bosses: Aaron McDade, "12% of Managers Say They've Fired a Gen Z Employee in Their First Week of Work—and Being Too Easily Offended Is Often to Blame, New Survey Finds," Business Insider, April 19, 2023.

230 "many high-quality surveys": Michael Dimock, "5 Things to Keep in Mind When You Hear About Gen Z, Millennials, Boomers and Other Generations," Pew Research Center, May 22, 2023.

230 "The field has been flooded": Kim Parker, "How Pew Research Center Will Report on Generations Moving Forward," Pew Research Center, May 22, 2023.

230 "When you're clicking": Kelli María Korducki, "Why We All Love to Hate Other Generations," Business Insider, July 26, 2023.

231 a lengthy advisory: Vivek H. Murthy, "Social Media and Youth Mental Health: The U.S. Surgeon General's Advisory," Office of the U.S. Surgeon General, 2023, https://www.hhs.gov/sites/default/files/sg-youth -mental-health-social-media-advisory.pdf, 10.

231 half of U.S. adults: Dipo Fadeyi and Juliana Menasce Horowitz, "Americans More Likely to Say It's a Bad Thing Than a Good Thing That More Young Adults Live with Their Parents," Pew Research Center, August 24, 2022.

232 "social isolation": Vivek H. Murthy, "Our Epidemic of Loneliness and Isolation: The U.S. Surgeon General's Advisory on the Healing Effects of Social Connection and Community," Office of the U.S. Surgeon General, 2023, https://www.hhs.gov/sites/default/files/surgeon-general-social -connection-advisory.pdf, 9.

232 They weren't alone: Bryce Ward, "Americans Are Choosing to Be Alone. Here's Why We Should Reverse That," *Washington Post*, November 23, 2022.

232 "the share of families living": Sean F. Reardon and Kendra Bischoff, "Growth in the Residential Segregation of Families by Income, 1970–2009," Stanford University, November 2011, https://s4.ad.brown.edu /Projects/Diversity/data/report/report111111.pdf.

232 "Cities with higher levels": Hannah Rubinton and Maggie Isaacson, "Income Segregation and Income Inequality," Federal Reserve Bank of St. Louis, March 27, 2023.

232 According to a 2020 study: Jacob Ausubel, "Older People Are More Likely to Live Alone in the U.S. than Elsewhere in the World," Pew Research Center, March 10, 2020.

233 "A large proportion": Jacob R. Brown and Ryan D. Enos, "The Measurement of Partisan Sorting for 180 Million Voters," *Nature Human Behavior* 5, no. 8 (2021): 998–1008.

234 "The realignment has increased": Greg Martin and Steven Webster, "The Real Culprit Behind Geographic Polarization," *The Atlantic*, November 26, 2018.

240 the number of sixteen- to nineteen-year-olds: Rainesford Stauffer, "Whatever Happened to the Summer Job?," Vox, July 22, 2020.

INDEX

A NOTE ABOUT THE AUTHOR

Adam Chandler is a journalist based in New York. He is the author of *Drive-Thru Dreams: A Journey Through the Heart of America's Fast-Food Kingdom*, a correspondent for the History Channel, and a former staff writer at *The Atlantic*. His work has appeared in *The New York Times*, *The Wall Street Journal*, *The Washington Post*, *WIRED*, *Vox*, *Slate*, *Texas Monthly*, *New York*, *Esquire*, *Time*, and other publications.

A NOTE ON THE TYPE

This book was set in Janson, a typeface long thought to have been made by the Dutchman Anton Janson, who was a practicing typefounder in Leipzig during the years 1668–1687. However, it has been conclusively demonstrated that these types are actually the work of Nicholas Kis (1650–1702), a Hungarian, who most probably learned his trade from the master Dutch typefounder Dirk Voskens. The type is an excellent example of the influential and sturdy Dutch types that prevailed in England up to the time William Caslon (1692–1766) developed his own incomparable designs from them.

Typeset by Scribe
Philadelphia, Pennsylvania

Printed and bound by Berryville Graphics
Berryville, Virginia

Designed by Soonyoung Kwon